THE SHAPING OF RATIONALITY

The Shaping of Rationality

TOWARD INTERDISCIPLINARITY
IN THEOLOGY AND SCIENCE

J. Wentzel van Huyssteen

WILLIAM B. EERDMANS PUBLISHING COMPANY
GRAND RAPIDS, MICHIGAN / CAMBRIDGE, U.K.

© 1999 Wm. B. Eerdmans Publishing Co.
255 Jefferson Ave. S.E., Grand Rapids, Michigan 49503 /
P.O. Box 163, Cambridge CB3 9PU U.K.

Printed in the United States of America

04 03 02 01 00 99   7 6 5 4 3 2 1

Library of Congress Cataloging-in-Publication Data

Van Huyssteen, Wentzel.
The shaping of rationality: toward interdisciplinarity in theology and science /
J. Wentzel Van Huyssteen.
p.   cm.
Includes bibliographical references.
ISBN 0-8028-3868-5 (cloth: alk. paper)
1. Religion and science.   2. Knowledge, Theory of.   I. Title.
BL240.2.V315   1999
261.5'5 — dc21   99-20793
                                        CIP

For Hester van Huyssteen

Contents

CONTENTS

Acknowledgments

During the past seven years Princeton Theological Seminary has become my intellectual and spiritual home, a place where wonderful friends, very special colleagues, and quite remarkable students have all contributed to create a near perfect ambience for discussion, teaching, and learning. I am deeply indebted to all my friends at Princeton Theological Seminary, and to the President and Administration for fully supporting my scholarly research and writing during these first demanding but happy years in a new country. I am especially indebted to so many of my students who have challenged and inspired me at various stages of a project that has consumed so much of my intellectual passion for quite a long time. This project now comes to an end with the publication of this book, and although it is impossible to thank each and every one for his or her constructive influence on the growth of this text, I have tried — where and when it was relevant — to acknowledge my gratitude in the text of this work.

In many ways my first probing into the problem of rationality in theology and science can be traced back as far as the Fall of 1990, when I was a Visiting Scholar at the Center of Theological Inquiry in Princeton. Much has happened in my life since those early days of research, not least of which was our move from South Africa to the United States of America. In a wonderful way, however, the location for my final work on this project has come full circle, and during 1998, a blessed sabbatical year, again at the Center of Theological Inquiry, I was finally able to finish a project that has dominated and inspired these busy and exciting years. I am deeply grateful to the Director and staff at the Center of Theological Inquiry for creating ideal circumstances for research and writing.

My wife Hester and I were also warmly welcomed at Clare Hall, Cambridge, where I was privileged to be a Visiting Fellow during the Summer of 1998, and could work on the final draft of this book. Furthermore, my work on this project has benefited greatly from a stimulating series of invitations to lecture as visiting professor at different universities and institutions over the past few years. It was a real privilege to share the emerging argument of this book with many colleagues and friends during public lectures or seminars at Tulane University, the University of Pennsylvania, Purdue University, the University of Aarhus (Denmark), the Universities of Utrecht and Groningen (The Netherlands), St. Petersburg (Russia), the University of Warwick (U.K.), and in South Africa, the Universities of Pretoria, Stellenbosch, Western Cape, and Port Elizabeth. I also lectured on early drafts of material from this book at the annual meeting of the American Academy of Religion (New Orleans 1996), at Workshops on Theology and Science organized by The Templeton Foundation at Oxford University, at conferences of the Highlands Institute of American Religious Thought in St. Andrews (Scotland) and Bad Boll (Germany), of the European Society for the Study of Science and Theology in Cracòw (Poland), and of the Swiss Theological Society in Emmeten, Switzerland. Some of these lectures were later reworked and published in journals or as parts of books. In a few cases where some of these earlier drafts were revised and incorporated into this book, it is referenced in the text. I do want to thank colleagues and friends, too many to mention here, who have made these stimulating and rewarding invitations possible.

I also want to mention, with much gratitude and appreciation, the ongoing support of Wm. Eerdmans Publishing Company for all the work that has gone into the writing of this book. I am happy and privileged to be associated with this publishing house, and especially thank Mr. William Eerdmans, Jr., for the way his energy and zest have been an inspiration for this project. I am very much indebted to Ernan McMullin for his important paper *Construction and Constraint: The Shaping of Scientific Rationality* (1988), which inspired the title for this book.

A special word of thanks must also go to my colleagues Jerome A. Stone, Helena Glanville, and LeRon Shults for their wonderful and unfailing support for this project, and for reading every single version or draft of this text during the past few years. A special word of thanks goes to LeRon Shults for his careful editing of the text, to Kirk Wegter-McNelly for his excellent research assistance during the early years of the project, and to Tomáš Hančil for doing such a great job of the Index.

In the last instance, however, this book belongs to my wife Hester. I dedicate it to her with love and appreciation. She was there when the problem of rationality began to haunt me, and she was there when it grew into a passion. That she put up with this, and that she could show me how the complexities of human rationality are deeply embedded in the joys and challenges of everyday life, has been an unforgettable lesson in what rationality really is about.

Introduction

Why rationality? The answer to this question has not been an easy one. I do know, however, that writing this book on *the problem of rationality* has been a life-changing experience that started a long time ago with a lingering fascination with a rather abstract, theoretical problem, and ends now with a profound and humble awareness of the deeply spiritual nature of the human self as embedded in the complexities of everyday life. My initial and ever-increasing fascination has been with the sheer fact of human intelligence, and with the spectacular difference its presence and almost limitless achievements have made in our time. As time went by, however, the contours of the problem shifted as the theologian in me pushed further and started wondering about the relationship between intelligence and rationality, and about how the uniquely human ability and skill of being rational in belief and action could ever be brought to bear upon what seemed to be a distant and remote world — the world of faith and religious commitment. From here it has been a short step to what has become one of the most pervasive and exciting problems of our time, the relationship of life-changing religious faith to the overwhelming and ongoing successes of contemporary science. It took me a long time, however, to grasp that in trying to *understand* what scientific reflection is about, and in trying to *understand* what theological reflection is about, the answer lay hidden in the understanding itself.

So, I do want to attempt an answer to the perplexing question *why rationality?* I now believe that the problem of rationality holds the key to understanding the forces that have shaped the radically differ-

1

ent domains of theology and of the sciences, today widely regarded as two of the most enduring, but also controversial, cultural achievements of our species. I also believe that the problematical relationship between these two cultural forces should be seen as the contemporary form of the age-old "faith and reason" problem *par excellence*. We are indeed the children of modernity, and the often stellar performances of the sciences in our time have again managed to elevate this mode of human knowledge to a status so special and superior that it just had to emerge as the paradigmatic example of what human rationality should be about. In stark contrast to this, religious faith, and theology as a reflection on religious faith, seems to be sliding down the lonely road toward irrationality as it increasingly has to come to terms with a breathtaking and bewildering pluralism of faiths, churches, doctrines, practices, and theologies.

Has science then finally claimed rationality, that most unique of our human abilities, at the expense of religious faith and theological reflection? This book will answer this question with a resounding "no," and will point the way to an unexpected, if not startling, discovery: rationality is alive and well in *all* the domains of our human lives. Rationality may turn out to have many faces, but rationality also ultimately defines who we are as a species, and rationality will hold the important and only key to bridging the different domains of our lives responsibly. In fact, rationality is all about responsibility: the responsibility to pursue clarity, intelligibility, and optimal understanding as ways to cope with ourselves and our world. The pursuit of intelligibility and optimal understanding will emerge here as possibly the most important epistemic goals that shape the way we interact with others, ourselves, and our worlds on a daily basis. And so we will discover that all the many faces of human rationality relate directly to a pre-theoretical reasonableness, a "common sense rationality" that informs and is present in all our everyday goal-directed actions. It is in the pursuit of these goals and ideals that we become rational persons as we learn the skills of responsible judgment and discernment, and when we articulate the best available reasons we have for making what we believe to be the right choices, those reasons we have for holding on to certain beliefs, and the strong convictions we have for acting in certain ways.

In the course of this book we will also see that we cannot talk abstractly and theoretically about the phenomenon of rationality anymore: it is only as individual human beings, living with other human beings in concrete situations and contexts, that we can claim some form of rationality. In this sense rationality will be revealed as always person- and domain-specific, as we discover it as present and operative in and through the dynamics of our words and deeds, and alive and well in our discourses and action. But as we turn rationality on itself and probe our various forms of understanding, we will find ourselves confronted with maybe the biggest challenge of all: both the traditional domains of science and religion have now woken up to find their identities challenged and changed by a new and pervasive postmodern culture. And in this postmodern world, should we not be taking seriously the "end of philosophy" talk, the jettisoning of all epistemology, and giving up our quest for finding the resources of rationality that our different domains of knowledge may share? More disturbingly, we will discover that it is *rationality itself* that has been the prime focus of the postmodern challenge. This is a challenge that has to be taken on directly, for if we let rationality slip away, we will be losing that which gives us our identity as human beings. The special focus of the postmodern challenge to human rationality will therefore be found in the challenge to revision the notion of rationality in such a way that all our reasoning strategies will ultimately again benefit from the rich resources of rationality. And it is precisely in trying to detect the presence of rationality in discourses as different as theology and the sciences that we will turn away from overly narrow and "rationalistic" notions of rationality: rationality will indeed turn out to have many faces, and is indeed as many-sided and wide-ranging as the domain of intelligence itself.

In the wake of the postmodern challenge to rationality we will therefore be pursuing the possibility that shared rational resources may actually be identified for the sciences, for theology, and for other forms of inquiry. Then we will proceed to ask what special link this may have opened up between different modes of human knowledge, and especially whether any form of interdisciplinary rationality can be credibly achieved — an interdisciplinary rationality that might finally support the claims by at least some in the theological epistemic community for a public voice in our complex, contemporary culture. On this view both theologians and scientists should be empowered to identify the rational integrity of their own disciplines by offering their own sources of critique and justification, and thereby answer to what will turn out to be one of postmodernism's most powerful challenges: neither theological reflection nor the many forms of contemporary scientific reflection require universal epistemological guarantees anymore. In this book I will therefore focus on the enduring problems resulting from theology's epistemic isolation in a pluralistic, postmodern world. And as we will see, it is the problem of pluralism that will provide us with the key to argue for the interdisciplinary nature and status of theological reflection.

In my recent *Duet or Duel? Theology and Science in a Postmodern World* (1998a) I argued that precisely in the interdisciplinary conversation between theology and the sciences of cosmology and evolutionary biology there are rich resources for retrieving an integrative approach to human knowledge that would be neither modernist nor foundationalist in nature. Moreover, I argued in this book that theological reflection is not only radically shaped by its social, historical, and cultural embeddedness, but also by the biological roots of human rationality. Especially in contemporary evolutionary epistemology we find surprising, if not startling, attempts to facilitate precisely the most difficult challenge of a constructive form of postmodern critique: the need for a more comprehensive and integrative approach to the problem of human knowledge that will not again totalize our views of human rationality into new and oppressive metanarratives.

I will not return here to this line of argument in my current attempt to explore the shaping of rationality, but much of what I argued in this recent book will be presupposed in this text. At this point it suffices to say that the basic assumption of evolutionary epistemology is that we humans, like all other living beings, result from evolutionary processes and that, consequently, our mental capacities are constrained and shaped by the mechanisms of biological evolution. I accept, at least in a minimalist sense, that all our knowledge, including our scientific and religious knowledge, is grounded in biological evolution. And if human knowledge results from, and is shaped by evolution, then the study of evolution should be of extreme importance for an understanding of the phenomenon of knowledge. Various philosophers have argued that it should not at all surprise us that as human beings we could have acquired intelligence, enabling us to secure information and survive in our world. As Nicholas Rescher has correctly pointed out, intelligence naturally arises through evolutionary processes because it provides one very effective means of survival. Rationality, seen in this broadest sense of the word as our particular human ability to cope with our world through optimal understanding, can therefore be seen as conducive to human survival, and the explanation for our cognitive resources as fundamentally Darwinian (cf. Rescher 1992:3f.). In fact, Rescher's observation here is sharp and to the point: the imperative to understand is something altogether basic for *homo sapiens*. In fact we cannot function, let alone thrive, without reliable information regarding what goes on about us. Intelligence is therefore our peculiar human instrumentality, a matter of our specific evolutionary heritage, and rationality will then primarily consist in the intelligent use of our unique ability for rational judgment, which ultimately determines the life-determining choices we make. We will see, then, that in this sense optimizing our ability for critical judgment regarding what we think, do, and value, indeed forms the crux of human rationality.

In *Duet or Duel?* I also argued that evolutionary epistemology — in spite of some of its inherent limitations — may facilitate a post-foundationalist notion of rationality that could actually take us beyond the confines of traditional disciplinary boundaries and modernist cultural domains. This notion of a postfoundationalist rationality will emerge as the central theme of this book. But what is presupposed here is that evolutionary epistemology, rightly understood, may indeed facilitate an interdisciplinary account of all our epistemic activities. An exploration into the interdisciplinary nature of specifically theological reflection will not only facilitate the revisioning of the nature and standards of theological reflection, but should also show how firmly religion and religious reflection are embedded in our culture today. Probing the problem of interdisciplinary reflection in a post-foundationalist mode will therefore lead to the important discovery that human rationality can never be adequately housed within any one specific reasoning strategy only. Therefore, to recognize that religious reflection may actually share in the rich resources of human rationality will be to open our eyes to the exciting fact that this rationality itself is operative among our different modes of knowledge and therefore links together the different domains of our lives, and therefore also different disciplines and reasoning strategies. The mere awareness of this fact, of course, already reveals the breakdown of the traditional modernist demarcation between science and religion/theology.

This book, therefore, should be read as an attempt to refigure the interdisciplinary nature and cross-contextual task of theological reflection. This book is also written with the strong conviction that talking about the nature and task of Christian theology today means talking about the complex set of values that shape the rationality of theological reflection. This quest for the rationality of theological reflection will be presented here in terms of two forceful claims: the rationality of theology, first of all, is definitively shaped by its location in the living context of interdisciplinary reflection; secondly, this interdisciplinary context is — epistemologically at least — significantly shaped by the dominant presence and influence of scientific rationality in our culture. Theologians, often focusing on the unique hermeneutics of theological reflection, are notorious for neglecting this profound epistemological challenge, ignoring or failing to recognize the pervasive influence of the sciences on the epistemic and other values that shape theological rationality today.

For theology, an all-important focus of its dialogue with our contemporary culture will therefore be found in two seemingly unrelated issues: on the one hand, the tremendous problems that arise if theology should choose to abandon its interdisciplinary, cross-contextual obligations and retreat to the insular comfort of sectarian notions of theological rationality; on the other hand, contemporary theology's enduring but uneasy relationship with what is often perceived to be a very superior scientific rationality. Both of these challenges, however, look different when we realize that theology and the sciences have also been profoundly influenced by postmodern culture. This gives an unexpected and complicating twist to the centuries-old theology and science problem: not only theology, but also postmodern science and postmodern philosophy of science have moved away quite dramatically from positivist and technocentric conceptions of scientific rationality with its closely aligned beliefs in linear progress, guaranteed success, deterministic predictability, absolute truths, and some uniform, standardized form of knowledge. As we will see, some contemporary philosophers of science now argue for a postmodern philosophy of science, which — along with feminist interpretations of science — rejects all global interpretations of science as well as the power-play implied by scientific progress, and focuses in stead on trust in local scientific practice. As will soon become clear, this kind of postmodernism in science not only sharply deconstructs and rejects the autonomy and cultural dominance of especially the natural sciences as the accepted paradigm for rationality in our time, but will also seriously challenge and deconstruct any attempt to develop a meaningful and intelligible relationship between science and Christian theology today. It is clear that the *problem of rationality* thus emerges as at the heart of the current dialogue between theology and the sciences. Furthermore, trying to find some kind of meaningful epistemological link between theology and the sciences also directly confronts us with the *problem of interdisciplinarity,* as we attempt to bring together two modes of knowledge as diverse as theology and science.

I hope to show in this book, then, that the theology and science dialogue today should be a crucial part of the broader discussion of the nature of theological reflection, and as such of the interdisciplinary status of theological reflection. Also, I hope to show that this cross-disciplinary debate is in fact dominated, and, in a sense, held together by what one may call a remarkable mutual quest for intelligibility and optimal understanding. This quest for intelligibility, as will become clear later, is at the heart of what human rationality and our various strategies of reasoning are about. Most of us would agree, of course, that God transcends any final intellectual grasp, and that encounters with God obviously involve deeper levels than that of the rational, inquiring mind alone. As many scientists and theologians today will acknowledge, the quest for intelligibility or optimal understanding will be incomplete if it does not include within itself the religious quest for ultimate meaning, purpose, and significance. This mutual quest for intelligibility has not only created exciting new areas of discussion between theology and the sciences, but also seems to bring these diverse modes of reflection closer together. In this mutual quest for intelligibility each of these modes of cognition will be seen as a very specific and disciplined attempt to understand our world of experience, and in the light of this experience, to identify possible points of consonance, but also possible points of difference between widely divergent reasoning strategies. The current theology and science dialogue, then, will turn out to be at the heart of the debate on the interdisciplinary nature and location of theological reflection, and presents itself as a plausible context for a contemporary apologetics for the Christian faith. As such it should not only fundamentally shape our expression of the Christian experience of God, but will also reveal the shared, as well as the distinct values that shape the rationality of theology and

7

the sciences respectively. This ongoing cross-disciplinary dialogue thus reveals itself as not just an esoteric intellectual hobby of a privileged few, but touches the heart of what theological reflection is about.

Reflecting on the relationship between theology and the sciences therefore reveals an important intellectual and spiritual incentive, which should also shape our reflective expression of the Christian faith, as well as caution us to greater epistemological and methodological sophistication in our reflection on the nature and status of theological reflection. One way to do this would be to first try to find and identify a model of rationality that would not only reveal the possibility of shared resources of rationality between theological and scientific forms of reflection, but which would lure us to move beyond the epistemological dichotomy of foundationalist objectivism and nonfoundationalist relativism. This option is what I have called *postfoundationalism,* an option that will reveal the shared rational resources of theology and the sciences, while at the same time creating a space for the very distinct knowledge claims of each of these reasoning strategies. A postfoundationalist model of rationality will take seriously the challenge of much of postmodern thinking, but will carefully distinguish between constructive and deconstructive modes of postmodern thinking. A postfoundationalist model of rationality will therefore especially incorporate into our reasoning strategies the relentless criticism of foundationalist assumptions: we all indeed exercise normative commitments, but the failure to acknowledge those commitments will leave us without any epistemological way of really taking them seriously (cf. Dean 1988:21f.).

A postfoundationalist notion of rationality will therefore provide a quite unique link between theology and the sciences, and will open our eyes to:

> *first,* fully acknowledge contextuality and the embeddedness of both theology and the sciences in the different domains of human culture;
>
> *second,* affirm the epistemically crucial role of interpreted experience and the way that tradition shapes the epistemic and nonepistemic values that inform our reflection about both God and our world;
>
> *third,* at the same time creatively point beyond the confines of

the local community, group, or culture, toward plausible forms of transcommunal and interdisciplinary conversation.

As we will see, this move toward a postfoundationalist notion of rationality in theology and science will therefore be held together by a twofold concern: *first,* recognizing that we always come to our cross-disciplinary conversations with strong beliefs, commitments, and even prejudices; and *second,* identifying the shared resources of human rationality in different modes of reflection, which allows us to reach beyond the walls of our own epistemic communities in cross-contextual, cross-cultural, and cross-disciplinary conversation (cf. van Huyssteen 1998a). Finally, reflecting on the relationship between theology and the sciences will therefore inevitably force us to reflect on the nature and task of theology as a form of rational inquiry too. We have to ask — also and especially of our own positions — what epistemic and other values lurk in the shadows of our tacit assumptions, and how these assumptions shape our epistemological and other judgments as we try to understand ourselves, our world, and what many of us believe to be God's presence in this world.

If the search for a more integrative model of human knowledge adequately reveals human rationality as our species' most distinguishing survival strategy, performatively present in all the various domains of our lives, then the seemingly remote epistemologies of our various reasoning strategies will be revealed to be integral parts of webs of theories about the world and ourselves. On this view religious and theological reflection can be equal partners in a democratic, interdisciplinary conversation where the voice of authentic religious commitment might actually be heard in a postmodern, pluralist situation. This kind of theological reflection will share in interdisciplinary standards of rationality which, although always socially and contextually shaped, will not be hopelessly culture and context bound; even with widely divergent personal, religious, or disciplinary viewpoints, we still share in the rich resources of human rationality.

Overview

This book consists of five chapters. In *Chapter One* I explore the complex and elusive phenomenon of postmodernism and its rather dramatic impact on the values that shape the rationality of postmodern philosophies of science, and of postmodern theologies. At the heart of the epistemological problem of defining the interdisciplinary location and the rationality of theology as a plausible form of critical reflection, we will discover the current theology and science dialogue, which in its own way will redefine the relationship of the Christian faith to contemporary postmodern culture. The crucial problem that will emerge here can be phrased as follows: in a cultural context so deeply affected by what many see as the fragmentation and even rampant pluralism of postmodernity, would some form of intelligible, cross-disciplinary conversation between theology and the sciences still be possible today? Surprisingly, however, it will be the blurring of traditional boundaries and the seemingly *cross-disciplinary character* of much of constructive postmodern thought that will present the problem of rationality in theology and science with the most intriguing challenge. Some postmodernists consider conventional tight definitions of academic disciplines simply as remnants of modernity and question the possibility of rigid disciplinary boundaries between the natural sciences, social sciences, humanities, art, literature, and religious reflection.

We will also see that postmodern philosophy of science understands science as a historically dynamic process in which there are conflicting and competing paradigm theories, research programs, and research traditions. On this view the reasons, arguments, and value judgments employed by the community of scientists are seen to be fundamentally related to, or "grounded" in, local, social practices. The very criteria and norms that guide and define scientific activity thus become open and vulnerable to criticism, as does the idea of philosophy of science itself. On postmodern views of science there is indeed no possibility of occupying a meta-standpoint from which to interpret science: all our interpretations of science imply a move within the contested terrain of scientific practice, i.e., the local contexts within which scientists themselves operate. But, and importantly, we will see that the claim is not that scientific knowledge, as local knowledge, has no universality, but rather that what universality it has is an achievement always first of all rooted in local know-how. We will also see, however, that it remains unclear how exactly this kind of postmodern science might relate to the broader issue of interdisciplinary reflection, and especially to such seemingly distinct cultural domains as religion, and theology as a reflection on religious experience.

The postmodern challenge, however, not only makes it virtually impossible to speak so generally about "rationality," "science," "theology," or "God"; as we will see, it is *rationality itself* that has been fundamentally challenged and problematized by postmodernism. *Chapter Two*, therefore, will explore the ramifications of this disturbing fact for some dominant forms of theological reflection, and will include a special focus on nonfoundationalism as one of the most important philosophical roots of postmodernism. Here I will begin my argument that, although nonfoundationalism seems to get us away from the dangers of overblown foundationalist epistemologies in theology and in the sciences, it does not really get us beyond relativism and the kind of "many rationalities" view, where incommensurability may finally stifle all meaningful cross-disciplinary dialogue. We will see that this kind of contextualism easily leads to a relativism of rationalities, where every social or human activity could in principle function as a framework for human rationality. The characteristics identified earlier as typical for a local form of postmodern science will now find remarkable parallels in other radically contextualized, nonfoundationalist modes of reflection. And as in the case of science as social practice, theological reflection in this mode will also emerge as a local practice, with strong contextual claims for its own internal criteria of rationality. For the rationality of science this isolationism, in its extremist form, might mean the actual loss of philosophy of science itself. For the rationality of theology, it might mean the dangerous reemergence of fideist, protective strategies and of crypto-foundationalism.

The postmodern challenge to both theology and the sciences will indeed leave us with serious problems as well as exciting challenges. Both in postmodern science and in nonfoundationalist theologies the powerful step beyond modernity was taken by a radical return to local, interpretative contexts. What is first required here is a trusting attitude toward local contexts of practice, toward scientific and theological traditions, respectively, where these are understood, not as representing an authoritative consensus, but rather a field of concerns within which both consensus and dissent acquire a local intelligibility. This will still leave us, however, with the question how nonfoundationalist theologies can be interdisciplinarily connected to other reasoning strategies via normative models of rationality that often still so clearly privilege the natural sciences.

In *Chapter Three* I proceed by focusing on various philosophical traits of the concept of rationality, while developing an argument for moving beyond the absolutism of foundationalism and the relativism of nonfoundationalism, to *a postfoundationalist notion of rationality* for which notions of intelligibility and optimal understanding, responsible judgment, progressive problem-solving, and experiential adequacy will be crucial. Here the contextual and pragmatic nature of diverse forms of rational inquiry will reveal important epistemological overlaps between natural scientific and nonnatural scientific modes of reflection. What this will mean for the challenge to theology's cross-disciplinary task, is that modes of inquiry as diverse and different as theology and the other sciences may actually share the same resources of human rationality without having to fall back on modernist, totalizing, or generic notions of human rationality.

To talk about the shaping of rationality, then, is to talk about the epistemic quest for optimal understanding and intelligibility, the epistemic skill of responsible judgment; it is furthermore to see the intellectual skill of rational judgment and theory choice as a fallibilist process of progressive problem-solving. Therefore, even if scientific rationality reveals itself as a very disciplined and manicured form of rationality, effective problem-solving and good judgment reach beyond the sciences and already form part of the common sense reasonableness by which we live our daily lives. My claim will be that these resources of rationality are not only shared by different and diverse modes of reflection, but are in fact revealed as rich resources only by a postfoundationalist notion of rationality. A postfoundationalist notion of rationality will help us to recognize the many faces of rationality as performatively present in our different modes of knowledge, and in the different domains of our lives.

Extremely significant for theology, however, is that on a postfoundationalist view, theological reflection not only can no longer be excluded from the broader epistemological endeavor, but epistemology itself will have to be creatively refigured. What will emerge here, therefore, is a broader and richer notion of human rationality: a notion of rationality that creates a safe space where our different discourses and actions are seen at times to link up with one another, and at times to contrast or conflict with one another. It is precisely in this hard struggle for interpersonal and interdisciplinary communication that the many faces of human rationality are revealed. A postfoundationalist notion of rationality thus manages to avoid the extremes of the modernist nostalgia for one, unified form of knowledge, as well as the relativism of extreme forms of postmodernism. On this view, it should become clear that a postfoundationalist notion of rationality could never function as a superimposed metanarrative, but develops, rather, as an emerging pattern that unifies and integrates our interpreted experience without totalizing it. With this broader view of rationality, and the shared resources that are revealed between often very diverse forms of intellectual inquiry, we will finally be in a position to claim a remarkable consonance between the shaping of scientific and theological rationality.

In *Chapter Four* I will argue that a postfoundationalist notion of rationality not only focuses on our experience of knowing, and thus on the experiential and hermeneutical dimension of rationality itself, but — for both theology and the sciences — very specifically implies an accountability to human experience, and thus will imply a postfoundationalist fusion of hermeneutics and epistemology. Despite important differences in epistemological focus and experiential scope, theology and other modes of inquiry all seem to be shaped by the epistemic value of experiential accountability. I see this experiential accountability playing out as only a gradual difference between empirical adequacy for science, and experiential adequacy for theological reflection. The fact that the rich resources of human rationality are shared by, and significantly overlap in, scientific and theological rationality will also reveal a significant breakdown of the traditional modernist demarcation between scientific and nonscientific rationality. Scientific knowing will thus turn out to differ from other forms of human knowing, and therefore from theological knowing, only in degree and emphasis. In this sense one could say that theology and the various sciences all grapple with what we perceive as real aspects of our *experience*.

Experiential accountability in theology and the sciences will also reveal another unexpected epistemological overlap between theology and other modes of intellectual inquiry: we relate to our world epistemically only through the mediation of interpreted experience. In theology this will be the final and decisive move beyond fideist strategies that claim theology's "internal logic" or self-authenticating notions of divine revelation as a basis for disciplinary integrity. This postfoundationalist move, moreover, should also enable us to transcend the kind of dualism that sets up naturalism against supernaturalism and then demands a reductionist choice between the two. In possibly the most crucial step beyond universalist and generic notions of rationality we will also discover that, as rational agents situated in the rich, narratival texture of our social practices, our self-awareness and our self-conceptions are not only intrinsically related to rationality, but are indeed indispensable starting points for any account of the values that shape human rationality. If the experiential bases of our rational decisions and actions are highlighted in this way, then the patterns of our ongoing experience are going to emerge as decisive for the way we rationally cope with our world. And precisely because rationality is so person-relative and thus requires that we attune our beliefs, decisions, and actions to our own self-awareness, rationality will also require that we attune our beliefs, decisions, and actions to the overall pattern of our experience. A postfoundationalist model of rationality is therefore accomplished when we find a careful balance between, on the one hand, the way our beliefs are anchored in interpreted experience, and, on the other hand, the broader networks of beliefs in which our rationally compelling experiences are already embedded.

In *Chapter Five* I will finally argue that, in a pluralist and cross-disciplinary dialogue, we begin our conversations by bringing our personal views and what we regard as our responsible judgments to those that make up our epistemic communities. The epistemic movement in a postfoundationalist evaluation of opinions and viewpoints therefore goes from individual judgment to expert evaluation to intersubjective conversation. Because each judgment always takes place in a community, and each community has a particular history, the broader research tradition(s) in which communities are embedded will now epistemically shape, but not completely determine, the questions one asks, the assumptions one makes, and the arguments one finds persuasive. What is epistemically relevant for us therefore finally depends on how we go about experiencing our world, and how we interact with what we presuppose as real in our experience. The many aspects of this experience will understandably lead to the problem of cognitive pluralism. But the only way to deal with this issue is to forge ahead through this pluralism, take it absolutely seriously, and instead of a nostalgia for modernist metanarratives, to rediscover rationality as alive and well in the many and varied domains of our discourses, practices, communities, art, sciences, religion, and also in our theological reflection. The refigured notion of rationality that I am arguing for will now emerge as a constructive response against any modernist attempts that would first want to carve out the different cultural domains of science, morality, art, and religion, and then afterwards search for some unifying perspective between them.

The main theme running through the entire book centers, therefore, on the broader, richer notion of human rationality which is revealed in the quest for the values that shape rationality in theology and the sciences. A postfoundationalist notion of rationality opens up the possibility for dialogue across disciplinary boundaries. And since rationality is always first of all person- and domain-specific, it heightens our understanding of the uniqueness of each of our discourses while at the same time enabling us to reach beyond the boundaries of our disciplines in cross-disciplinary dialogue. The hazy intersection between the diverse fields of theology and the sciences is therefore not in the first place to be determined by exploring possible methodological parallels or degrees of consonance. What should be explored first is the shared epistemic resources found in a richer notion of human rationality.

Chapter One

Rationality and the Postmodern Challenge in Science

"These are trying times for truth seekers."

John Horgan,
*The End of Science. Facing the Limits
of Knowledge in the Twilight of the Scientific Age*
(Reading, MA: Addison-Wesley, 1996:5)

It is common knowledge today, and widely accepted, that we have inherited from modernity a possibly overemphasized but still burdensome dilemma in which "science" has long emerged triumphantly as a superior form of rational thinking, and "religion" has faded into a rather privatized form of subjective, if not irrational, experience. The ramifications of this modernist heritage have been all-consuming, and certainly devastating for religion: the division between science and religion (and theology, as a reflection on religious experience) has led to sharp distinctions between objective descriptions and subjective experiences, between scientific and symbolic uses of language, between scientific truth and religious opinion, and finally to an all-consuming worldview in which science is taken to be more enduringly true than religion precisely because it is empirically based on observation and

17

repeatable experimentation. As a result science, in many ways, has therefore become a test case for rationality: if rationality cannot survive here, it will survive nowhere (cf. Trigg 1993:11). Over against this view where science, as the paradigm of rationality, is seen to progress through time, accumulating knowledge and even aspiring to a complete account of all that is genuinely knowable, religion was often forced to retreat to symbol and art as expressions of personal and communal experience. In this way religion — and theological reflection — would still create communities of shared symbols and practices through which the meanings and aspirations of our lives could be expressed, but one thing remained certain: religion, and reflections on religious experience, did not yield any "knowledge" (cf. Bowker 1998:115).

With this situation in mind, Fraser Watts has correctly argued that the resulting image of an enduring "conflict" between science and religion has indeed been the received wisdom in the ongoing reflection on the nature of the relationship between religion and science (cf. Watts 1998:1ff.). This conflict image was extended to include troubling conflicts on philosophical, historical, and some quite substantive content issues, about which scientists and theologians would continue to differ sharply. Theologians and believing scientists to this day try to resolve these differences through well-known attempts to construct wide-ranging typologies that have now creatively emerged to give "names" to the kind of relationship one might want to see between these two dominant, conflicting forces in our culture. The ongoing conversation about the relationship between religion and science is also, however, revealing some important new nuances in this age-old relationship: it has become increasingly clear that, contrary to popular misconceptions, the dialogue between theology and the sciences rarely is about conflict and dissensus only. Furthermore, the idea that science and religion have always been in conflict, is increasingly seen as an invention of the late nineteenth century, while at the same time scholars in this field are realizing that the truth about the historical relationship between theology/religion and science has always been much more complex (cf. Gregersen and van Huyssteen 1998:1ff.; Watts 1998:2f.). Moreover, for many participants in this discussion the whole idea of a "conflict" has become somewhat of a moot issue once one realizes how really different the questions are that science and religion are answering: science and religion are indeed giving different answers to different questions, rather than different and conflicting answers to the same questions (cf. Watts 1998:2).

Clearly important shifts in this troubled but exciting relationship are occurring when Fraser Watts can go on to claim "that both science and religion are rational in their somewhat different ways and that there can be mutual respect between them" (cf. Watts 1998:2). For Watts the task now is to find a place for religion and theological reflection "within the broad family of rationalities" after coming face to face with the fact that there is no single scientific method anymore, no sharp dividing line between the natural sciences and other forms of inquiry (1998:5). This is a strong statement, and we are warranted to ask what it is about our culture that is causing us to ask "new questions" about some very "old problems." It is from this strong and provocative claim that I want to take my cue and ask what it is about the current state of affairs in "theology and science" that now forces us back to the problem of rationality. As we will see, part of our current state of affairs certainly is the enduring attempt to maintain science's alleged priority as the paradigmatic way of establishing true knowledge. Our contemporary culture, however, has also been radically redefined by a new, all-pervasive mood that we have come to know as *postmodernity.* As we will soon see, the confusing co-presence in our intellectual culture of both superior notions of natural scientific rationality and pluralist, postmodern views that radically reject all notions of neutrality and universality, will emerge as the most defining challenge to anyone trying to come to terms with the values that shape the rationality of theological and scientific reflection today.

In a recent and provocative paper, this radical contemporary revisioning of the theology and science question is anticipated in an intriguing way when John Bowker asks: What would happen if we look at the relationship between science and religion in an entirely different way? Bowker then proceeds to argue that this relationship looks entirely different when one realizes that the really persistent issue between religion and science is not so much one of *propositions,* but one of *power* (cf. 1998:116f.). Although he never identifies this important shift as a *postmodern* one, we will soon see what some of the ramifications of this epistemic shift might imply for reflecting on a possible interdisciplinary relationship between theology and science. For John Bowker the real challenge of science to religion and theology is not so much a conflicting of competing propositions and worldviews, but much rather a ruthless challenge to the independence of religion's own authority. In doing this, science takes over areas where religion traditionally has its authority and control. Against the background of this argument Mary Hesse has recently also critically asked whether science is the "new religion" (cf. 1998:120ff.). By asking this question Hesse too wants to alert us that issues of power and authority are indeed crucial as we try to rescue the fact that religious faith may have an essential function in human life, a function that cannot be allowed to be taken over by the ever-increasing power of scientism. The power of science today is certainly inherent in the technology without which society would collapse. But the focus of the power of science certainly is found in its claims to *rational authority* (cf. Hesse 1998:122), and is vividly present in the often spectacular metaphysical claims of contemporary cosmology and evolutionary biology (cf. van Huyssteen 1998a).

The challenge to the intellectual integrity of theological reflection in our time is indeed serious. A theology that takes seriously, first, its embeddedness in the life of faith, and, second, its responsibility of publicly relating that faith to the important and challenging claims of science, will first of all avoid strategies of irrationality where the rationality of theological reflection is either sacrificed to the rational authority of science or protected from interdisciplinary conversation by withdrawing to the private world of fideism. At the heart of the challenge to the interdisciplinary identity, the intellectual integrity, and thus the rationality of theology as a credible form of human reflection, we therefore again discover the problem of the relation of theology to the sciences, which in its own very special way will redefine the problem of how the Christian faith relates to contemporary postmodern culture. Behind this problem, however, is hidden the even more complex issue of how the epistemic and nonepistemic values that shape the rationality of religion and of theological reflection will be different from, or similar to, those that shape the rationality of science. As will become clear, the challenge of a postmodernist pluralism, of course, makes it extremely difficult to speak so generally about "rationality," "theology," "science," or even of a "dialogue" between "theology" and "science." And yet, even if we were to acknowledge the possibility of radically separate or different forms of rationality (which is, as will become clear later, highly problematical and therefore unlikely), the crucial question will still remain whether the rationality of science is in any significant way superior to, or normative for, other forms of rationality.

The contemporary postmodern challenge not only makes it impossible, however, to speak so generally about "rationality," "science," "religion," or "God": it is finally *the idea of rationality itself,* and particularly rationality as it figures in the philosophical discourse of modernity, that has been challenged and problematized by postmodernist thought. As we will see, however, it is also possible to argue that most of contemporary postmodernism has actually been unable to come to terms with the issue of rationality from a more positive, constructive point of view (cf. Schrag 1992:155). As a result the issue of rationality and the values that shape human rationality appear to have become some of the most elusive of all the ingredients that make up our contemporary intellectual and social lives (cf. Schrag 1989:84).

Rationality and the Postmodern Challenge

Modern thought has left those of us who are theologians, and who are concerned with the rationality of theological reflection and, consequently, with theology's interdisciplinary status, with little or no choice when it comes to finding a plausible starting point for our critical reflection. Whether we like it or not, we have all become part of modernity's pervasive "flight from authority" (cf. Stout 1981). In theological reflection today, "fleeing from authority" would also have tremendous epistemological ramifications for those theologians who are trying to map out some credible form of participation of theology in today's interdisciplinary dialogue. At the very least it implies — as we will soon see — liberating ourselves from all the different types of foundationalisms that we have come to associate with the broad spectrum of traditional, political, doctrinal, and even biblically inspired ideologies that used to be so helpful and readily available in attempts to justify and secure the truth of our varied and often conflicting theological claims. But for both theology and the sciences the postmodern challenge to rationality, however, will imply more than this: it implies a specific reaction to the narrow and troubling constraints of rationality within modernity.

Much has been written on modernity as a complex and heterogeneous phenomenon, and I will not explore it in detail here (cf.

21

Toulmin 1990). Robert C. Neville has argued eloquently that the beginnings of modernity, or the modern age, can be dated from the scientific, political, and literary revolutions of the sixteenth and seventeenth centuries, and that our popular sense of the "modern" normally refers to societies that have been transformed by industrial technology and the economic, educational, military, and communications systems that accompany industrialization. *Modernism* as a cultural movement, however, is a specific nineteenth- and twentieth-century movement in the arts, letters, and philosophy (Neville 1992:4). It is this much more focused sense of modernism that we often imply when we speak of "modernity," and when we indicate that which postmodernism is reacting against today. And it is this specific sense of modernism as a cultural movement that I will imply when I use the terms "modernism" or "modernity" alternatively in this text. Looking back, it is at least clear that modernity, in its response to premodernity, entered history as a progressive force promising to liberate humankind from ignorance and irrationality (cf. Rosenau 1992:5). To say this is of course already to understand the hugely and pervasively influential phenomenon of modernity in fairly minimalist terms as dynamic and progressive. But this minimum dimension already has a maximal significance: as a flight from authority, modernism certainly means the abandonment of guidance by the past, even the immediate past and its presupposed traditions (cf. Cahoone 1995:19). Closely aligned with this is modernity's plea for the rationality of the autonomous subject. To believe that there even is such a thing as "modernity," however, one would have to believe that there is/was a cluster of social phenomena of different kinds (intellectual, political, cultural, economic, technological, artistic) which is more or less coherent, exhibits common traits, and which can finally be seen as the cumulative product of an historical process called the "modern" era (cf. Cahoone 1995:9).

Understanding the complex era called modernism, and finding some form of identifiable common trait for that era, finally turns on the principle of subjectivity, which is seen as grounding the human subject as at once rational and free, and liberated from the fetters of authoritative tradition (cf. Schrag 1989:83). The rationality of modernity thus resides in a centered human subject, functioning as an epistemological foundation from which all justification of knowledge claims proceeds. The classical period of modernity, from Descartes though Kant and Hegel to Husserl, therefore portrayed a rather distinct and profound confidence in the claims of human reason. The subject-centered epistemological paradigm of modernity thus marked the modern age as not only an age of representational knowledge, but also as an age of individualism, rationalization, technical control, and secularization (cf. Schrag 1989:84f.). In this sense modernity not only characteristically represents the name for a comprehensive, meta-narrative strategy that describes the historical construction of the modern world, but even more fundamentally represents a widespread cultural understanding. This is perhaps most clearly exemplified in the phenomenon of secularization, so often cited as one of the most distinctive aspects of the modern. Secularization typically points to the decline of religious belief and practice. It also, however, exemplifies the separation of various realms of human life from religion and theology, and in a fearless polarization of the "true" knowledge yielded by a superior natural scientific rationality and the "mere" opinions yielded by subjective, religious beliefs, would ultimately lead to the intellectual marginalization of theological reflection, and the privatization of religious beliefs into (irrational) beliefs and commitments.

Closely related to this is another crucially important aspect of modernity: the development, on the one hand, of distinct domains of knowledge and practices whose disciplinary autonomy was ultimately institutionally recognized and protected, but which, on the other hand, at the same time were unified by a formal and universal notion of human rationality (cf. Rouse 1996:49). In a sense the domains of science, morality, art, and religion can certainly be seen as the most distinct cultural achievements of our species throughout its historical development. These cultural domains, however, also comprise those configurations of human experience that are generally referenced in the literature as the "culture-spheres" of modernity (cf. Schrag 1997:5). Of these different cultural spheres, it is especially science, morality, and art that have received particular attention in current literature: Jürgen Habermas, especially — as is well-known — has defined modernity as typified by this differentiation of culture into the spheres of science, morality, and art. David Tracy has recently criticized Habermas's relative lack of attention to religious thought and practice, which flows so directly from his rigorous division of the modern intellectual world into only three strictly autonomous

23

spheres, namely the scientific, ethical, and aesthetic (cf. Tracy 1992: 34f.). Calvin Schrag has also argued that what Habermas may have overlooked is precisely the contribution of *religion* as a legitimate fourth culture-sphere of modern thought (cf. Schrag 1997:6). This goes together closely with Habermas's definition of modernity, which highlights the splitting apart of the three domains of science, morality, and art. Habermas's project can certainly be seen as precisely that of solving the problem of the fragmented culture spheres with a doctrine of communicative rationality (cf. Habermas 1984; 1987). Postmodernists, of course, see this whole project of modernity as contrived, and reject any need to unify these culture spheres. In fact, the whole idea of unity, totality, identity, sameness, and consensus, is — as will soon become clear — radically rejected by postmodernity in all its various constructive and deconstructive forms. Instead, pluralism, heterogeneity, multiplicity, diversity, incommensurability, and dissensus became the chief interpretative categories of the postmodern mind (cf. Schrag 1997:8). In addition, the very notion of rationality, along with the project of epistemology, has been jettisoned by most postmodern thinkers. For all of these reasons modern culture and society is often seen as not only dynamic and progressive, but as a globally integrated environment held together by precisely the kind of intellectual and political metanarratives that postmodernity would rebel against (cf. Cahoone 1995:12). This would also explain why the rapid growth of science and technology and the correlated understanding of nature as an inert object of knowledge is seen today by many as effects of quintessentially modernist human practices.

In the recent history of philosophy of science, positivism most clearly exemplifies a typically modernist view of science (cf. van Huyssteen 1989). Like modernist movements in painting, music, architecture, and literature, the positivists' view of mathematics and science emphasized disciplinary purity, and the application of formal (scientific) rules and methods to the domain of that which is regarded as objective (cf. Rouse 1991a:145). The direct result of all of this for positivism was the crucial importance of scientific rationality and method, of unified science as objective knowledge, and of the primacy of mathematics and mathematical physics within the whole of culture. For the greater part of the twentieth century, philosophy of science has therefore operated with the following explicit assumptions: true to the modernist mold, philosophers of science just assumed that is possible to make rational reconstructions of what "the" scientific method consists of, and then to proceed to provide a unitary explanation of how science progresses (cf. Lötter 1997:4f.). "Science" was thus treated as a single intellectual enterprise with one reliable method for all its different disciplines and research programs. As we will see in the final chapter, this typically modernist search for a rigorous and unifying scheme for "science" has lately been revived in a rather startling way by sociobiologist E. O. Wilson. For Wilson this search for the unification of all knowledge already found its apex in the Enlightenment, where we saw best illustrated the "greatest enterprise of the mind," i.e., the attempted linkage of the sciences and the humanities. For Wilson the current (postmodern) fragmentation of knowledge and the resulting "chaos in philosophy" are not reflections of the real world but "artifacts of scholarship" (cf. 1998:8). The way out of this fragmentation, the key to unification, Wilson finds in *consilience*. The concept "consilience," he claims, through its rarity of use, has retained a precision that a concept like "coherence" does not have anymore. Consilience points to an integration, literally a "jumping together" of knowledge by the linking of facts and fact-based theory across disciplines to create a common groundwork of explanation (cf. 1998:8). Wilson's massive and reductionist scientism, however, shines through when he proceeds to argue that the only way to either establish this kind of unified knowledge by consilience would be in terms of methods developed in the natural sciences (1998:9).

Roger Trigg has eloquently argued that precisely the idea that science is the source of all explanation runs deep in the modern world: modernity and science certainly sit very happily together, and confidence in science as the arbiter and exemplar of human rationality indeed lies at the heart of the modern world (cf. Trigg 1993:25f.). Attempts at unifying our human knowledge on the basis of a narrow vision of an allegedly superior natural scientific rationality notwithstanding, it will soon become clear that it is not going to be possible anymore to so narrowly and rationalistically reconstruct what the scientific method and scientific progress consist of. As traditional disciplinary boundaries blur in contemporary interdisciplinary research, no philosopher of science can even begin to claim an adequate overview of the multitude of highly specialized scientific disciplines and research fields contained within just one domain of contemporary science, or to have an overview of the ever-increasing number of sciences. On the contrary, the postmodern challenge to contemporary notions of rationality has already exploded all easy attempts to unify human knowledge on natural scientific terms alone.

The modernist attempt at defining all knowledge in terms of the credibility of scientific knowledge has had further ramifications for interdisciplinary reflection. Much of modernist, twentieth-century philosophy of science also worked with the assumption that the rational reconstruction of scientific method and progress had to be based on the exemplary example of physics (cf. Lötter 1997:4). The superiority of the rationality of physics, however, is today challenged as strong hierarchical models of an interdisciplinary organization of the various sciences must make way for a more democratic acknowledgment that each field of research has its own group of experts, its specific body of knowledge, techniques, and methods appropriate to its particular field of investigation. The idea that physics could be presented as a paradigm case of empirical science has also led to the widely influential fact that in contemporary philosophy of science philosophically reconstructed models of science were generally accepted as normative for other disciplines too. This led to a kind of "physics envy" that is clearly demonstrated when not only other sciences but also the social and the human sciences would work from the assumption that to do proper scientific work one had to appropriate the rigorous standards that could help a discipline to be more "physics-like" (cf. Kline 1995:214). However, not only have postmodern philosophies of science now shattered the prestige and alleged unifying power of this kind of natural scientific rationality, but the emergence of new and richer notions of rationality are sensitizing us to broader definitions of (even scientific) rationality, and to the fact that the standards of what we accept as rational thought or behavior may, in very important ways, be radically domain- and person-dependent.

In highly reductionist views of scientific rationality the consistent focus would still, in typically modernist fashion, be on the human subject as a knowing entity and source of values. For this reason science could easily be seen to take the traditional place of theology in a new secularized culture, transforming and marginalizing theological reflection into privatized matters of individual belief and desire (cf. Rouse 1991a:147). Because of this kind of metanarrativical legitimation of modernity, science and technology — as paradigm examples of secularized domains of knowledge — would of course escape this kind of privatization. Indeed, positivism's classical program of unified science was both the technical consolidation and purification of the domain of objective knowledge, constituted by a formal, theoretical rationality, and the assertion of universal, internationalist, progressive values. Joseph Rouse puts it well: modernism celebrates both the epistemic autonomy of increasingly specialized domains of knowledge and social practice, and their unification by formal rules and procedures of reasoning and justification (cf. Rouse 1991a:148).

Modernist notions of a superior scientific rationality has in the meantime very much become part and parcel of the way in which we live our everyday lives. "Science" and "scientific" are frequently appealed to as a means of bestowing respectability on a subject, thus always implying connotations of reliability, utility, and rationality. In direct contrast, "religion" and "theology" for many in our culture have come to imply irrationality, ideological thinking, confusion, and even irrelevance. This has had serious consequences for theological thinking and takes many forms (cf. Murray 1999):

- science is generally seen as a truly modern form of knowing, while theology represents at most a premodern throwback;
- science is really useful, public, and reliable, whereas theology promotes the retreat into a private world of subjective faith and esoteric commitment;
- science is objective and value-free, whereas theology is fatally compromised by the highly personal values originating in personal commitment;
- science is open to various modes of justification or falsification, while theological reflection is by definition ideologically and dogmatically entrenched;
- science is based on empirical data and a methodology that assures objectivity, while theology focuses on spiritual and highly speculative matters and as such deals only in subjective meaning.

As we will see, these traditional stereotypes caricature both theology and the sciences and are certainly offensive to the way that rationality, as maybe the most unique and human of our mental skills, is present in all of our cultural domains and in our diverse (and often very different) modes of knowledge. Of course, the well-documented gradual collapse of positivism in the 1950s and 1960s introduced a whole new set of themes and problems to the philosophy of science. Post-positivist philosophy of science, prominently associated with the work of Paul Feyerabend, Thomas S. Kuhn, and Larry Laudan, very specifically emphasized antimodernist themes: dethroning the sciences from their cultural preeminence, recognizing the profound and pervasive influence of dogmatic or irrational belief, as well as the distinctive role of particularistic communities in scientific practice, and replacing formal rules, methods, and rational criticism with the language of religious conversion and unanalyzable holistic Gestalt switches (cf. van Huyssteen 1989:24-71; also Rouse 1991a:148). In a broader cultural context it would be precisely the end of metaphysics, the "death of God," the disappearance of the author, the crisis of reason, and the dissipation of all metanarratives that would mark the definite demise of the modern (cf. Byrne 1992:335).

The way that these challenging issues have now been phrased reveals much about the fact that we can never deal with the problem of modernity in isolation, but that we have in fact already moved on to the even more complex challenge of postmodern thought. For theological reflection this challenge seems to be especially harrowing. If, as we will see, one of the most distinguishing characteristics of the postmodern is a jettisoning of all attempts at the unification of knowledge, a rejection of metanarratives, and a crisis of continuity as the role of traditions are reevaluated, then the implications of this view for history and tradition would indeed present a radical challenge to a Christian faith that lives out of continuity with the event and person of Jesus Christ. For the problem of the shaping of rationality in theological reflection, this challenge to tradition, continuity, and commitment will eventually be distilled into one crucial question: In a context deeply affected by what many see as the fragmentation and rampant pluralism of postmodernity, would some form of intelligible, cross-disciplinary conversation between theology and the sciences be at all possible today? For the interdisciplinary dialogue between theology and the sciences this question obviously is of extreme importance. Several authors, however, have recently shown how notoriously difficult it has become to even begin to define what postmodernism might mean today (cf. Schrag 1992).

Gary L. Comstock has correctly argued that any attempt to successfully explain the term "postmodernism" can only be reached by initially contrasting it with modernism, and modernism — as we saw — reveals itself especially in the (foundationalist) belief that the rationality of science is superior to that of other domains and as such is the sole road to truth (cf. 1989:196). This kind of scientific knowledge, moreover, tries to legitimize itself by reference to various metanarratives: in epistemology it is the conviction or "story" that knowledge rests on a few unquestionably certain beliefs; in ethics it is the conviction that morality rests on unquestionable rational principles; in science itself it is the belief that scientific progress and true discoveries are the result of adhering to a universally accepted, value-free, and objective methodology. This not only implies that truth results from an adherence to objectivity, but also reveals the foundationalist assumption that all true knowledge rests on a few unquestionable beliefs. This typical epistemological model of modernity would thus provide a grand metanarrative for which its own foundationalist beliefs would be crucial. It would also prove to be irresistible to foundationalist theologies, even while it sets them apart and isolates them from the sciences. For many, of course, the shift from a modern to a postmodern culture, and the implied new understanding of the self and the world, is still in the making (cf. Rossouw 1993:984ff.). Most of us would agree, however, that the "postmodern phenomenon" eludes all clear conceptual definition. In a sense postmodernism is more of a cultural attitude and a point of view, and never a doctrinal platform that might lend itself to some kind of systematic survey. In this sense postmodernity then escapes any and all linear characterizations (cf. Schrag 1989:84). Difficulties in defining postmodernism are, furthermore, highlighted by the interdisciplinary ramifications of the problem: there is today, e.g., postmodern philosophy, postmodern art, postmodern architecture, postmodern literature, postmodern politics, postmodern science, postmodern philosophy of science, and finally postmodern theology.

In trying to come to terms with the shaping of rationality between modernity and postmodernity, efforts by some to "sharpen the fuzzy edges of the phenomenon" (cf. Schrag 1989:84) by giving it some form of philosophical expression have been very helpful, and we will appropriate critically some of these as the argument for cross-disciplinary dialogue between theology and the sciences unfolds. Nancey Murphy, for instance, has correctly pointed out that the move beyond modernity is always a move beyond epistemological foundationalism, the representational or referential view of language, and the typical individualism of modernity which takes the individual to be prior to the community. Beyond this typical conceptual space of modernity, postmodern thought for Murphy presents itself clearly in:

- a focus on holism in epistemology
- a focus on meaning as use in philosophy of language, and
- a focus on tradition and community in ethics (cf. Murphy and McClendon 1989:191ff.).

These typical traits of postmodernity, as identified by Murphy, are complemented and enhanced further by what Calvin O. Schrag has identified as the five interrelated marks of postmodernity:

- the decentering of the subject as epistemological foundation
- the recognition of the social and contextual resources of rationality
- the embeddedness of power and desire within the claims of reason
- the undecidability of meaning and the inscrutability of reference, and
- a celebration of radical historicism and pluralism (cf. Schrag 1989:84ff.).

Some of the more prominent ideas developed by postmodern thinkers include, of course, Jean-François Lyotard's now famous notion of an incredulity toward all metanarratives (Lyotard 1984:xxiv). Metanarratives function as overarching and totalizing explanations and as such legitimate what people do and how they justify their choices. Precisely these grand narratives that also purport to interpret history, Lyotard claims, have now been revealed as incredulous by postmodernity. Closely aligned with this is Jacques Derrida's idea of deconstruction and its signification of a postmodern way of reading texts. Closely associated with this style of reading texts is the idea that no authoritative interpretation of any text is possible, and that multiple readings of texts are not only possible, but also justified. The concept of text here also becomes metaphorically extended to include persons, events, and institutions (cf. Lötter 1994:153). The challenges postmodernism poses thus indeed seem endless: it rejects episte-mological assumptions, refutes methodological conventions, resists knowledge claims, and obscures all versions of truth. Because it espe-cially challenges authoritative notions of tradition and all global, all-encompassing worldviews, it actually succeeds in reducing move-ments as diverse as Marxism, Christianity, capitalism, liberal democ-racy, secular humanism, feminism, and modern science to the same order and fundamentally challenges them all as totalizing meta-narratives that anticipate all questions and provide predetermined an-swers (cf. Rosenau 1992:3ff.).

While it has become highly unlikely that anyone could ever demonstrate some final and generally accepted demarcation between modern and postmodern thought, it is the blurring of traditional boundaries and the seemingly *cross-disciplinary character* of much of constructive postmodern thought that will present the problem of ra-tionality in theology and science with the most intriguing challenge. Postmodernists consider conventional tight definitions of academic disciplines simply as remnants of modernity and question the possi-bility of rigid disciplinary boundaries between the natural sciences, so-cial sciences, humanities, art, and literature; between culture and life, fiction and theory, image and reality in nearly every field of human endeavor (cf. Rosenau 1992:6f.). It is, however, the reaction against the typical *epistemological* paradigm of modernity that has become possibly the most explicit feature of the postmodern attitude. With this, some of the most spectacular features of postmodernity are re-vealed as direct challenges to, and problematizations of, *rationality as such*. With this in mind, Calvin O. Schrag now follows Lyotard (1984:79) and convincingly argues for seeing the postmodern as not only a strong reaction against modernity, but rather as part of the modern, and the project of refiguring rationality as an exploration of rationality *between* modernity and postmodernity (cf. Schrag 1992:7). Without this to-and-fro movement between modern and postmodern thought, and without the relentless critical return to modernist as-sumptions, the postmodern challenge by itself would indeed only be a farewell to reason, a jettisoning of any drive for integration, a mere toleration of the incommensurable, a waging of war on totality, and an endless celebration of *différance,* plurality, and ambiguity.

Whatever notion of postmodernism we eventually opt for, all postmodern thinkers see the modernist quest for epistemic certainty, and the accompanying program of laying foundations for our knowledge, as a dream for the impossible, a contemporary version of the quest for the Holy Grail (cf. Schrag 1989:84). Postmodern thinkers from Foucault to Rorty have also coupled this deconstruction of the epistemological paradigm of modern philosophy with a marked recognition of the social and pragmatic resources of rationality. On this view human reason no longer issues from an isolated, epistemic consciousness, but unfolds in a variety of sociopolitical functions in a focused attention for the marginalized, that which is left out and those who are constructed as the other (cf. Rossouw 1993:902). Michel Foucault in particular, in his celebrated attack on a totalizing and hierarchical rationality, has made much of "regimes of knowledge" as forms of social practices that reflect — consciously or unconsciously — certain power relations within the existing social order (cf. van Huyssteen 1998b). For Foucault it is precisely *tradition,* and the progressivist perspective of uninterrupted continuity we project onto it, which preserves the power-relations that underlie all conventions and oppressions (cf. Foucault 1980:49). For Foucault power is the fundamental characteristic of human culture and tradition, and as such produces knowledge. But power and knowledge are so integrated with one another that there would be no point in dreaming of a time when knowledge will cease to depend on power: it is not possible for power to be exercised without knowledge; it is impossible for knowledge not to engender power (cf. Foucault 1980:52).

Later we will have to evaluate whether Foucault's view enables a distinction between legitimate and illegitimate uses of power, and whether his radical view of the discontinuities of tradition allows for some form of continuity at all. What is clear, however, is his sharp criticism of all thinking that uncritically situates itself in the context of a tradition (cf. Byrne 1992:335), and especially of all modernist notions of progress. In his own words: "I adopt the methodical precaution and the radical but unaggressive skepticism which makes it a principle not to regard the point in time where we are now standing as the outcome of a teleological progression which it would be one's business to reconstruct historically" (cf. Foucault 1980:49). This rupture of the modern epistemological paradigm would therefore highlight the play of power in the domain of reason, and have far-reaching consequences for "meaning" and "reference" as the two linchpins of modern epistemological thought. Against the backdrop of the pluralization of social practices that congeal into regimes of knowledge, meaning escapes the constraints of decidability and reference remains inscrutable (cf. Schrag 1989:35ff., 85f.; also Murphy and McClendon 1989). In Richard Rorty's neopragmatist version of postmodernism, the discourse of modernity is ruptured with the proclamation that we are at the end of philosophy. With this Rorty wants to move away from all foundationalist and epistemological reflection that yearns for a reconstruction of knowledge, and thus move from an epistemology where reality was supposedly pictured or mirrored via one's favorite representation, to a hermeneutics that would pragmatically aid us in living with plurality, change, and incommensurable discourse (cf. Rorty 1979:315-94).

It is now already clear why postmodernism's celebration of pluralism and radical historicism presents such a challenge to epistemology, and specifically to the problem of rationality as such. If this challenge is to be taken seriously at all, then the notion and the resources of rationality will have to be refigured and redescribed in a way that will enrich our rational communal and social practices, but also in a way that will hopefully avoid the nihilism and blatant relativism of what Schrag has called the "antireason postmodernists" (cf. Schrag 1989:86). But is there a way to talk about epistemology and rationality that would take very seriously the critical concerns of postmodernity without succumbing to its extremes? I believe there is, and this refigured notion of rationality is what I have called a *postfoundationalist rationality:* a model of rationality, as we will see, where a fusion of epistemological and hermeneutical concerns will enable a focused (though fallibilist) quest for intelligibility through the epistemic skills of responsible, critical judgment and discernment. This notion of rationality will be discovered as alive and well in all our domains of living, and also in modes of knowledge as diverse as theology and the sciences. There we will discover the richness of shared resources of rationality even as we carefully distinguish between the focus and interpretative scope of these very different domains of knowledge.

Postmodernism and Science

Several theologians have recently analyzed and commented on the ramifications of both constructive and deconstructive forms of postmodern critique for theological reflection and how postmodern themes have been either constructively appropriated in various forms of narrative, political, or liberation theology, or deconstructively developed into extreme forms of a/theologies (cf. Tilley 1995; Griffin, Beardslee, and Holland 1989; Murphy and McClendon 1989). Despite the current flood of philosophical texts on postmodernism, relatively few attempts have been made to measure the importance of postmodern ideas for science.[1] Of course, Lyotard's influential *The Postmodern Condition* (1984) focused on science and knowledge and reads like a postmodern philosophy-of-science text most of the time (cf. Lötter 1994:154). Lyotard distinguishes between narrative and scientific knowledge as two distinct species of discourse that can each fulfill legitimate functions (1984:29f.). He claims, however, that narratives provide a certain kind of knowledge that cannot be had in any other way. This narrative knowledge can also function as a legitimation for scientific knowledge instead of the "grand narratives" that previously were necessary to legitimate science in the modern world (Lyotard 1984:18ff.). Without this kind of narrative legitimation science would just presuppose its own epistemic validity, and proceed on prejudice (Lyotard 1984:29).

As we saw, the modernist view of science found its apex in the positivistic view of science: objective, true scientific knowledge is grounded in empirical facts which are uninterpreted, indubitable, and fixed in meaning; theories are derived from these facts by induction or deduction and are accepted or rejected solely on their ability to survive objective experimentation; finally, science progresses by the gradual accumulation of facts (cf. van Huyssteen 1989:3ff.; Jones 1994:3). *Postmodern science,* however, finds its best expression in postpositivist, historicist, and even post-Kuhnian philosophy of science, and has revealed the theory-ladenness of all data, the underdetermination of scientific theories by facts, and the shaping role of epistemic and nonepistemic value judgments in the scientific process. Postmodern philosophy of science also reveals the hermeneutical dimension of science to us by acknowledging that science itself is a cultural and social phenomenon (cf. Bernstein 1983:30ff.). As will become clear, this not only results in the cross-disciplinary breakdown of traditional boundaries between scientific rationality and other forms of rational inquiry,

---

1. For a brief discussion of issues in postmodern science, cf. my *Duet or Duel? Theology and Science in a Postmodern World* (1998a).

but also in the inevitable move from being objective spectators to being participants or agents in the very activities that were initially thought to be observed objectively. Stephen Toulmin puts it succinctly: all postmodern science must start by reinserting humanity back into nature, and then integrate our understanding of humanity and nature with practice in view (cf. Toulmin 1985:210, 237f., 257). Epistemologically this is what ultimately is recognized as *the turn from foundationalism to holism,* and also as the move away from a modernist notion of individualism to the indispensable role of the community in postmodern thought. In Nancey Murphy's terms: it is the community of scientists that decides when to take anomalous facts seriously; it is the community — and not merely a tyrannical majority — that must decide when to make changes in the accepted web of beliefs (cf. Murphy and McClendon 1989:201, 205). In Murphy's brand of postmodernism the conventions, the language games, in which one participates precede individual speech and in fact determine what can and cannot be said by individuals in that community. In this context both language and the search for knowledge, therefore, are practices, and as communal achievements, dependent directly on tradition (Murphy and McClendon 1989:205).

Philosophical theologians who are engaged in dialogue, not only with other religions but also with the sciences, will find the postmodernist rejection of grand, legitimizing metanarratives and the acceptance of pluralism formidable challenges for the theology and science dialogue. A crucial and increasingly controversial theme throughout the development of twentieth-century philosophy of science has therefore been precisely the justification for interpreting the history of science in terms of a modernist story of progress or rational development (cf. Rouse 1991b:610). Postmodern philosophy of science challenges the ubiquitous notion of progress in science as an imposed metanarrative, and combines with this challenge a new respect for the local context of inquiry and a resistance to any global interpretation of science that could constrain local inquiry. As such it refuses any overall pictures or grand narratives that would want to explain science as the kind of modernist, unified endeavor with an underlying essence that we discussed earlier, and makes sense of the everyday praxis of science by seeing it as unfolding within a set of narrative enterprises that will give scientific endeavor its focused, local intelligibility (cf. Lötter 1994:160). At the same time, of course, it also raises serious political issues by sharply focusing on the role of power and knowledge in science, and on the pervasive autonomy and cultural authority of the sciences that was so much part of the modernist worldview.

The concern to uphold the political autonomy and cultural authority of successful scientific practice is, of course, part of the modernist legacy of logical positivism, which had always claimed — as we saw — the epistemic and cultural primacy of mathematical physics by asserting that mathematics exemplifies the very structure of rational thought, and that our sense experience can be the only basis for knowledge of the world (cf. van Huyssteen 1989:3-10; also Rouse 1991b:613). Postmodern philosophy of science, on the other hand, realizes that science must be understood as a historically dynamic process in which there are conflicting and competing paradigm theories, research programs, and research traditions (cf. Bernstein 1983:171ff.). This important fact reveals that the reasons, arguments, and value judgments employed by the community of scientists are also fundamentally related to or "grounded" in social practices. The very criteria and norms that guide and define scientific activity thus become open and vulnerable to criticism, as does the idea of philosophy of science itself. Postmodern science in this mode therefore rejects any attempts at legitimating science by means of allegedly superior metanarratives based on its own history of objective success and progress, and urges scientists rather to locally resolve philosophical issues pertinent to their own work. At first blush it therefore seems obvious that what postmodern philosophy of science is willing to sacrifice in the name of postmodern pluralism is precisely those tenets of scientific research that have come to be accepted as defining the very nature of science, namely the *objectivity* of science and the *reality* of the empirical world that science is supposed to gain a deeper understanding about.

A now celebrated case that succeeded in bringing postmodern science to our doorsteps via the front page of *The New York Times* (cf. Scott 1996:A1, 22) was the publication of Alan Sokal's hoax article "Transgressing the Boundaries: Toward a Transformative Hermeneutics of Quantum Gravity" in 1996. Alan Sokal, controversial New York University physicist, fed up with what he saw as the excesses of the academic left, tricked the social science journal *Social Text* into publishing a paper, written as a parody on postmodern science, as a serious scholarly work (cf. Sokal 1996a:217-52). In this paper Sokal pretends to join the ranks of those postmodern scientists whom he typically, albeit naively, sees as epistemic relativists and antirealists. In this hoax he pretends to show how apparent it has become that physical reality, no less than social reality, is at bottom a social and linguistic construct and that scientific knowledge, far from ever being objective, reflects and encodes the dominant ideologies and power relations of the culture that produces it (cf. Scott 1996:22). At the same time, however, professor Sokal succeeded in publishing another article, this time in the journal *Lingua Franca*. In this article he cheerfully reveals that the *Social Text* article was written as a satirical hoax in which he wanted to expose the hollowness of postmodernism as it "sacrifices" objectivity and reality (cf. Sokal 1996a:22), two of the most crucially important tenets of natural scientific knowledge. This philosophically rather naive view of postmodern science was publicly and eerily echoed just a few weeks later when — again in *The New York Times* — John Horgan wrote that, like a mutant virus, postmodernism has infected not only philosophy and the social sciences but even such alleged bastions of truth and objectivity as physics and chemistry. Horgan then takes up an earlier theme from his own writing (cf. Horgan 1996a) and goes on to label postmodern science as "ironic science" (ironic in the sense that science *too* has now been set free from the "tyranny of truth" and is revealed to have multiple meanings, none of which is definite. Horgan includes in this category contemporary chaos theory, superstring theory, and quantum theory, which unlike conventional science — which gives us "truth" — allegedly function to keep us in awe, and to induce wonder for the many mysteries that conventional science has left unsolved (cf. Horgan 1996b).

While some of us may want to salute the fact that postmodernism in science, along with the problem of interdisciplinary dialogue, has now apparently made it into the media, it is still true that these popular versions of postmodernism remain fundamentally misguided and serve to confuse the issue of postmodernism in science, especially what the postmodern challenge to the science and theology dialogue may entail. To understand, therefore, what a postmodern perspective might mean for the complex interdisciplinary dialogue of which theology and science form a part, we will have to move beyond these rather naive stereotypes of rampant relativism, and the loss of all objectivity and reality. I will argue instead that a positive appropriation of constructive forms of postmodern critique in both theology and the sciences will reveal the resources of rationality shared by these two seemingly very different reasoning strategies. In this way, too, a truly postfoundationalist space for the interdisciplinary conversation between theology and science will open up.

At this point, however, it may be worthwhile to return to Alan Sokal and his developing views on postmodern science. In the wake of all the controversy surrounding his hoax article, Sokal has now collaborated with his Belgian colleague Jean Bricmont and recently published *Intellectual Impostures* (1998). In this book Sokal and Bricmont return to the now famous hoax and to what they see as postmodern philosophers' shocking abuse of science. Their special target remains famous French deconstructivist intellectuals such as Lacan, Kristeva, Irigaray, Baudrillard, and Deleuze, who are now unmasked as consistently and repeatedly abusing scientific concepts and terminology, an abuse that could have serious consequences for the very nature of science itself. The fact that deconstructive postmodernists are here accused of using scientific ideas out of context, and without the slightest justification extrapolating concepts from one field to another, makes for fascinating reading but falls outside the focus of my argument in this book for an interdisciplinary space where theology and the sciences could communicate in cross-disciplinary conversation. What is of direct importance, however, is Sokal and Bricmont's argument against postmodern relativism in science — an argument that now is made with much more integrity than in the original "hoax" publication.

Sokal and Bricmont now want to limit their discussion of postmodern issues in science to the problem of *epistemic* or *cognitive* relativism, and qualify this relativism as based on the idea that contemporary science is deep down nothing more that a "myth," a "narration," or a "social construction" (cf. 1998:x). This relativism, furthermore, designates any philosophy that claims that the truth or falsity of a statement is relative to an individual or a social group (cf. Sokal and Bricmont 1998:50). This eventually forms the heart of what Sokal and Bricmont see as "postmodernism": the explicit rejection of the rationalist tradition of the Enlightenment, theoretical discourses presented as science but disconnected from any empirical test, and a cognitive and cultural relativism that regards "science" as just one more story/narrative among many others (cf. 1998:1ff.). The authors are, furthermore, deeply worried that the well-known Kuhnian idea of the underdetermination of theory by evidence/data to the theory-ladenness of observation, although essentially correct, could be misconstrued to support radical relativism in science. What I see as the overall and very serious concern of this book, however, is the concern for the nature and integrity of science itself: indeed, if postmodern science was only about radical relativism, and if one then were to willingly accept extreme forms of epistemic relativism, there would be no reason to be upset by the misrepresentation of scientific ideas, since all they would represent would be just another "discourse" (cf. 1998:x). What Sokal and Bricmont want to communicate, then, is the *mystification,* the deliberately obscure language that here affects what natural science really is about. And in uncovering this abuse of science, they see themselves as defending the canons of scientific rationality, and of the kind of intellectual honesty that should be common to all scholarly disciplines.

In a distinctly more nuanced and higher-level view than the original hoax article and the direct follow-up discussion, Sokal and Bricmont approach the practice of science by linking the rationality of scientific thinking and practice to other domains of human knowledge, and even to the rationality of everyday life. The basis for this argument is found in the thesis that the scientific method is not radically different from the rational attitude in everyday life or in other domains of human knowing. It is worthwhile to quote at length here:

> Historians, detectives and plumbers — indeed, all human beings — use the same basic methods of induction, deduction and assessment of evidence as do physicists or biochemists. Modern science tries to carry out these operations in a more careful and systematic way, by using controls and statistical tests, insisting on replication, and so forth. Moreover, scientific measurements are often much more precise than everyday observations; they allow us to discover hitherto unknown phenomena; and they often conflict with "common sense." But the conflict is at the level of conclusions, not the basic approach. (cf. 1998:54)

What seems to be emerging here is the idea that scientific rationality, although not a unique and superior form of rationality, certainly emerges as in "methodological continuity" with other forms of knowledge, especially everyday knowledge, but at the same time seems to achieve a clarity that might reveal it as one of the most exemplary forms of human rationality around. Whether this is a viable idea or not, we will return to it later. At this point it is significant that Sokal and Bricmont back away from contentious realist or instrumentalist interpretations of scientific theories, and in opposition to "postmodern relativism in science," propose as the main reason for believing scientific theories (at least the best-verified ones), *that they explain the coherence of our experience* (cf. 1998:55) — a statement that will be, as we will see later, in complete consonance with what *constructive* forms of postmodern philosophy of science are claiming, and with the fact that scientific forms of explanation may differ from other forms of explanation only by degree. With this strong statement Sokal and Bricmont reveal their position as already decisively critical of modernist, superior natural scientific claims to rationality. And their claim, furthermore, that "rationality is always an adaptation to a new situation" (cf. 1998:56) shows that some of the crucial tenets of a postmodern philosophy of science may already be at work in the position they are taking here — something that unfortunately is scarcely acknowledged, due to the ongoing identification of postmodern science with extreme forms of epistemic relativism.

In fact, Sokal and Bricmont are at their most "postmodern" when they proceed to argue openly for a scientific praxis that is local and often highly contextual. What is rigorously argued here is that the absence of any "absolutist," context-independent criteria for scientific rationality precisely implies that there can be no general justification, for instance, for the principle of induction: some inductions are justified and others are not; or, to be more precise, some inductions are more reasonable and others are less so. In science too, everything may depend on context, on locality, on the case at hand (cf. Sokal and Bricmont 1998:57). Toward the end of their book Sokal and Bricmont are, therefore, honest enough to admit that what they are criticizing in their protective argument for the integrity of science, are only extreme or radical versions of postmodernism (cf. 1998:174).

The fascinating emergence of postmodernism in the domains of science and philosophy of science may of course be said simply to reflect intellectual currents in the larger society, but even so it still presents a sharp rejection of the uncritical confidence in much of modern science, and especially the smugness about objective knowledge and progress. Postmodernists indeed sharply critique the uncritical acceptance of foundationalism, the Enlightenment heritage, and the methodological suppositions of modernist science (cf. Rosenau 1992:9). Although it is extremely difficult to try to fit postmodern ideas into some coherent conceptual scheme, as has already become clear, it is helpful to take note of an important distinction that has surfaced in at least some of the recent literature on postmodernism. When Calvin O. Schrag referred to "antireason postmodernists" (Schrag 1989:86), it already seemed to imply that some postmodernists, at least, may not be so eager to jettison rationality and epistemology. Zuzana Parusnikova similarly distinguishes *deconstructive* postmodernists from other more *constructive* postmodernists (1992:36; cf. also Neville 1992:4f.), an idea that is clearly developed by Pauline Marie Rosenau when she tentatively distinguishes two broad strands within the current postmodern debate: *affirmative* and *skeptical* postmodernism. Skeptical postmodernism is the dark and deconstructive side of postmodernism (cf. also Lötter 1994:55) and offers a pessimistic, negative, gloomy assessment by arguing that the postmodern age, in its complete break with modernity, is an age of fragmentation, discontinuity, disintegration, and meaninglessness, with a vagueness or even absence of moral parameters, a postmodernism of despair. Affirmative postmodernists, on the other hand, although they agree with skeptical postmodernists in their critique of modernity, have a more hopeful and optimistic view of the postmodern age. This kind of postmodernism is open to positive political action and the making of responsible normative choices, and it seeks an intellectual practice that is relentlessly critical, and therefore nondogmatic, nonideological, and tentative. Many affirmative or constructive postmodernists would also argue that some of our values and some of our epistemic choices could indeed be superior to others, and therefore warranted (cf. Rosenau 1992:16).

The postmodern challenge to the problem of rationality is further complicated by the fact that not all postmodernists agree on whether a postmodern philosophy of science is even possible at all. This obviously would have serious implications for the shaping of scientific rationality, and thus for any attempt to bring theological reflection into a meaningful interdisciplinary discussion with contemporary notions of scientific rationality. In a careful and intriguing analysis, Zuzana Parusnikova focuses on the difficult issue of trying to bring together an enigmatic phenomenon such as postmodernism with something as positive and concrete as science (1992:21-37). Parusnikova's question: "Is a postmodern philosophy of science possible?" is eventually answered with a tentative "no" (1992:36), and she reaches this negative conclusion by analyzing how a philosophy of science would look if developed along the lines of the two most important postmodern tendencies of our time. The first tendency is directly related to Lyotard's idea that our world is fragmented into a plurality of worlds constituted by local discourses that can no longer be unified by any grand metanarrative. Parusnikova engagingly relates how scientists that she talked to would respond quite positively to a popularized version of Lyotardian postmodernism: scientists often turn out to appreciate the anti-authoritarian and anti-dogmatic component inherent in postmodernism, identifying it with a rejection of any methodological normativism, of any constraints imposed by the rules and goals of their research. Postmodernism in this interpretation allows for unconventional approaches in doing science and for greater flexibility in various organizational and administrative arrangements concerning scientific life (cf. Parusnikova 1992:22).

Parusnikova is right in claiming that these views reflect some highly relevant features of postmodernism, namely the focus on imagination, and the rejection of any higher authority for the legitimation of the rules and goals of science. The same kind of anti-authoritarianism is claimed for science by Sokal and Bricmont (cf. 1998:178), an anti-authoritarianism that especially implies a rejection of any possibility of defending the universal validity of scientific discourse itself, and with that its alleged supremacy over other kinds of discourse. In a postmodern world, however, which has been fragmented into a collage of many isolated worlds that cannot be unified by any "grand" metanarrative, what is to become of science, philosophy, and any possible philosophy of science? From a postmodern attitude both science and philosophy of science are just two specific discourses among many others. Furthermore, from a postmodern view "science" as such does not exist anymore; instead there now exists a plurality of sciences playing their own games and generating their own local rules for what they do (cf. Parusnikova 1992:23). In this postmodern space where science displays its own diversity and plurality, there seems to be little room for the philosopher of science to initiate a metadiscourse for elucidating what is going on in science, or what the rationality of science should be about. In this postmodern pluralism of local discourses, postmodern philosophy of science can either attempt to develop as an ironical conversation about science, or becomes superfluous because a philosophy of science that appears to be merely parasitic on science might in any case best be carried out by the experts, viz., the scientists themselves (cf. Parusnikova 1992:37).

The second postmodern tendency that Parusnikova considers as relevant for science is the deconstructionist one, the poststructuralist idea of meaning as fundamentally elusive, slippery, and ungraspable, normally associated with Derrida, and other French theorists such as Barthes, Lacan, Kristeva, Deleuze, and Foucault (cf. Parusnikova 1992:31f.). The Lyotardian version of postmodernism tried to remove the problem of meaning from a universal to a local dimension. In a deconstructive postmodernism, however, it is already fundamentally impossible to make meaning present, regardless of the scope within which meaning is situated and analyzed. Deconstructive postmodernism thus turns out to be even more damaging to philosophy of science, since it could only lead to a literary deconstruction of scientific texts in which any authority of meaning would be destabilized (cf. Parusnikova 1992:37). Parusnikova thus presents us with a rather bleak vision for a postmodern reflection on scientific rationality: in both its Lyotardian and deconstructionist versions, postmodern philosophy of science would therefore dissolve into other activities performed by academics better equipped than philosophers (cf. Lötter 1994:154). Philosophers would here no longer provide any unique philosophical insight relevant to science.

Clearly, this could not be the last word on the rationality of science from a postmodern perspective. The possibility of at least some creative implications of a constructive postmodern view of science for the notion of rationality should again be carefully unpacked. It is to this task that we now turn.

Rationality and Science

A more positive appropriation of some of the far-reaching implications of postmodernism for scientific reflection is found in the recent work of Joseph Rouse (cf. 1987; 1990; 1991a; 1991b; 1996). In his rather compelling project for reconstructing the project of science beyond modernity, Rouse starts out by classifying most twentieth-century philosophers of science as still being quintessentially modernist and as such concerned mainly with some form of global legitimation of science (cf. 1991a:141f.). Because a truly postmodern philosophy of science — for Rouse at least — would have to completely break away from all modernist notions (cf. 1991a:161), even Kuhnian and post-Kuhnian philosophy of science is still seen here as exemplifying what he calls the "persistent narratives of modernity" (Rouse 1991a). In developing his own constructive vision of science as a dynamic social practice, Rouse takes up some of the most important themes of Lyotardian postmodernism and confidently moves beyond a narrow epistemologically conceived notion of theoretical scientific rationality. Crucial for this reconstructed postmodern view of science is, of course, the complete rejection of any global, or grand-narrative legitimation of the history of science as a history of rationality, progress, success, or of the search for truth. Rouse also very clearly warns, however, against the debunking of science in some of the more extreme reactions against modernist science, and then goes on to claim that any postmodernist legitimation of scientific practices and beliefs is always going to be local and partial, within specific contexts, and for specific purposes (cf. 1991a:161). Also the idea that there is a "natural world" for natural science to be about, entirely distinct from the ways human beings as knowers and agents interact with it, must similarly be abandoned. On this view scientists are recognized as situated agents with inescapably partial and local positions, and instead of thinking of the sciences as in some sense being "representations" of the world, we should look at the actions and practices they involve and to the way they transform specific situations for further action (cf. Rouse 1991a:162).

The purpose of Joseph Rouse's revisioning a constructive form of postmodern science is ultimately to develop a view of science that takes into account the power relations involved in the practice of science itself, and how these applications of power affect human life outside of the laboratory.[2] In doing this Rouse very consciously wants to break through typical modernist distinctions that oppose understanding to explanation, and hermeneutics to epistemology, and develops his own interpretation of science as *practical hermeneutics*. Ultimately, and importantly, this understanding of science also will lead to a blurred distinction between the natural and the human sciences, since

2. I am grateful to Ginny Landgraf for valuable issues raised in our discussion of Rouse's work.

44

the same kind of interpretative procedures is at work in all our varied, and often widely divergent, reasoning strategies (cf. Rouse 1987:5). This will also mean that the natural sciences cannot be compartmentalized and elevated to a "higher," more objective and value-free level as if there is always something at stake politically and culturally in the human sciences, but never in the natural sciences. Rouse thus opens the door for a revisioned look at a more holistic form of interdisciplinary reflection, and wants to show why we must regard the natural sciences as fundamental to our human self-understanding, and also to what is at issue politically in our lives (cf. 1987:xiv).

For the interdisciplinary dialogue between theology and the sciences Rouse's rejection of traditional, modernist distinctions between (empirical) natural science and (interpretive) human science will have important ramifications. It will also help us to directly challenge all modernist notions that oppose objective, empirical science to subjective, irrational religious faith, and to theology as a privatized reflection on this experience of faith. This well-known polarization between science and religion is also (epistemologically, at least) deeply embedded in what, on a modernist view, is normally seen as typical differences between the natural and the human sciences. To fully grasp this widely accepted and almost hermetic distinction between our different domains of knowledge, it is helpful to first consider Rouse's list of what these alleged differences (cf. Rouse 1987:45ff.) between the natural sciences and the human sciences are normally considered to be:

1. On a modernist view the natural sciences are seen to work with data that either are given identically to all observers, or, in more sophisticated accounts, have conventional interpretations that normally are not disputed. Moreover, over against the way in which scientific data are objectively determinable by empirical testing, the human sciences have no indisputable data. They deal with meaningful objects and situations, whose interpretation is always potentially open to challenge based on the interests, situations, or prior beliefs of different interpreters.

2. Theories in the natural sciences are explanatory constructs from which observation statements are deducible. The human sciences do not produce these kinds of explanatory theories but rather interpretative redescriptions of the data. As such they do

45

not strive for explanation, but only for clearer, more coherent understanding.

3. The human sciences cannot avoid using the ordinary, everyday language within which objects are constituted, complete with all its ambiguities and connotations. Natural scientific language, however, is highly theoretical, and can in principle be formulated as a formal, uninterpreted calculus whose elements could then acquire univocal meaning.

4. Natural scientific theories are either confirmed or falsified by data that can be identified and described without reference to theory. In the human sciences, "data" are manifested only within an ongoing process of interpretation. The natural sciences thus leave their data as they are, while the human sciences continually reinterpret and remake theirs.

5. The natural sciences aim to eliminate anthropocentric references and connotations that may obscure the objectivity of their concepts, whereas the human sciences inevitably refer to the interests, goals, beliefs, and feelings of their practitioners.

6. The objects of the natural sciences are significant only in terms of their use for universally valid knowledge. The human sciences do not avoid generality, but in their concern for the particular event, the individual life, the local situation or culture, they also typically aim for local knowledge.

7. The natural scientist is in principle normally seen to be anonymous: whoever makes a specific claim within a specific research program really is irrelevant for its validity or justification. The human sciences, however, always bear distinct marks of their authorship, however implicitly. In fact, the experiences, cultural background, interest, and purposes of the scientist guide and even help to justify specific interpretations.

These alleged "standard" differences between the natural and the human sciences again and clearly reveal why natural scientific rationality, on a modernist view, is normally seen to be such a superior form of human rationality. On this classically modernist view the human sciences are firmly embedded in and continuous with the practices and concerns of everyday life, while the natural sciences mark a very distinct theoretical, reflective break with these same concerns and practices. Rouse is, of course, correct in arguing that these alleged distinctions between the natural and human sciences clearly presuppose a now largely discredited empiricist account of the natural sciences: post-empiricist philosophies of science today in many ways more resemble the epistemology of interpretative human science than of their own empiricist predecessors (cf. Rouse 1987:47). Exactly this point will later enable me to argue that, whether in the natural sciences, the human sciences, or in theology as a reflection on religious experience, we relate to our world(s) only through interpreted experience. At the same time, however, all our knowledge, including direct experiential knowledge, must be expressed in languages that always already embody theoretical presuppositions. What we interpret is the world we are embedded in, and which on an everyday level is taken to be a universe of objects and events that exists independent of what we do and say, but which at the same time is manifest to us only through our previously understood beliefs and values. It is clear that on such an account there is going to be no significant epistemological difference between the interpretations of the empirical world and interpretations of human beings and their practices and institutions; all of these belong in the same way to our theoretical networks of beliefs about the world, and both are shaped by our worldviews, by social practices of language use, and by the same epistemic and non-epistemic values that shape our behavior. What we have here in Rouse's argument is a position that already points toward a fusion of epistemological and hermeneutical concerns that will transcend the traditional modernist distinction between the domains of the natural sciences and the human sciences. There will certainly still be important differences between the natural world and the social world as we understand them. But these would be empirical differences that are established by our theories and by the way we interrelate to the world of our experience, and not some kind of transcendental difference between two different kinds of knowledge about two different kinds of objects (cf. Rouse 1987:57f.).

For Rouse the recognition of this kind of embeddedness of all our knowledge, also our natural scientific knowledge, is a distinct non-foundationalist move beyond any appeal to grand metanarratives that should enable philosophy of science to finally move beyond the rigid structures of modernity. This does not mean, however, that it gets us beyond the telling of stories and the recognition of interpretative patterns, which can now be revealed to play an important role in science too. There is indeed no possibility of occupying a meta-standpoint from which to interpret science; all our interpretations of science imply a move within the contested terrain of scientific practice, i.e., the local contexts within which scientists themselves operate. Rouse then goes on to argue for a narrative reconstruction of science by taking up another Lyotardian idea, namely the importance of narratives in everyday life (cf. Lötter 1994:157). In an important article, "The Narrative Reconstruction of Science" (1990), Rouse develops this further by arguing for the epistemic significance of narrative, and by explaining why narrative is important in natural scientific knowledge. To grasp this fully, we must understand narrative here not as a literary form into which knowledge is written, but as the temporal organization of the understanding of practical activity, i.e., as a way of comprehending the temporality and locatedness of one's own actions in their very enactment. Scientific research on this view clearly is an ongoing social practice through which researchers structure the narrative context in which past work is interpreted and significant possibilities for future work are projected. For Rouse this narrative field of science displays a constant tension between a need for a coherent, shared understanding of the field, and the incoherence threatened by divergent projects and interpretations (cf. Rouse 1990:179). In this sense scientists of various stripes make sense of their practice by understanding it first as a response to situations and emerging traditions presented by past research, and then also as a quite specific narrative anticipation of future developments.

Rouse's understanding of the praxis of science is therefore thoroughly postmodern: this narrative reconstruction of science as action does not need the modernist global legitimation, since scientists in their everyday work do not need philosophical explications of the epistemic and ontological standing of scientific research. The reason for this is found in the fact that most scientists have a strong developing sense of what counts as adequate explanations, of when a claim is well confirmed, even if interpretations of these concepts are local rather than general (1990:193). In this narrative reconstruction of science Rouse shows that any attempt to impose a grand narrative scheme on science should be rejected, since even in science we all live within various ongoing stories embedded in our local contexts. In the narratives of science there are multiple authors engaged in an ongoing struggle to determine the configuration of the narrative within which they are situated. In fact, scientists compete with one another to influence the direction of research in their field and to create an important place for their results in the unfolding narratives of their field.

For Rouse all of this leads to one important conclusion: the intelligibility, significance, and justification of scientific knowledge stem from the fact that it already belongs to continually reconstructed narrative contexts supplied by the ongoing social practices and developing traditions of scientific research (cf. 1990:181). Scientific knowledge on this view clearly and fundamentally is an important form of *local* knowledge: through experimentation scientists artificially create "microworlds" in their laboratories which enable them to isolate, manipulate, and monitor phenomena, and construct theories with which to reciprocally interpret these microworlds (cf. 1987:99-106). Rouse also thinks that the belief that scientific knowledge is always nonlocal, objective, universal knowledge arises from its wide technological applicability and the universal dissemination of scientific research in scientific literature. Scientific knowledge, however, is always first of all local knowledge, and whatever universal applicability it may also have, arises not from some form of theoretical decontextualization that may be seen to be "typical" of scientific knowledge, but rather arises from a very conscious and sophisticated process of *standardization* (cf. Rouse 1987:113). This standardization of scientific knowledge is actually closer to the transformation of a tool originally designed for a highly specific task within a particular context, into a more general-purpose item of equipment.

I believe this "process of standardization" could be interpreted as Rouse's answer to views like those of E. O. Wilson, who recently protested against postmodernism in science by saying that the mathematical formulae of natural science cannot be given "Chinese or Ethiopian or Mayan nuances, or be interpreted in masculinist or feminist variations" (cf. Wilson 1998:49). For Rouse, on the contrary, the language of science, in fact scientific problems, results, procedures, and tools, become applicable and accessible outside of their original setting or local contexts, only through the kind of standardization found in the ongoing process of interdisciplinary and cross-contextual interpretation. Virtually every kind of scientific practice and achievement can in fact be standardized and can thereby circulate outside its original more specific context. After successfully collapsing the modernist distinction between natural and human sciences by a powerful fusion of epistemology and hermeneutics, Rouse now opens a door to cross-contextual conversation by his description of the extension of scientific knowledge outside the local laboratory as a "translation" of local practices to adapt to new local situations. The claim is not that scientific knowledge, as local knowledge, has no universality, but rather that what universality it has is an achievement always first of all rooted in local know-how. And in this sense the empirical character of scientific knowledge is the result of an irreducibly local construction of empirical reference rather than the discovery of abstract, universal laws that can be instantiated in any local situation (cf. 1987:119).

Rouse strengthens his position on postmodern science by also critically endorsing what Arthur Fine has called the *natural ontological attitude* (Fine 1984). This proposal by Fine is another example of a development of Lyotardian postmodernism, although Fine does not present his views as being explicitly postmodern (cf. Lötter 1994:156). In this postrealist proposal Fine, too, wants to develop a philosophy of science without any grand metanarratives that might be expected to justify scientific practices, and he does this by arguing for a "natural ontological attitude" as a "common sense epistemology" (cf. Fine 1984:98). What a natural ontological attitude would imply for philosophy of science is a move beyond all realist and instrumentalist attempts to make sense of science in a global or totalizing way. This does not mean that science has no broader meaning or even universal aims, but it does mean that such questions can only be asked *locally*, that is, what meaning or goals a specific investigation or research program may have in specific circumstances. Fine thus also rejects the idea that science, or scientific rationality, has an essence other than its contingent, historical existence which of course changes continually. The natural ontological attitude's rejection of global explanations and its choice to first follow scientific practice, now presents us with a minimal standard for contemporary philosophy of science (cf. Fine 1984:100). This minimalist stance, which shows just how minimal an adequate philosophy can be, thus implies a trusting attitude toward the overall good sense of science. It also implies, however, a trusting attitude in our own good sense in which scientific truths as well as everyday truths are accepted.

In Fine's — and Rouse's — revisioning of philosophy of science, "truth" will therefore function only in a pragmatic way and in local scientific contexts where scientists themselves negotiate their meaning for use in those specific contexts. This pragmatic trust in the local activity and traditions of actual scientific practices exemplifies the kind of practical hermeneutics that rejects the need for any "added" unifying philosophical interpretation or legitimation of science (the problem, for Fine, with both realist and antirealist interpretations of science). The "naturalness" of the natural ontological attitude is precisely the fact that we would do better to take scientific claims *on their own terms,* with no felt need for further interpretations, no further additives — a naturalness that Rouse, following Fine, has wittily called "California naturalism" (Rouse 1991b:611; cf. van Huyssteen 1997a: 274). Underlying Fine's California naturalism is the claim that science can do for itself what the various philosophical additives were supposed to do for it, namely, situate scientific practice within local, interpretative contexts. Fine's natural ontological attitude, then, is part of a generally trusting attitude toward local contexts of practice, and what the natural ontological attitude is asking us to trust are scientific narratives or *traditions,* where these are understood, not as an authoritative or prescriptive authority, but rather as a creative field of concerns within which both consensus and dissensus acquire a local intelligibility (Rouse 1991b:614; 1987:120). Scientific claims are thus established within a rhetorical space rather than a logical space, and scientific arguments settle for rational persuasion of peers instead of context-independent "truth."

Rouse escapes the radically contextualist and relativist implications of Fine's position on the local nature of scientific praxis precisely by his innovative grasp of the role of *standardization* in the natural sciences. In his strong argument for the local nature of scientific praxis, Rouse has vividly sketched the local domain of inquiry, especially the laboratory where scientists do their work, as a structure of expectations and surveillances, and science as a complex of practical activities rather than a mere form of clinical and empirical observations (cf. Rouse 1987:108ff.). The implications of this shift point directly to the implicit recognition that — instead of seeing objectivity and truth as the hallmarks of scientific research — *power* is an issue that is alive in the forces that shape the rationality of science too. And power does not merely impinge on science and scientific knowledge from outside, but power relations permeate the most ordinary activities in the praxis of science. Scientific knowledge in this sense is never removed from "power issues" but actually arises out of these power relations.[3] In this sense, then, Rouse can affirm the Foucaultian maxim that knowledge is power and power is knowledge (cf. Rouse 1987:24). In this sense science is now revealed as a powerful force that shapes us as well as the world around us, and scientific laboratories as places where scientists make things happen rather than just observing what goes on around them (cf. 1987:102). And if scientists are practitioners rather than observers (1987:38), and therefore socialized into their skills, scientific rationality too emerges here as a context-bound skill.

At this point it may be useful to evaluate some of the outlines of Rouse's postmodern philosophy of science in order to eventually bring it into the broader discussion of the shaping of rationality in theology and science. In two recent articles Hennie Lötter presents us with a clear and helpful analysis of some of the Lyotardian postmodern themes in Joseph Rouse's work by looking critically at Rouse's use of narratives, his critical endorsement of Arthur Fine's philosophy of science, his sharp distinction between modern and postmodern, and finally the role he assigns to philosophers of science (cf. Lötter 1994). Rouse certainly manages to move beyond Parusnikova's negative assessment of the possibility for a postmodern philosophy of science, which we discussed earlier. His use of the idea of narratives and tradition for providing a deeper understanding of science is clearly successful: it provides us with insight into the way scientists judge the significance of any new scientific work, while reevaluating previous work. It also deepens our understanding of the fierce competition among scientists for getting their results accepted (cf. Lötter 1994:63). Rouse's endorsement of Fine's philosophy of science also helps him to describe science as having no overall aim, no typical or exclusive rationality, and no general theory of truth. Scientists are furthermore urged to answer their own conceptual questions, while philosophers are cautioned to resist interpreting science through their own philosophical categories or theories.

3. I am grateful to Gregor Etzelmüller for an excellent example on exactly this important point: Joseph Rouse's *Knowledge and Power* was originally published in 1987; ten years later the successful cloning of Dolly the sheep has now made abundantly clear how important it is (especially for an understanding of scientific rationality) to draw our attention to the scientific laboratory as a place of constructive power where scientists make things happen with enormous and controversial consequences.

Rouse's assumptions about postmodernism itself, however, shine through in all his work. As such it eventually creates some problems for refiguring our notion of rationality, and for identifying what the ramifications of interdisciplinary reflection in a postfoundationalist context might be. In trying to move toward a plausible notion of postmodern scientific rationality, Rouse assumes, most importantly, but ultimately inconsistently, a complete break between modernity and postmodernity (1991a), and ends up with articulating a too rigid and narrow definition of postmodernism as a mindset or attitude that has to help us *overcome* and radically move beyond modernity. Lötter correctly finds that at this stage of the debate, with so much controversy on the characteristics of postmodernism, Rouse would have done better to rather recognize and acknowledge the positive value of various modern as well as postmodern characteristics, to see postmodernism as a critical reflection on the nature, potential, and shortcomings of modernity, and therefore place different philosophies of science on a continuum somewhere between being completely modern or, alternatively, completely postmodern (Lötter 1994:64). To this I would add that, without this kind of corrective critical suggestion, even a constructive postmodern philosophy of science would have a hard time taking the typical cross-disciplinary challenge of postmodernism seriously; precisely the local, narrative reconstruction of science as social practice could easily slide into an incommensurability of disparate and isolated language games, and a relativism of localized, disciplinary rationalities. Rouse avoided this by introducing his notion of *standardization,* which helped him to extend local scientific knowledge to other locations where sciences are being practiced. This certainly enabled him to avoid the epistemic sovereignty and the dominance of a culturally superior natural scientific rationality, which might so easily have led to science relentlessly policing its own epistemic boundaries (cf. Rouse 1996:241). It remains unclear, however, how exactly these kinds of postmodern science studies will now relate to the broader issue of interdisciplinary reflection, to such a seemingly distinct cultural domain as religion, and to theology as a reflection on religious experience.

In some of his latest work Rouse does seem to give us some important pointers to what the interdisciplinary ramifications might be of collapsing the stark modernist distinction between the natural and human sciences. He does this by introducing the phrase "cultural studies of science" (Rouse 1996:237f.), which as such again confirms the thoroughly hermeneutical dimensions of science as social practice, and its epistemic affinity to other forms of intellectual endeavor. On this view, "cultural studies of science" could therefore cut across some very important methodological, theoretical, and political differences between the different disciplines, and is actually an important acknowledgment that some of our most important scholarly work today takes place across the boundaries of different reasoning strategies. It also manages to situate the natural sciences within a heterogeneous body of scholarship in history, philosophy, sociology, anthropology, feminist theory, and literary criticism, in a context where disciplinary boundaries have become so much more fluid.

Rouse clearly is developing a very promising notion of postmodernist interdisciplinary reflection. And although he never refers to religion, philosophy of religion, or theology, his revisioning of science as "cultural studies of science" is very specifically concerned with the interface between science and culture, and with "the traffic between scientific inquiry and those cultural practices that philosophers of science have often regarded as 'external' to knowledge" (Rouse 1996:239). What this may imply philosophically for the shaping of rationality in various disciplines and different cultural domains, and what this tells us about the nature and resources of human rationality, is left unexplored. What has become clear, however, is that natural science can no longer claim epistemic autonomy in the interdisciplinary conversation; this notion of a revisioned cultural studies of science would reject out of hand the existence of an "essence" of science, or of a single essential aim to which all genuinely scientific work must aspire.

For an interdisciplinary conversation between theology and the sciences this again reveals how dangerously simplistic it will be to continue talking about "the" dialogue between "theology" and "science" today. Postmodernism has indeed radically pluralized each of these concepts. Moreover, the practices of scientific investigation, its norms, and its products are historically variant and also vary considerably across and within disciplines. Scientific work is also culturally variant even within the same field. Rouse points to the fact that there are even important national differences in the style, standards, and goals of scientific work (cf. Rouse 1996:243). But as we saw earlier, this does not mean that different scientific cultures are self-enclosed or mutually uncomprehending, or that individual scientists or groups cannot navigate their borders quite effectively. Nor does it mean that epistemically interesting differences in scientific cultures neatly map onto national, linguistic, or other cultural boundaries. For Rouse an insensitivity to this kind of heterogeneity of the sciences is exactly what was wrong with modernity's global legitimation of the rationality of science in terms of its success or progress.

This does leave us, once more, with the important question: How then could a *constructive* form of postmodern thought influence and shape our understanding of science, and how would this help us shape an interdisciplinary space for the dialogue between theology and the sciences? One plausible set of answers to this important question would read as follows (cf. Lötter 1994:65f.):

- postmodern thought makes us conscious of the metanarratives that are uncritically used to justify the cultural authority of the natural sciences in the Western world;
- instead of the attempted overall legitimation of science by metanarratives like rational development, success, or progress, postmodern thought suggests that scientists themselves give a localized, partial legitimation of their own scientific practices within specific contexts and for particular purposes;
- postmodern thought rejects any unified explanations of the "essential" nature of science: scientists themselves must reach a local consensus on the definition of their discipline or on the aims of their projects. Only then can the results of this reflection be standardized and translated to other contexts;
- postmodernists would encourage scientists to be aware not only of the diversity of science itself, but also of the diversity of various conceptions and practices of science within their own discipline;
- postmodern thought presents us also with the hermeneutical dimension of all scientific reflection: scientists share a narrative field in which their narratives compete for dominance;
- postmodern thought presents scientists with an ethical and political imperative as well: it urges scientists to become aware of the voices of those who are voiceless in our culture, those who are often on the receiving end of our powerful scientific expertise;

- postmodern thought necessarily collapses stark distinctions between the natural and human sciences and sets the stage for a creative fusion between hermeneutics and epistemology.

These characteristics of postmodern science will have to be taken up creatively into the interdisciplinary problem of relating religion, or theological reflection, to the sciences. Along with these typical traits of postmodern science, however, it is especially postmodernism's general embracing of pluralism and the rejection of all grand or unifying metanarratives that still seem to have serious implications for retrieving an interdisciplinary location for theology, and thus also a safe epistemological space for the theology and science discussion. The fundamental question, "Is postmodern religious dialogue possible today?" (cf. Comstock 1989:189ff.), now translates into an even more complex question: Is any meaningful dialogue between postmodern science and postmodern theology possible, or does the pluralism and localization of postmodern discourse throw theologians, philosophers, and scientists who share some common quest for human understanding into near-complete epistemological incommensurability?

Disturbingly enough, some postmodern theologians seem to accept just this in their enthusiastic embracing of a postmodernism of reaction (cf. Hodgson 1989:29) that calls for a "postliberal" return to orthodox or neo-orthodox epistemic values and confessional traditions. Nothing will be gained, however, by asserting the epistemic sovereignty of theological reflection in such a reactionary way. This should again alert us to the fact that postmodernism is a complex phenomenon and that no position in either theology or philosophy of science — just because it claims to be postmodern — should be accepted uncritically. Moving from the sciences to religious and theological issues, postmodern thought will certainly challenge theologians to account for what the Christian faith stands for, for the impact of its ancient narratives on its ongoing tradition, and to somehow also rediscover the explanatory function of religious experience in theology. In this sense, the postmodern theological project can actually be seen as an attempt to reaffirm and revision faith in God *without* abandoning the powers of reason (cf. D. Harvey 1989:41). Obviously this will imply a careful revisioning of what "the powers of reason" and rational reflection might mean as we negotiate our way through the space created by modernist assumptions

56

and postmodernist challenges today. Also, the postmodern challenge to the theology and science dialogue invites a serious counter-critique: if postmodernism's antimetanarrative stance should be uncritically equated with a bias toward the broader epistemological problem of the shaping of rationality in *religious* reflection (even in Joseph Rouse's broad interdisciplinary notion of cultural studies of science, religion and religious reflection are notoriously absent) a few epistemological eyebrows would have to be raised. Even a postmodern attitude can inadvertently manage to still mask a repressive and intolerant neopositivist epistemology.

Eventually, of course, in refiguring theological rationality in the light of the postmodern challenge to interdisciplinary reflection, certain crucial questions will have to be answered: How does not only science, but how does theology move beyond modernist notions of rationality, and what would be the epistemic role of religious experience in any move beyond foundationalism? What, from an epistemological point of view, is the status of an ultimate religious commitment and thus of one's preferred religion? How, and why, do some of us hang on to faith in a postmodern age? What becomes of the problem of religious certainty within a postmodern context that celebrates pluralism? Can theology, as a reflection on religious experience, indeed claim to be a credible partner in the postmodern conversation, and if so, what will the effect of this conversation be on theology's claim to knowledge and some form of religious truth? And last but not least: How does all of this relate back to the shaping of scientific rationality? If it is unacceptable today to continue seeing the sciences as the ultimate paradigm for human rationality, why are some continuing to claim that scientific rationality may still be our best or, at least, our clearest example of human rationality at work? And if this is still in some way true, how normative should scientific rationality be for the rationality of theological reflection?

As in the case of scientific knowledge, the question here will ultimately focus on what the aims of religious reflection are, and also on how much we should believe when we accept a theory or doctrine: Is the proper form of theory acceptance the belief that the theory as a whole is really "true," or could it also be something else (cf. van Fraassen 1989:17f.)? I will eventually argue that the acceptance of theories in theology, as in science, should only be determined by responsible rational judgment as a carefully developed and local epistemic skill, that this skill will enable us to determine contextually the theoretical and experiential adequacy of a specific theology, and that these epistemic skills might open up an exciting epistemological link to the complex and broad spectrum of contemporary interdisciplinary reflection on scientific rationality.

In Conclusion

In this chapter I have argued that the dilemma in which a superior, rational scientific rationality is opposed to religious faith as a seemingly very privatized form of subjective experience and opinion, is thoroughly embedded in the stark, modernist separation between understanding and explanation, human and natural sciences, hermeneutics and epistemology. In this context theology, as a reflection on religious experience, can only suffer complete marginalization. A constructive appropriation of some of the issues raised by the postmodern challenge to science will make it possible, however, to collapse these rigid distinctions into more comprehensive, interdisciplinary spaces where traditional disciplinary boundaries and distinctions are blurred and we realize that the same kind of interpretive procedures are in fact at work in all our various reasoning strategies — even those as divergent as theology and the sciences. This already suggests, as will soon become clear, that reasoning strategies as different as theology and the sciences may not only share similar interpretative strategies, but may in fact share the same resources of human rationality.

The central problem addressed in this book can now be restated as follows: Can we successfully deal with the problem of the shaping of rationality, and in the process also identify the epistemic and nonepistemic values that shape religious and scientific reflection within a postmodern context? As we now turn to the postmodern challenge in theology, and to *nonfoundationalism* as one of the most important philosophical roots of postmodernism, a first step in the right direction again will be to rule out one of the most important and influential misconceptions about postmodern thought, i.e., the assumption that it is always and radically opposed to modern thought. Rather, as we saw, it is important to view the postmodern challenge as an opportunity for an ongoing and relentless critical return to precisely the questions raised by modernity. From this perspective,

58

postmodern thought is undoubtedly part of the modern, and not only modern thought coming to its end. Seen in this way, the modern and the postmodern are also unthinkable apart from one another, because the postmodern shows itself best in the to-and-fro movement between the modern and the postmodern (cf. Schrag 1992:7), i.e., in the relentless interrogation of our foundationalist assumptions in all our reasoning strategies, also in theology and the sciences. Following Lyotard's (1984:79) initial lead, it has indeed become possible to acknowledge the postmodern as part of the modern, or to see to it that "the discourse of modernity remains within the web of the discourse of postmodernity" (cf. Schrag 1992:17). Exactly for this reason epistemology, and epistemological issues like rationality, progress, and truth — issues that have become so controversial in current "end of philosophy" postmodern talk — will remain in our focus as we try to determine the values that shape the way we think, and rationally cope with our worlds.

It is, therefore, indeed possible to appropriate postmodern thought in a more constructive way by interpreting it as a reflection on the strong potential, nature, or the shortcomings and darker sides of modernity (cf. Lötter 1994:159). This positive appropriation of a constructive form of postmodern reflection will be pursued in more detail in the third chapter, but here we have already seen it tentatively emerge in the recent writings of Alan Sokal and Jean Bricmont, and in an even stronger sense in Joseph Rouse's postmodern philosophy of science. By focusing so radically on context and praxis, while at the same time developing a revisioned model for interdisciplinary reflection, Rouse has successfully taken on the breakdown of traditional barriers between the natural sciences and other reasoning strategies. In the blurring of distinctions between reasoning strategies as diverse as the natural and the human sciences, and the need, furthermore, to articulate scientific practices as arenas of the exercise of power, Rouse has shown that our understanding of science has a direct impact on our understanding of knowledge, and of rationality itself. In so doing, he has certainly anticipated the argument for the kind of postfoundationalist model of rationality that is emerging here.

For theology a constructive shift to postmodern thought will be equally far-reaching; it will immediately, as will become clear, imply that central theological terms like *religious experience, revelation,* and *tradition* can no longer be discussed within the generalized terminology of a metanarrative that ignores the sociohistorical location of the theologian as an interpreter of experience and an appropriator of tradition. Within the context of a revisioned postfoundationalist epistemology it will eventually prove to be impossible for theologians to see central issues like religious experience and tradition (which includes theological interpretations of divine revelation) as two opposing poles that somehow have to be related to one another (cf. Dean 1988:20). Trying to think through the troubled and confused relationship between theology and the sciences, as well as the complex set of epistemic values that shapes the rationality of each, we might begin to realize that a postmodern faith need not be so heavy and serious, and that we can indeed readjust our thinking to resist the excessive "weight" of any form of foundationalism, religious conflict, and intellectual isolation. Gary Percesepe says it well: when seen in this way, we may eventually get to the point where we can celebrate the truth behind truth, the God behind God, and the religious behind religion (Percesepe 1991:134).

Chapter Two

Rationality and Nonfoundationalism in Theology

"It does seem that Wittgenstein was right: when we find the foundations, it turns out they are being held up by the rest of the house."

William C. Placher, *Unapologetic Theology*
(Louisville: Westminster/John Knox Press, 1989:34)

I t has now become clear that in any evaluation of what the interdisciplinary relationship between the theology and the sciences might be, modernist views of the rationalities of either theology or the sciences would be fatal. In this quite specific (epistemological) sense both theological and scientific reflection now find themselves at the end, or at the outer boundaries, of modernity. As the Enlightenment challenged appeals to authority and tradition, so the radical historical consciousness of the postmodern attitude is now repudiating the atemporal character of the modern quest for certitude, truth, and sure foundations (cf. Davaney 1991:4f.). It is in this quest for sure foundations for the claims of our knowledge that modernity has found a dubious identity in what today is widely regarded as *foundationalism*. Foundationalism today understandably is a pejorative label, and can broadly be defined as the view that *mediately* justified beliefs require epistemic support for their validity in *immediately* justified beliefs, or alternatively, as the view that systems of knowledge, in content or method, always require first principles (cf. Thiel 1994:2.). Philosophically it is quite clear that it is precisely foundationalist views that finally transform the narratives we live by into the typical grand or totalizing metanarratives of modernity. Foundationalism also typically holds that, in the process of trying to justify our knowledge claims, the chain of justifying evidence cannot go on *ad infinitum* if we are ever to be in a position to claim that we have actually justified our knowledge (cf. Steuer 1987:237). Thus, foundationalists specify what they take to be the ultimate foundations on which the evidential support-systems for various beliefs are constructed. The most typical or frequently mentioned epistemic features of these foundational beliefs are self-evidence, incorrigibility, indubitability, being evident to the senses, and thus being self-authenticating and properly basic (i.e., foundational) for our wider networks of belief.

Foundationalism, as the powerful thesis that our beliefs can indeed be warranted or justified by appealing to some item of knowledge that is self-evident or beyond doubt, certainly eliminates any possibility of discovering a meaningful epistemological link between theology and the other sciences. To claim that our knowledge rests on foundations is to claim that there is a privileged class of "aristocratic" beliefs (cf. Rescher 1992:161) which as such are intrinsically credible and which are able, therefore, to serve as ultimate terminating points for chains of justification. These basic "givens" could be anything from sense data to universals, essences, experience (also religious experience), and, in the case of theology, certain notions of divine revelation. In this sense the "doctrine of the given" can indeed be called the comrade-in-arms of all foundationalism (cf. Frankenberry 1987:6). In the natural sciences, as we saw, modernist notions of foundationalism gave rise to a positivist empiricism or scientific materialism that by definition renders all religion, and certainly all theology and theological reflection, as radically subjective, if not meaningless (cf. Barbour 1990:4). In theology, foundationalism most often implies biblical literalism, or the positing of religious experience as an unmediated and unique dimension of experience, or, on a more sophisticated theoretical level, a self-authenticating "positivism of revelation" which ultimately isolates theology from other reasoning strategies because it denies the crucial role of interpreted religious experience in theological reflection. Here the theologian is left speaking a language whose conceptuality might be internally coherent, but which at the same time is powerless to communicate its content because it is unrelated to and cut off from all nontheological discourse (cf. Green 1989:34). The way philosophical foundationalism worked itself out in modernity's opposing views on religion and science is very clear: while science gained ascendancy as the model for truth and superior rationality, traditional arguments for the existence of God were eclipsed and theologians increasingly turned to the depths of human subjectivity as the source of religious experience and belief. Schleiermacher and a long line of successors would find a protective location in the foundationalist retreat to experiential subjectivity, a refuge for religious experience and its theological interpretation in the modern world (cf. Davaney 1991:2-16).

Nonfoundationalism

Whatever its virtues might have been, modernity has certainly not been hospitable to religion, let alone to theology, and thus consigned both to the private realm where "opinion," not "knowledge," reigns supreme. It should therefore really not surprise us at all that theologians today are so attracted to postmodernism, and thereby inevitably also to *non-* or *antifoundationalism,* as one of the most crucially important philosophical roots of postmodernism (cf. Cahoone 1995:13). As will soon become clear, nonfoundationalism, in a strong reaction against modernist and universalist notions of rationality, highlights the fact that every historical context, and every cultural or social group, has its own distinct rationality. This kind of contextualism easily leads to a relativism of rationalities, where every social or human activity could in principle function as a framework for human rationality. In his distinctive nonfoundationalist view of postmodern rationality, the characteristics that Joseph Rouse identified as typical for a local form of postmodern science will now find remarkable parallels in other radically contextualized, nonfoundationalist modes of reflection. And as in the case of science as social practice, theological reflection in this mode will also emerge as a local practice, with strong contextual claims for its own internal criteria of rationality.

Philosophers like Ludwig Wittgenstein, and contemporary philosophers like Thomas S. Kuhn, Willard V. O. Quine, and Richard Rorty, represent a strong nonfoundationalist (and some would argue, even postmodern) response to traditional epistemological questions. The early pragmatists all already rejected the traditional rationalist or empiricist definition of truth as an isolated correspondence between the self and the world, as well as the concept that either sense experience or ideas were privileged as the authoritative basis of human knowing (cf. Thiel 1994:10f.). Instead of a model where knowledge is seen as an entity resting on fixed and immutable foundations, nonfoundationalists offer a picture of human knowledge as an evolving social phenomenon shaped by the practical implications of ideas within a larger web of beliefs. This contextual and foundationless conception of truth can today be seen as the most characteristic mark of the philosophies of pragmatism, and would find remarkable parallels in Wittgenstein's appeal to language as a vehicle of contextual meaning. The view of meaning as use, and thus as a network of practically justified beliefs, was held in common by the forerunners of contemporary nonfoundationalist philosophers, and would later find its special focus in both Quine's holism and Rorty's neopragmatist rejection of traditional epistemology. Belief systems are here constructed within a contextual matrix that is itself groundless, and justification becomes a matter of accommodating those beliefs that are being questioned to another body of accepted beliefs. Whatever theories we might have about anything that might be "given" in religious or scientific experience, epistemic justification can certainly no longer have an unproblematic, uninterpreted "given" at its foundation.

The antifoundationalist move to a more local and functionalist perspective on meaning, where meaning is the use to which sentences are put contextually, not only reveals how senseless it would be to speak of foundations for such meaning, but also how easily foundationalism can steal into our broader conceptual schemes and epistemic claims. This is vividly illustrated in Quine's fascinating description of the metaphor of the "myth of the museum" (cf. Quine 1969:27). On this (foundationalist) view a conceptual scheme is revealed to be like a "museum" in which the exhibits are objective meanings and the words are the labels we use to describe them. Like exhibits in a museum, meanings in our conceptual schemes are taken to be part of a permanent collection and regarded as independent, objective realities with values of their own. An awareness of the power of the "myth of the museum" thus reveals the disturbing fact that epistemic foundationalism is not just found in given, first principles of knowledge, but can in fact be spread or distributed throughout the network of beliefs that make up any conceptual scheme. On this view meanings are thought to have a mental life of their own, quite apart from their use and applicability in language (cf. Thiel 1994:19f.). In this case not just the first founding principles of our knowledge claims function as foundationalist beliefs, but whole networks of belief acquire a doctrinal aura and thus assume foundationalist status. For Quine, however, there can be no privileged meanings that provide foundations for expression in language, and therefore there can be no conceptual scheme like the illusory museum that houses independent, fixed meanings outside of the actual use of language. Meaning is therefore never fixed objectively or apprehended in context-free theories, but (because it is found in use) is always local or contextual, and these theories as such are always holistically located in ever-widening language contexts.

Quine's nonfoundationalist holism is closely aligned to Richard Rorty's sweeping criticism of the Western metaphysical tradition (cf. especially Rorty 1979), and his view of foundationalist epistemologies as mere sophisticated variants of fundamentalism. The attractiveness of foundationalist epistemologies and of "museums of fixed meaning" indeed lies in their promise of ready and reliable answers, and the banishing, therefore, of doubt in favor of absolute certainty (cf. Thiel 1994:24). The most significant postmodern challenge to this kind of epistemological foundationalism certainly comes from what is now called the "new historicism" (Dean 1988:1), with Rorty's neopragmatism as its most important representative. Rorty seems to take the (skeptical) postmodern critique of modernity, and postmodernity's insistence on incommensurability, historicity, linguisticality, and difference, to its logical and most radical conclusion. With this is rejected all modernist attempts to construct an overarching "theory of rationality" in terms of which claims to truth and genuine knowledge could be adjudicated (cf. Pieterse 1996:26). The denial by the new historicists of any reality beyond the contingencies of history thus logically implies the rejection of foundationalism, realism, and of the transcendentalized subject: the self is capable of experiencing only that which can be experienced within historical space and time. It can know neither foundations transcending history, nor realities that can be known objectively, nor universal subjective structures inherent in all persons. With this complete rejection of foundationalism, new historicists like Richard Rorty therefore embrace pluralism and pragmatism: a *pluralism* that is unlimited because, as long as foundational realities are not experienced, there are no things beyond the plurality of particulars that could be experienced; a *pragmatism* that is an answer to the confusion introduced by the absence of criteria for truth formerly provided by foundationalism, realism, and the transcendentalized subject (cf. Dean 1988:6f.).

The special postmodern challenge of Rortian neopragmatism to theology should immediately be obvious: all theology, all God-talk, represents a typically modernist, foundationalist attempt to first escape from contingency, history, and time, and to then embrace ahistorical, eternal realities beyond history. Like the Platonic tradition of which it is a part, theology has outlived its usefulness and is now best abandoned (Rorty 1982:xiv). The fate of theology is therefore so entangled in the whole onto-theological tradition of Western "Philosophy" (Rorty's term for foundationalism generally) that the demise of metaphysics and foundationalism also is the demise of meaningful theological language as such (cf. Pieterse 1996:171). For Rorty the failure of foundationalism therefore gives us an opening to see everything — our language, our conscience, our community — as products of time and chance (cf. Rorty 1989:22). This obviously implies the radical temporalizing and historicizing of rationality. Also, the justification of any claims to knowledge now becomes a matter of social practice only: for the neopragmatist all criteria are only "temporary resting places constructed for specific utilitarian ends" (cf. Rorty 1982:xli), and all justification of knowledge can happen only in terms of what we already accept as plausible networks of belief to cope with our worlds. In this sense Rorty can therefore claim that any notion of objectivity should now be seen only as reflecting conformity to the accepted norms of justification we find about us (cf. Rorty 1979:361). Rorty's nonfoundationalist neopragmatism thus shows remarkable parallels with Joseph Rouse's postmodernist views of science as social practice: "truth" here too becomes a function of the coherence of a particular social practice, a function of the historical standards of the inquirers involved in a particular language game.

From this it should also be quite clear that Rorty shares Lyotard's incredulity toward all metanarratives. As we saw in the preceding chapter, just the mere fact that a postmodern society has no need for grounding its ongoing conversations in any overarching theory of rationality, always will have direct consequences for the way it perceives science and the rationality of scientific reflection. In Rorty's post-Philosophical society, what is needed is not more narratives — and certainly no superior natural scientific narratives — but rather a sort of intellectual analogue of civic virtue, with tolerance and the willingness to let spheres of culture flourish without worrying too much about their "common ground" or any "intrinsic" or unifying ideals they may presuppose or need. This too therefore represents a distinct move away from any notions of superior scientific rationality, and naturally leads to an "epistemological leveling" which rests on the assumption that scientific, political, and other discourses are continuous and that there are no significant epistemological differences between the aims and procedures of science and those of other modes of reflection (cf. Pieterse 1996:202). As in Joseph Rouse's cultural studies of science, the natural sciences are in no way to be granted any form of epistemic sovereignty and are not to be elevated above other discourses as *the* paradigm of rationality. They are to be viewed, rather, as *one genre of literature* (cf. Rorty 1982:xliii), helping us cope in the same way that the social sciences or literature do. On this view the sciences, along with morals, religion, and art, are revealed as tools for coping with our world. As tools for coping, the vocabularies for these various strategies are never "more objective" or "less objective," or more or less "scientific," but they are useful or useless, good or bad, helpful or misleading (cf. Rorty 1982:203). In Rorty's postmodern culture too, the strict boundaries between disciplines thus fall away and no form of discourse, not even religion, could as such be ruled as "subjective" or "merely expressive," or "less rational," because there would be no metanarrative in terms of which these kinds of distinctions could be framed to still have a point (cf. Pieterse 1996:204). In such a society religious inquiry could apparently coexist peacefully with scientific and all other forms of inquiry; there would be no need to look for an encompassing theory of rationality, or for a common ground in terms of which one form of inquiry could be reduced to another.

As this brief overview shows, in the philosophical work of Quine and Rorty, we find some of the most influential contemporary nonfoundationalist attacks on the modernist idea of necessary foundations for knowledge. In this they are also revealed as important allies for Joseph Rouse's revisioning of postmodern philosophy of science. The objectivist expectations of modern knowledge are now finally exposed for what they are: fearful of the ever-receding horizon of an infinite regress of justification, the foundationalist arbitrarily draws a boundary where none could possibly exist and then designates that boundary as the true foundation for all knowledge (cf. Thiel 1994:30-35). The foundationalist belief that sufficient reasons for knowledge depend in the end on the existence of other beliefs that require no justifying themselves, is in fact an expression of the epistemic worry, or the "Cartesian anxiety" (cf. Bernstein 1983: 8-20) that without foundations knowledge can in fact never be more than mere opinion.

The increasing attacks on modernity and its characteristic foundationalist assumptions have also emboldened a number of contemporary theologians to embrace nonfoundationalist philosophy as a critical resource for revisioning their own discipline. In a sense the amorphous postmodern attitude, in moving beyond the modernist dilemma of opposing objective science to radically subjective religion, does seem to create a more receptive context for theological reflection. Nonfoundationalism can, however, also be co-opted by theologians only for confessional purposes, and in an attempt to legitimate the theological enterprise, can often generate theologies with little or no real resonance to postmodern sensibilities. It would be relatively easy today to understand why theology could so easily be guilty of foundationalism: a theological model would be foundationalist if its argumentation is tainted by questionable philosophical premises, or if its disciplinary integrity is subverted by its ongoing appeals to foundational construals of theoretical explanation. This is especially the case when theology — exactly like in Quine's "myth of the museum" — constructs and identifies a "true," objectivist conceptual scheme, only to then spread its foundationalism throughout the whole conceptual network, where theological meanings then acquire a doctrinal life of their own apart from their use and applicability in language.

With this in mind, it will soon become clear that not only in theology all forms of foundationalism and fideism always go hand in hand, but that also the relativism implied by postmodern nonfoundationalism will present a very special epistemological challenge to Christian theology. All nonfoundationalist philosophies, as we saw before, would argue that no authoritative givenness exists in experience or reason, and this challenge to the viability of authoritative, justifying foundations is as consequential for theology as it is for philosophy. So both foundationalism and nonfoundationalism seem to present theology with an unenviable dilemma, especially when theological claims are presented as reasoned attempts to understand the authoritative givenness of God's revelation in scripture, or in the sanctioned tradition of its interpretation in history. John Thiel puts it well: theology seems to be a discipline shaped by the kind of epistemological commitments that most contemporary philosophers would identify as blatantly foundational, and therefore seems to be susceptible through and through to nonfoundationalist critique (cf. 1994:41). From this perspective even the classical Augustinian definition of theology as "faith seeking understanding" seems to subordinate rational inquiry to the given authority of faith in God's revelation. Can a theology with postmodern sensibilities then even manage to credibly adopt a philosophical position like nonfoundationalism, or is it already and always doomed to foundationalism and fideism? It does seem that a non- or antifoundationalist critique of human rationality extends to the most authoritative claims of theology itself, and this seems to warrant Thiel's insightful comment that "nonfoundational criticism and theology seem to represent completely incompatible modes of argumentation and stances on the possibilities, limitation, and authority of human knowing" (Thiel 1994:41). But is there a positive and constructive way of appropriating postmodern nonfoundationalist critique for theology without succumbing to the epistemic hazards of nonfoundationalism? It is precisely as a way out of the dilemma posed by foundationalism *vis-à-vis* nonfoundationalism, that I will eventually argue for *a postfoundationalist* notion of rationality.

Nonfoundationalism and Narrative Theologies

Surprisingly enough, nonfoundationalism has nevertheless very successfully managed to inform theologies with postmodern sensibilities. This is especially true for various types of current narrative and postliberal theologies, which indeed claim to take the postmodern nonfoundationalist challenge seriously. What happens, in a quite remarkable parallel with postmodern philosophy of science, is that the Lyotardian idea of the importance of narrative knowledge is taken up in a serious attempt to refigure the identity of Christian theology. The category of narrative has of course been used to explain human action, to articulate the structures of human consciousness, to depict strategies of reading, to account for the historical development of traditions, and to provide an alternative to foundationalist and/or other scientific epistemologies (cf. Hauerwas and Jones 1989:2f.). Nonfoundationalist narrative theology develops these themes further by recognizing that rationality itself, and therefore all methods of argument, all reasoning strategies, and all historical explanation, has a fundamentally narrative form and texture.

As a paradigm for postmodern theology, narrative theology thus grows directly from the deep conviction that temporal narrativity constitutes the substance of personal human identity. As such it is a reflection on the religious claims embedded in stories, and on the basic narrative condition of what it means to be human. Narrative theology takes this basic narrativity seriously in order to think through the nature of specifically religious knowledge. Today prominent although diverse theologians are associated with some form of narrative theology: Paul Ricoeur, Hans Frei, George Lindbeck, Johann Baptist Metz, Ronald F. Thiemann, Stanley Hauerwas, and James McClendon, to mention just a few. Elsewhere I have briefly discussed an intriguing attempt by Gary L. Comstock (1987) to try and find some methodological link between the extremes of revisionist and postliberal forms of contemporary American theology (cf. van Huyssteen 1997a:180ff.) and would now like to return to this discussion in some greater detail. Comstock has suggested dividing narrative theologians into two distinct groups, each with a more or less definable set of theological presuppositions and methodology. Comstock identifies these two groups of narrative theologians as "pure narrativists" and "impure narrativists": pure narrativists can be described as nonfoundational, cultural-linguistic, Wittgensteinian-inspired descriptivists (cf. Comstock 1987:688f.). For theologians like Frei, Lindbeck, and Hauerwas, narrative as an autonomous literary form is particularly suited to nonfoundationalist theological reflection. Narrative here has a special status in the construction of theological statements, while abstract reasoning and philosophical categories do not belong to the essential task of what it means to do theology. Christian faith is here best understood by grasping the grammatical rules and concepts of its texts and practices. Impure narrativists, on the other hand, find their inspiration in the circle of revisionist, hermeneutical, Gadamerian-inspired correlationists (cf. Comstock 1987: 688). Theologians like David Tracy, Sallie McFague, and Paul Ricoeur, while agreeing with "pure narrativists" on the central role of narrative in the communication of the Christian story, deny it any exclusive or autonomous theological function in theological theorizing. For them narrative does indeed exhibit philosophical, historical, and psychological claims — claims that need to be evaluated in interdisciplinary discussion. In addition, pure narrative theologians very consciously want to construct a postmodern paradigm for theology, while revisionists creatively revise the paradigms of language, reason, and practice of the liberal tradition in diverse attempts to justify the cognitive claims of theological reflection.

Regardless of Comstock's attempt to link postliberal and revisionist theologies via narrative, it does seem to be clear now that narrative theology's attempt at a nonfoundationalist rejection of all global, modernist legitimation in favor of a focus on doing theology locally, could turn out to be thoroughly postmodern in nature. This narrative reconstruction of a postmodern theology becomes especially interesting when we take a look at the way in which three specific features — description, explanation, and justification — are shared within the family of narrative theologians (cf. Comstock 1987). All narrative theologians agree that in theology acceptable description should be conducted in terms of Scripture's own narratives and biographies, and not in categories alien to the biblical stories. Narrative theologians, of course, do not at all reject critical thinking, but in the attempt to construct a radically contextual Christian theology, they are wary of speculative reason and of any attempts at foundationalist epistemology. Because Christian theology is seen to be fundamentally descriptive and regulative, it should therefore not step outside the boundaries of the confessing community where the biblical narratives ultimately determine the pattern of what can be said and done in theological reflection.

It is obvious that in this version of a nonfoundationalist narrative theology, any adequate explanation of the Christian story should be arrived at only in terms of the internal rules and logic of the biblical language game, and not in terms of "imported" philosophical theories (cf. Pieterse 1989:2f.). The Christian story here apparently posits a kind of language game *sui generis,* a language game that has its own unique rules and procedures. In the Lindbeckian version of this model, Christian doctrines become regulative rules for a confessing community and as such make no factual or ontological claims (cf. Lindbeck 1984). Any claims for justification in this insulated context could only take the form of a pragmatic demonstration that this tradition indeed entails a liberating and authenticating form of life — a form of life that is already beyond the need for (foundationalist) philosophical criteria for rationality. Nonfoundationalist narrative theologians therefore seem to bring theology to a complete halt once it has narratively described, narratively explained, and narratively justified the Christian faith (cf. Comstock 1987:703f.). For any attempt to find a plausible interdisciplinary location for theological reflection, at least two serious problems *vis-à-vis* a postmodern narrative theology can now be identified: the hermeneutical problem of finding adequate criteria for distinguishing between good or bad receptions of Christianity's classic text, and the epistemological problem of determining criteria for assessing, in some way or other, the truth claims and the cognitive status of theological statements.

Narrative theology, as a reflection on the religious claims embedded in stories, is touched at its heart by this last problem: What indeed is the *epistemic status* of theological theories if they are based on a nonfoundationalist discourse which is fundamentally narrative and metaphorical? The postmodern focus on the limitations and contextuality of human thought, as well as on the paradigmatic value of truth (cf. Glanville 1989:3), could of course challenge this kind of question as just the wrong question to ask in a nonfoundationalist situation. It is therefore perfectly understandable that a narrative theologian like Ronald F. Thiemann can caution theology not to formulate a specific theory for understanding faith, because on a postmodern/nonfoundationalist view all such theories obscure the diversity and the mystery of human response to the Christian gospel. In Thiemann's words: "to acknowledge the biblical narrative as God's promise is to believe that the crucified Jesus lives" (Thiemann 1987a:38). In this sense a postmodern narrative theology can even be seen as a call for a "new Reformation" — a Reformation that would free Scripture once more, but this time from the papacy of the scholar (cf. Wiles 1986:44).

It is clear that this isolationist move could be the first step toward a headlong plunge into epistemological isolation and incommensurability; what started out as a well-intended protective strategy could backfire and reduce theological reflection to a form of fideism. Foundationalism and fideism seem to go together very well, but — amazingly enough — a distinct fideist move could also be at the heart of nonfoundationalism. The specter of an even more disturbing possibility, reminiscent of Quine's "myth of the museum," now raises its head here: *Would it be possible to actually epistemically extend a sophisticated form of foundationalism over a whole conceptual network of nonfoundationalist beliefs?* This problem touches the heart not only of theory choice in nonfoundationalist theology, but also of the nature and role of faith and commitment in theological reflection as such. Does, therefore, a postmodern, nonfoundationalist theology necessarily imply an irrational, esoteric commitment to the Christian faith? If so, this theological paradigm would not only be giving up on any interdisciplinary location, but it would willingly embrace incommensurability, and thus firmly bar its own ability to make responsible and intelligible judgments.

One narrative theologian, whose work has become especially interesting because of his specific claims to break away from all foundationalism, while at the same time constructing a nonfoundationalist "public" (and not an esoteric, privatized) theology, is Ronald F. Thiemann. These claims are especially prominent in Thiemann's recent work (1987a; 1987b; 1991), where he has argued repeatedly that the category of "narrated promise" not only offers a nonfoundationalist way of reconceptualizing Christian theology, but also enables a descriptive, nonfoundationalist theology which at the same time would be a genuinely public theology. Thiemann sees theology as primarily a descriptive activity, and descriptive is contrasted with explanatory, which for him always directly implies a foundationalist epistemology. Thiemann thus wants to show that a theology shaped by the biblical narratives, and grounded in the practices of the Christian community, can provide resources to enable people of faith to regain a public voice in our pluralistic culture — a culture where contemporary Christians are socialized into a world littered with the fragments of previously coherent traditions and formerly intact communities (cf. Thiemann 1991:18). Epistemologically, however, the true nature of Thiemann's "public" theology is quickly revealed here: the public character of theology is found not in any attempt to identify theology's interdisciplinary voice or status, or in the extent to which theological reflection might share important resources of rationality with other modes of reflection. The challenge for a public theology is to remain based in the particularities of the Christian faith while genuinely attempting to address issues of public significance. Thiemann's postliberal aversion to apologetics also shines through when he warns against what he sees as a very real danger for theology today: too often, theologies that seek to address a broad, secular culture lose touch with the distinctive beliefs and practices of the Christian tradition (cf. 1991:19). What is lost, for Thiemann, is the prophetic "bite" of the Christian witness when concepts and theories foreign to the Christian faith are adopted. Thiemann does, in all fairness, warn against going too far on this point. Theologies can become so obsessed with the characteristic language and patterns of Christian narrative and practice that they often fail to engage in the public realm in an effective and responsible fashion; either they eschew public discourse altogether in order to preserve what they see as the uniqueness of Christian life, or they enter the public fray with single-minded ferocity, heedless of the pluralistic traditions of our democratic polity (cf. Thiemann 1991:19).

Theologians, of course, remain notoriously divided on the question of what criteria for a public theology would look like. Thiemann has been very critical of, and has rejected as foundationalist, David Tracy's well-known proposal for a public theology that addresses the three "publics" of society, academy, and the church (cf. Tracy 1981). Thiemann feels that Tracy, by identifying genuine publicness with general rational, philosophical argument, severely undercuts the ability of Christians to employ the specific resources of their own traditions to engage in public conversation (cf. Thiemann 1991:21). In a remarkable parallel to Joseph Rouse's argument for a postmodern philosophy of science, Thiemann also rejects any pursuit of a general notion of human rationality, and urges theological reflection to become consciously local and contextual, and thereby to enter the living context of the Christian faith by engaging in what Clifford Geertz has called "thick description": a detailed understanding of social, cultural, and moral issues that begins with extremely small matters or concrete issues, and then moves slowly to broader interpretations and abstract analyses (cf. Geertz 1973:10f.). For Thiemann this "thick description" would, for theological reflection at least, encompass the specific beliefs, rituals, and practices of the Christian community from which a form of public theology can then arise. Part of Thiemann's version of a "thick description" à la Geertz will therefore be a careful attention to the form and substance of biblical narratives, the practices of Christian worship and piety, the institutional life of church and academy, and the pluralism of contemporary society. Using Geertz's notion of a "thick description" is not about again providing an overarching, modernist theory that explains how church and world relate to one another. Rather, the goal is to identify the particular places where Christian convictions intersect with the practices that characterize contemporary public life (cf. Thiemann 1991:21).

A nonfoundationalist public theology for Thiemann thus begins from the standpoint of faith, and the theologian launches his or her inquiry with the conviction that its most crucial questions have been answered positively through the revelation of God in Jesus Christ. The theologian thus enters the public realm with the confidence that Christian convictions do have relevance for public life. In Thiemann's case, however, faith — as a "starting point" for argument and reflection — is clearly contrasted with rational argument, and in this nonfoundationalist theology, theological reflection is dubiously rewarded with its own, exclusive, internal, and protected form of rationality. This kind of theology seeks to provide a justification for Christian belief that is specific to the Christian faith, community, and tradition. In this attempt, however, the reasons for conceptually holding on to certain religious beliefs are ultimately collapsed into, and confused with, a comprehensive faith commitment which as such cannot, and need not, be justified. Not the faith commitment as such, however, but rather the conceptual structure in which we hold this faith commitment, thus turns into a protective and fideist strategy. In fact, nonfoundationalist theology wants to be located squarely within the Christian tradition and community, and as such its first interest is never epistemology, but the redescription of the Christian faith's own internal logic (cf. Thiemann 1987a:74ff.). This is accomplished by the argument that biblical narratives do illuminate what Thiemann has called a "followable world" for the readers of Christian texts (cf. 1991:48). Thiemann truly believes that multi-interpretable biblical narratives get us beyond the objectivism of a modernist foundationalism. He is certainly right in suggesting that the act of coming to believe is always an individual person's specific act, with both reasons and causes related to that person's individual history (cf. 1991:60).

Theology, on this view, is indeed not able to devise a general explanatory theory for the subjective conditions for the making of a religious faith commitment. However, because — as will be argued later — we always relate to our world (and therefore also to texts and narratives) epistemically through interpreted and traditioned experience, we have our faith and religious commitment only in terms of the beliefs in which we hold them. To completely collapse a faith commitment into the conceptual structure in which we hold that commitment, epistemically transforms faith into fideism, and the conceptual structure of our religious and theological beliefs into a sophisticated, but nevertheless still crypto-foundationalist belief system. With this in mind, it now seems that Thiemann too inevitably slides into contextualism: a "many rationalities" position where postmodern pluralism is taken to its extreme, and different autonomous domains of knowledge function only according to their own internal rationality. In this sense nonfoundationalism indeed does not seem to be a move beyond foundationalism: identifying an esoteric and unique form of theological rationality, and constructing autonomous domains of knowledge and practice that can be rationally administered in accordance with internal goals and standards, may thus turn out to not really be an appropriation of the postmodern emphasis on heterogeneity and pluralism, but rather a promotion of the kind of disciplinary closure and intellectual autonomy which is just the other side of a typically modernist rationalization (cf. Rouse 1991a:157).

It is interesting (although also obvious) that Thiemann has accepted as his own the Barthian view that theology should be located squarely within the Christian community and begin its reflection with the "objective credo" of the Christian church, its confession that God is known only in Jesus Christ (cf. Thiemann 1991:88). For both Barth and Thiemann, theology is a hermeneutical task that begins with a text which has to be interpreted in the context of a living tradition. And within this context contemporary philosophical and cultural resources can be used, but only in a way that allows for the distinctive logic of the Christian gospel to guide and shape that use. On this view, however, all hope of finding a cross-disciplinary location for theological reflection as a plausible reasoning strategy is lost forever. The best we can now hope for is a series of temporary and *ad hoc* alliances between theology and the other intellectual resources of our culture (cf. Thiemann 1991:91; cf. also Werpehowski 1986:282-301). For Thiemann, then, no positive link between Christian belief and rational inquiry seems to be possible because, in his words, "rational inquiry has increasingly sought to identify itself with unbelief" (1991:91). With this controversial claim all attempts at a truly public theology are surely and finally lost. In fact, even if we should agree that belief in God is no longer (was it ever?) part of our common human heritage, it certainly does not mean that *human rationality as such* is not part of this common heritage. Thiemann's nonfoundationalist theology at this point reveals at least a very inadequate and reductionist notion of rationality, and finally proliferates into the typical "many rationalities" view held by most forms of nonfoundationalist theology. This "many rationalities" view, however, in spite of its brave attempt to be a "public" theology, actually successfully isolates the rationality of theological reflection from the way human rationality functions in all other domains of knowledge, since it is so oblivious to the great extent to which theological reflection shares the rich resources of human rationality with other reasoning strategies.

Thiemann's nonfoundationalist theology is reminiscent of a peculiar brand of neo-Wittgensteinian fideism, where religious beliefs have no need for explanatory support and in the end can be seen as a groundless language game. In fact these beliefs become a species of belief whose truth is discovered by means of criteria internal only to the language game itself (cf. Steuer 1987:241). Even more disturbing, however, is the idea that the whole conceptual network of a narrative, nonfoundationalist theology can epistemically begin to function in a crypto-foundationalist way. To counter this, theologians would have to realize the epistemological and hermeneutical implications of the fact that biblical narratives are already interpretations, that so-called biblical concepts in themselves are mini-theories that reveal the complex way in which these texts have been received, experienced, and interpreted through the long history of the Christian tradition. Moreover, Janet Martin Soskice's apt remark, that "to narrate is to explain" (cf. Soskice 1988:130), correctly exposes the fine division between narrative and discursive forms of theology as a naive and even potentially dangerous illusion (cf. also Jeanrond 1988:158). Of course narrative is always going to be crucially important for Christian theology. For this reason Soskice, in answer to the question, "What would the epistemological status of theological concepts be if they were not based on a discourse which is fundamentally narrative and metaphorical?", can claim: whatever they would be, they would not be Christian (cf. Soskice 1988:131). For the same reason, however, a "pure" form of non- or antifoundationalist theology that consciously brackets the question of truth can only be seen as a kind of sectarian instrumentalism — a narrative theology that achieves a meaningful Christian story at the cost of detaching this story from any meaningful dialogue with other Christians, with other scientific and nonscientific modes of reflection, and with the secular world. Against this background it would be rather naive, epistemologically at least, to think that narrative, as a nonfoundationalist biblical genre, is precritical and preinterpretative, and thus always preferable to interpretation, justification, and argumentation (cf. Jeanrond 1988:151). Although narrative is an essential genre for communicating the Christian gospel, no form of "pure" narrative theological nonfoundationalism seems to be able to solve the epistemological problem of the shaping of rationality in contemporary theology. Nonfoundational narrative theology, therefore, not only leads to relativistic and incommensurabilist understandings of justification, truth, and rationality, but also to an epistemic fideism that would be quite fatal for the cognitive claims of interdisciplinary theological reflection.

What nonfoundationalist theologians therefore confidently see as the logical integrity of theology (cf. Thiel 1994:74) is thus (epistemologically at least) rather easily revealed as a first-rate isolationist move, a protective strategy in which the belief, worship, and the practice of the Christian tradition is seen as sufficient to internally justify its own theological claims. Appealing to the Quinean idea of knowledge as an intricate web of justifying explanations whose meaningfulness is always relational, nonfoundationalist theologians thus understand the intelligibility of their claims to be rooted only in the local context of ecclesial belief, worship, and practice. Remarkable similarities with Rouse's call for science as a very local social practice are thus revealed. Postmodern science, however, still allows for cross-disciplinary conversation through a process of translation and standardization. In nonfoundationalist theology, however, this kind of interdisciplinary conversation and blurring of disciplinary boundaries is seriously suspect. In this holistic approach to theological knowledge, apologetics as such is therefore understandably suspect, and even seen as a dysfunctional form of theology. In apologetics nonfoundationalist theologians actually see other (foundationalist) theologians succumb to the Cartesian anxiety by seeking closure to the task of justifying theological claims (cf. Thiel 1994:36, 76f.). In a legitimate move beyond foundationalism, nonfoundationalist theologians correctly see knowledge and understanding not as fixed points at the beginning or the end of inferential justification, and therefore not as independent of context and its tightly woven "thick fabric" of epistemic, cultural, and pragmatic particularities. A postfoundationalist move beyond the objectivism of modernist foundationalism and the relativism of postmodern nonfoundationalism will indeed have to take this contextuality of disciplines seriously. Joseph Rouse, as we saw earlier, has convincingly argued that all disciplines are indeed contextually bound, and are also contexts in their own right. And in this sense a theology that wants to move beyond foundationalism should indeed, and first of all, recognize and acknowledge the disciplinary commitments of reason (cf. Thiel 1994:77). It is, however, when theology takes the next step and wants to assure its own rational integrity *only* through the contextuality of its own disciplinary reasoning that a few epistemological eyebrows have to be raised.

The philosophical inconsistency of such a radical nonfoundationalist contextualism has recently been argued eloquently by Mikael Stenmark. Stenmark identifies as the "contextual principle" the fact that for contextualists (read: nonfoundationalists), what is to be regarded as rational or irrational can only be determined internally, from within a practice or context, since there exist no context-independent standards of rationality (cf. Stenmark 1995:303-10). In the light of this fundamental assumption, contextualists make three basic claims that ultimately structure this model of rationality: first, rationality is always internal to some practice (the *internal thesis*). Second, the beliefs of a specific practice cannot be used intercontextually to assess another practice (the *incompatibility thesis*). Third, there are no standards of rationality that are applicable across all practices, nor may the rationality of a practice be assessed from outside the practice itself (the *autonomy thesis*). Although Stenmark never directly addresses the impact of the postmodern challenge to epistemology, his analysis clearly supports the argument that in nonfoundationalism all common standards of rationality are prematurely jettisoned. A contextualist nonfoundationalism thus clearly opens the way for seeing the rationality of religion as radically different from the rationality of science (or of any other human activity) — a protective strategy required as a first epistemic move for any irrational retreat to commitment. The most important inconsistency in this nonfoundationalist view is revealed, however, when contextualists claim that different practices have their own rationalities and their own truth, and then proceed to deny any universal or cross-contextual truth (also the cross-contextual truth-claim that different practices each have their own rationalities and truth).

Nonfoundationalism, then, in fact claims that any social or human activity — including theological reflection — could in principle function as a legitimate test case for human rationality. Nonfoundationalism therefore finally leaves us with an extreme relativism of rationalities, a relativism that not only forms the opposite of foundationalism's objectivism, but an epistemic contextualism that would also be devastating for any attempt at interdisciplinary conversation between reasoning strategies as diverse as theology and the sciences. Proponents of the relativism of this "many rationalities" view hold that the rules which govern the natural or social sciences are indeed internal to those sciences in the same way that other human activities (cf. religion, business, magic, etc.) are also governed by rules internal to them. In the relativism that flows from this contextualist nonfoundationalism, it is consistently maintained, as we saw, that each area of human activity finds its own criteria for rational belief and behaviors only within the inner logic of a specific culture or social group. Since each context can therefore claim its own criteria of rationality, there can obviously be no independent, cross-contextual framework for deciding whether or not one framework is more rational than another (cf. H. Brown 1990:113). On this view, science (along with religion) is seen as just one among many of the features of postmodern Western society, where all cultures or societies create cognitive structures that try to explain the world around them. What is also denied is that the body of beliefs developed by science could be in any way cognitively superior to other beliefs. On this view, then, neither the rationality of the natural nor of the social or human sciences could seriously threaten the rationality of theological reflection. It is extremely ironical, then, that non-

foundationalist theology should feel the need to employ an epistemic protective strategy that — amazingly — allows theological reflection to claim again, and unabashedly, a form of epistemic
sovereignty that will allow only the practitioners of theology to po-
lice their own protective epistemic boundaries.

The ramifications and complexities of such a radically contextualist view of rationality are very well illustrated in John Milbank's influential *Theology and Social Theory* (1990). Milbank's book clearly is
breathtaking just by virtue of its comprehensive, intellectual scope. I
think this exciting book in many ways, and maybe even first of all,
represents a seriously problematic epistemic move to esotericism and
sectarian rationality: behind the impressive grasp of contemporary
postmodern thought, the resulting rejection of "secular reason," and
finally the elevation of Christian faith and theology as the only adequate social and intellectual project for our postmodern times, is hidden a massive and spectacular fideist claim — a protective strategy so
effective, and of such enormity, that it catapults the Christian faith
out of its context in the real world into complete and splendid isolation. Milbank wants to restore, for our postmodern times, the possibility of theology as a metadiscourse. In the process of doing so, he exposes scientific social theories as "theologies" or "antitheologies" in
disguise, and goes on to assert theology's epistemic sovereignty by
even reclaiming for theology the startling title of "queen of the sciences" (cf. 1990:380ff.).

However, this kind of theology quickly seems to turn into a
"Theory of Everything," a social science on a triumphant pilgrimage
through this temporary world of ours. What is revealed, though, is not
the nature of theology's epistemic location in contemporary interdisciplinary thought, but the following: first, a tacit acceptance of modernist notions of the superiority of natural scientific rationality; second, the assumption that the rationality of theological reflection
therefore has to be retrieved only through a battle with the social sciences; and third, an argument that theology has to turn into social science to attain some form of intellectual credibility. This theology is
epistemologically identified as a "metanarrative realism," which now
replaces theology as mediated by (and reduced to) the social sciences
(cf. 1990:251). Milbank's alarming retreat to this kind of commitment
to a metanarrative realism not only reveals traits of epistemological
positivism and foundationalism — in spite of his claims to the con-

trary (cf. 1990:163) — but also goes completely against the epistemic grain of what I think the Christian faith should be about: a positive, constructive, and even corrective engagement with the culture of its day. This cross-disciplinary space for theological reflection should indeed be possible, not because theology should assimilate the mood of a culture uncritically, or even in terms of a general/modernist notion of rationality, but, *theologically,* because of the Christian faith's remarkable universal claims, and, *epistemologically,* because of our biocultural heritage as human beings, where the shared resources of human rationality, and our quest for intelligibility and understanding, necessarily overlap in all the various fields of our intellectual endeavor.

In a review of Milbank's book, Aidan Nichols persuasively argued that the Christian faith is not helped at all by this kind of intellectual and spiritual isolation, or "hermeticism" (cf. 1992:327). I believe that with Milbank we have a sophisticated brand of postliberal narrative theology whose only claim to nonfoundationalism may be found in the fideist way in which the Christian narrative is not argued for in a critical encounter with contemporary culture, but is confessed over against secular culture in a retelling of the Christian narrative for its persuasive power. The price for these stark choices, and for this kind of isolationist theology, however, is high. The successful retreat to a sectarian form of rationality will be won only at the price of never again being able to criticize others who think differently because they inhabit different epistemic communities. The cost of the heroic, but fundamentally problematical choice for complete incommensurability will be the complete (and to my view fatal) loss of true intersubjectivity and cross-disciplinary engagement. On this point Milbank's theology could indeed easily become both a caricature and a victim of his own critique of certain forms of neo-orthodox theology: a theology which speaks only of itself, which does not seem to penetrate the realm of human symbolic constructions without getting tainted and distorted, and which must continue to be without any impact upon our world (cf. 1990:101).

John Milbank's simple but ingenious thesis is that, far from being two separate and self-sustaining disciplines, *theology* already contains a great deal of social theory, while the *social sciences,* on the other hand, are already steeped in theology (cf. Kerr 1992:305f.). Milbank is therefore struck by the fact that recent developments in social theory seem to suggest that — *vis-à-vis* Marxism — there is no socioeconomic reality more basic than the reality of religion. Theologians who place themselves under the rule of methodological atheism therefore uncritically accept the autonomy of secular reason. Theology's task then becomes to lay bare the theology, and anti-theology, that is at work in supposedly nontheological disciplines like sociology.

In the final part of the book it becomes clear that Milbank wants his project to be nothing less than a creative retrieval of Augustine's *De Civitate Dei:* the true peace of the heavenly city (the church) is a state of harmonious agreement, a community of love and a realization of justice for all. Christianity here is committed to the ontological priority of nonviolence, harmony, and peace over anarchy, aggression, and war. For Milbank this crucial notion of Christian theology is played off against the views of post-Nietzschean philosophers like Heidegger, Derrida, Deleuze, Foucault, and Lyotard, who are all caught under the label of "nihilism": reality ultimately is anarchy, which in the absence of God cannot be controlled except by subjecting it to the "will to power" in some form or another (cf. Milbank 1990:278ff.; also Kerr 1992:309). Milbank also deals with the views of Alasdair MacIntyre who has sought, over against this position, to retrieve a Christian moral philosophy that breaks with this kind of modern nihilism. Milbank, however, wants to radicalize the thought of MacIntyre, which he in the end finds to be far too close to Aristotle, and therefore insufficiently Christian (cf. 1990:326ff.).

Milbank's own proposal, finally, is that, in contrast to other views, Christianity alone, properly understood, is able to deny the ultimacy of chaos and conflict. Christianity alone is capable of exposing and overcoming the liberalism, positivism, dialectics, and nihilism that has infiltrated so much of Western theology (cf. Kerr 1992:310). In Graham Ward's words: Milbank deconstructs secular discourses and reveals their dependence on metaphysical and theological assumptions (cf. 1992:311). At the same time, however, he constructs a grand narrative in which a premodern theological perspective is recovered, but — again in Ward's striking words — theologically there really is no moment of revelation, no epiphany, no epistemological rupture; there is only mediation and mythologies, and his own omniscience becomes a rhetorical structure also (cf. Ward 1992:311).

Milbank will of course have to accept that, in a postmodern and nonfoundationalist context, his own account of the rationality of theological reflection is just one more story, one more way of retelling and reappropriating Christian traditions. The "truth" of this (or any other) position can indeed never again be "verified." In a sense this does not really seem to be an argument *for* Christianity, but narrative and rhetoric become, rather, the foundational categories of knowledge in Christianity's intellectual testimony to the world (cf. Ward 1992:312). I would put it as follows: the superior claim for the epistemic sovereignty and the truth of this kind of faith and this kind of theological reflection is so massive that it becomes virtually impossible not to see the fideist and crypto-foundationalist basis of its epistemological structure. The fideism implied in this version of the Christian metanarrative does not concern itself at all with the pragmatic, evaluative, or cognitive reasons for why it may still be meaningful for the Christian to live from within the realist assumptions of this faith. Ultimately a theological antirealism, where language creates all reality — including the reality of faith — rears its head here. Christianity offers a better story, has greater persuasive power as a metanarrative, because of its discourse for peace and non-mastering. Or, put differently, *Theology and Social Theory* is both an argument for the greater persuasive power of the Christian mythos and an exercise in the creation of such persuasiveness (cf. Ward 1992:313). Milbank's hope, then, is for a rhetorical victory over secular reason. In this version of a Christian narrative theology, faith becomes reason's all-pervasive context: all reasoning is an act of faith within a particular mythos, a particular story that transcends reasoning. What emerges is a theological "realism" in which language and interpreted experience do not give us epistemic access to any reality that may transcend language, but rather presuppose a sharing of God's participation in the world, a relationship that is also seen as rhetorical and narratological (cf. Milbank 1990:430). In all of this the church, which reads, retells, reenacts, and promotes the Christian mythos, is crucial to the process of a Christian social praxis, and theology becomes the narrative of that praxis. This is also Milbank's move from a "malignant" to a "benign" form of postmodernism (1990:326).

Milbank's resentment of theologies that are mediated by and reduced to social theory, and his subsequent isolationist choice for the "inner logic" of this faith, leaves unanswered, however, some of the most crucial questions about the epistemic and nonepistemic values that shape the rationality of theological reflection. He ignores not only theology's cross-disciplinary commitments, but also the epistemic role of the rationality of scientific reflection in this important interdisciplinary conversation. Some important questions, therefore, remain unanswered: What, for instance, does religious *faith* mean for Milbank? What enables us to be open to the persuasiveness of the Christian story, and then to choose for a specific form of belief or conceptual structure in which we then hold this faith commitment? Surely not "just" faith, but also the crucial and responsible judgments we make for the best possible reasons available to us. Faith and narrative practice clearly play axiomatic roles in Milbank's views, but what is the relationship between the dynamics of faith and the other epistemic and nonepistemic values that shape human rationality? Milbank certainly tells us nothing about this. And because of this, even more questions remain unanswered: In the light of the current postmodern challenge to Christian faith, what does it mean that the event of Jesus Christ, and the retelling of that event, is "foundational" for the Christian life and for the decisions we make daily? Also, there are so many versions of the Christian story: How does *one version* of this story not become yet another foundationalist ground for the appeal of this faith, and thereby reveal itself as a form of theological positivism? Milbank's view of theology as social theory in the end does not seem to take us beyond the impasse of having to choose between the absolutism of foundationalism and the relativism of nonfoundationalism.

A postfoundationalist view of rationality would reject not only modernity's marginalization and privatization of theological reflection, but also any position that would exploit this privatization by declaring a completely isolated theology the "queen of the sciences." The intellectual aloofness of Milbank's theology is thus revealed as part of a protective strategy in which first the stage seems to be set by a tacit acceptance of a typically modernist notion of superior natural scientific rationality, which is then completely *ignored,* however, as a shaping epistemological force in pursuit of this splendid theological isolation. I believe that the interdisciplinary location of theological reflection, and its relationship with the social and natural sciences, is secured only when a constructive postmodernist critique allows us to discover the shared resources of rationality between our various and diverse reasoning strategies. This kind of theology will not be marginalized or willingly isolated, nor would it want again to ascend

85

to the epistemic throne as "queen of the sciences." On the contrary, a postfoundationalist theology wants to be an *equal partner* in a democratic, interdisciplinary conversation where an authentic Christian voice might actually be heard in a postmodern, pluralist conversation.

Our discussion of postmodernism has now revealed that neither theology nor the sciences are ever based on incontrovertible, secure grounds of knowledge. What is demanded in each of these reasoning strategies is a fallibilist commitment to a corrigible point of view and to the fact that an element of the unexplained will always remain in our ongoing epistemological quest for intelligibility (cf. Russell 1989: 201). Both theology and the sciences, furthermore, have to speak of entities that are not always directly observable, and both must therefore be prepared to use models and metaphors as heuristic devices in their reflection. In science this epistemological move beyond foundationalism also points to the biggest revolution in physics since the days of Newton: the discovery of the elusive and fitful subatomic world of quantum theory. Here our world has been proved to be strange beyond our epistemological powers of imagination. If this is true for physics, it undoubtedly may be true for theology as well. In theology, the rejection of foundationalism will not, however, imply the embracing of anti- or nonfoundationalism *per se:* in any case not a type of nonfoundationalism which claims that one can engage in theological reflection without attention to the explanatory nature and interdisciplinary status of theological claims. In fact, it can be convincingly argued that the whole debate between foundationalism and nonfoundationalism is ultimately based on the false dichotomy of an outdated epistemological dilemma (cf. Bernstein 1983; also Clayton 1989:152). Moreover, I will argue that a postfoundationalist shift to a fallibilist epistemology, which honestly embraces the role of traditioned experience, personal commitment, interpretation, and the provisional and fallibilist nature of all of our knowledge claims, ultimately avoids the alleged necessity of having to choose only between foundationalism or nonfoundationalism at all.

Rationality and Postmodern Faith

Leaving behind the dichotomy that frames the foundationalism/nonfoundationalism debate opens the way to a postfoundationalist epistemology which as such may have important ramifications for theological methodology: it is, first of all, no longer necessary to hold that the traditional project of theological prolegomena is always ancillary to theology, functioning (as in "fundamental" theology) as a foundation to be dealt with prior to theological reflection and then always assumed in what follows (cf. van Huyssteen 1989:xi). Second, in a postfoundationalist theology the epistemological link between theology and other reasoning strategies will be left open and flexible because theological reflection will now necessarily be shaped by the fact that the epistemic boundaries between theology and other modes of reflection have now become so fluid. The project of a theological methodology or "prolegomena" now becomes an integral part of theological reflection as such, i.e., as part of the ramifications that an ongoing interdisciplinary inquiry will have for the practice of theology itself. What will be needed in this cross-disciplinary conversation is a methodological approach that not only recognizes theology as an explanatory discipline, but also takes seriously the epistemological problem of the shaping of rationality in theology and the sciences, the hermeneutical problem of relating context and meaning, the explanatory role of religious experience and beliefs, and the fallibilist and provisional nature of both theological and scientific truth claims. To this end the discussion of the problem of rationality in contemporary philosophy of science has recently more and more proved to be an important guide to theology, and perhaps the most fruitful theology and science link to date. This discussion not only opens up broader definitions of rationality and indicates the sort of criteria needed to govern theological assertions; it also highlights the centrality of experiential and pragmatic factors in rational judgment and explanation, and therefore in rationality in general.

In the current dialogue between theology and the sciences, only a few scholars have shown sensitivity for the difficult challenge and special demands posed to both theology and science by current postmodern, nonfoundationalist thought. One such scholar, who is both a theologian and a philosopher of science, is Nancey Murphy. Especially the publication of her acclaimed *Theology in the Age of Scientific Reasoning* (1990)[1] and subsequent publications have been very

1. For an earlier detailed discussion of this work, see J. Wentzel van Huyssteen 1997a:73ff.

welcome and crucially important additions to the growing literature on "theology and science," and in more than one way illustrate the complexity of trying to relate theological reflection to other modes of reflection in a postmodern world. I now want to return briefly, but in some more detail, to this first important work by Murphy before moving on to evaluate the implications for the rationality of theological reflection in some of her more recent work. This book is still unique in its attempt to bridge directly the gap between nonfoundationalist theology and nonfoundationalist, postmodern philosophy of science. She not only convincingly demonstrates that both theologians and philosophers of religion need a thorough knowledge of the cognitive aspects of religion, but also shows us why contemporary philosophy of science has become such an important methodological link in the current theology and science dialogue. In arguing for the epistemological integrity of theological reflection in an age dominated by scientific reasoning, Murphy wants to vindicate her claim that theology too, in its reflection on religious experience, can actually qualify as a scientific research program. Moreover, her own creative revisioning of the Lakatosian model of rationality for theology — as is now well-known — in itself becomes a novel and challenging postmodern paradigm for dealing with the troubled relationship between theology and the sciences.

True to her postmodern sensibilities, Murphy's more recent work (cf. especially Murphy 1996a; Murphy and Ellis 1996) also espouses a holist epistemology that transcends the traditional modernist boundaries between theology, philosophical theology, and philosophy of religion and eventually (although she never explicitly deals with the problem of rationality as such) centers on the problem of assessing the theologian's claims to rationality. It is especially significant to note that Murphy apparently wants to avoid the fideism of some forms of postmodern "narrative theologies," as demonstrated by her stated assumption that in this age of agnosticism and atheism, the Christian community indeed has an obligation to provide "rational support" for its belief in God "in accord with the going standards of evidence" (1990:192). What is meant by "rational support" and "the going standards of evidence," and whether her model lives up to this claim, will eventually have to be evaluated carefully. Only then will we be able to determine the validity and credibility of the promising program that is presented to us in her work.

The model that Nancey Murphy presents to us (cf. 1990) certainly is consistent with her explicit arguments against foundationalism in work published before and after this book (cf. Murphy and McClendon 1989; also Murphy 1994). Murphy has argued eloquently, along with other nonfoundationalist philosophers and theologians, that the decisive break with foundationalism came with the philosophical work of Willard V. O. Quine. In "Two Dogmas of Empiricism" Quine argued against the empiricist "dogma" that each meaningful statement is equivalent to or can always be reduced to terms that refer to immediate experience. The other "dogma" was the analytic-synthetic distinction, which provided justification for a sharp differentiation between the sciences as empirical disciplines and philosophy as purely conceptual (cf. Quine 1951:42f.). Quine's most important influence on Nancey Murphy's own holist epistemology, however, is found in his introduction of what was then a new picture of knowledge: not a building built on a sure foundation of indubitable first principles, but rather a nonfoundationalist web of beliefs (cf. Murphy 1994:12f.). It was Quine's judgment that statements are still too small a unit to be reducible to experience; it is, rather, the whole fabric of our knowledge that "faces the tribunal of experience." Therefore, changes in the total network of our beliefs are finally made on the basis of pragmatic considerations only (cf. Murphy 1990:294).

For Murphy, holism in epistemology goes together very closely with the influence of Wittgenstein and Austin on theories of language and their well-known recognition that the meaning of language is tied in so directly with its use, and that there is no more basic foundation for language than the conventions of the community that uses it. For Murphy this focus on *use* in language reveals the relation of language with its context, both to the system of linguistic conventions that govern its use, and to the social context that makes it meaningful (cf. Murphy 1994:15). This move includes her attempt to move beyond referential theories in philosophy of language, which turn out to be the equivalent of foundationalism in epistemology. On Murphy's nonfoundationalist view, then, what is true for the various religions is also true for Christian theology: religious beliefs cannot be understood or evaluated in abstraction from the practices of specific communities. There is indeed no universal, conviction-free place to stand from which convictional disputes can be adjudicated. This does not mean, however, that no rational assessment of our beliefs is possible (cf. Murphy 1994:22). This now leads to the important question: Will Nancey Murphy's nonfoundationalist philosophical theology be more successful in its claim to be truly interdisciplinary and public than Ronald Thiemann's "public" theology was? It is clear that the retrieval of the irreducible importance of the community will have epistemological, ethical as well as linguistic ramifications in Murphy's theology. As a reasoning strategy this theology will claim a "modest sort of reasonableness" that will be tolerant of diversity and ambiguity, modest about its own powers, and ultimately concerned with the practical (cf. Murphy 1994:31).

In *Theology in the Age of Scientific Reasoning* (1990), Murphy set out to dispel skepticism regarding Christian belief, so widespread since Hume and the rise of modern science. She accepts Jeffrey Stout's (1981) verdict that theology can no longer validly appeal to traditional sources of authority in order to establish its credibility, and attempts to demonstrate theology's commensurability with current scientific nonfoundationalist, "probable reasoning." Murphy argues for the rationality of Christian belief by carefully demonstrating the similarities between theological and scientific modes of reflection, and true to her postmodern, holistic sensibilities, even claims that theology is (potentially, at least) methodologically indistinguishable from the sciences (cf. Murphy 1990:198). She finally concludes that a nonfoundationalist approach to theology, when guided by important trends in contemporary philosophy of science, is indeed possible, and then justifies this by drawing on new historicist accounts of the history of science, relying heavily on philosopher of science Imre Lakatos. According to Lakatos, scientists normally work within a research program consisting of a fixed core theory and a series of changing auxiliary hypotheses that allow for prediction and for the explanation of novel facts. Furthermore, Lakatos claimed that the history of science is best understood — not in terms of successive paradigms, as it is for Thomas Kuhn — but rather in terms of competing research programs, which as such could be either progressive or degenerating (cf. Murphy 1990:59). On Lakatos's view, scientific rationality requires a specification of a criterion for choice between competing research programs. A research program always consists of a set of theories and a body of data, and one such theory, called the "hard core," is central to the research program. Next to this crucially important core theory is a set of auxiliary hypotheses that together add enough information to allow the data to be related to the hard core theory. These auxiliary hypotheses form a "protective belt" around the hard core theory and can as such be modified when potentially falsifying data are found (cf. Lakatos 1970:132ff.). Murphy competently summarizes this when she says "a research program, then, is a series of complex theories whose core remains the same while auxiliary hypotheses are successfully modified, replaced, or amplified in order to account for problematic observations" (1990:59).

Like Kuhn, Lakatos distinguished between mature and immature science. In mature science a research program includes both a negative and a positive heuristic. The negative heuristic is simply the plan to avoid falsification of the hard core, and as such implies a "hard core" of basic beliefs that could either be tacitly assumed without question, or could be treated as if they were irrefutable. The positive heuristic includes plans for the future development of the program and thus implies a long-term research policy. This gives rise, in the course of research, to a protective belt of auxiliary hypotheses (e.g., scientific models and answers to possible refutations) which, as such, are falsifiable (cf. Clayton 1989:50f.). Against this background, programs of research can over a long period of time be either fruitful or unfruitful. Hence Lakatos's distinction between progressive and degenerating research programs. For Murphy, Lakatos's answer to two of the main problems in philosophy of science can now be stated as follows:

1. Regarding *demarcation,* Lakatos claimed that we have "science" whenever there is a series of theories whose empirical content increases as the auxiliary hypotheses are modified to avoid falsification; and we have "mature science" whenever these content-increasing modifications are in accordance with a preconceived plan.
2. Regarding *justification,* Lakatos claimed there are objective reasons for choosing one program over another when the former has a more progressive record than its rival, i.e., a greater demonstrated ability to anticipate novel facts (cf. Murphy 1990b:61).

In a move that is crucial to her overall approach, Murphy then argues that similar patterns of probable reasoning can be used to justify theological claims. Lakatos's idea of a research program with its own distinctive hard core, negative and positive heuristic, now becomes central to her proposal for a nonfoundationalist theology. Following Lakatos, Murphy argues that theologians also need an imaginative judgment, an organizing idea regarding what Christianity is about, before they start. This idea would be the hard core of the program, and should contain the theologian's judgment about how to sum up the very minimum of the relevant community's faith. As the hard core of her own nonfoundationalist theology, Nancey Murphy wants to begin with a minimal doctrine of God, including the trinitarian nature of God, God's holiness, and God's revelation in Jesus Christ (cf. Murphy 1990:184). In addition to this Lakatosian idea of a hard core, the negative heuristic is simply the plan to protect the hard core from falsification by making additions or changes in the belt of supporting clusters of theories called auxiliary hypotheses. The positive heuristic consists of those methodological and doctrinal commitments called upon to guide a specific theology along a consciously chosen programmatic path.

In what may be the most original part of this specific book, however, Murphy develops a characterization and analysis of what could be regarded as "theological data" for a postmodern Lakatosian theological model. This indeed focuses Murphy's program on what I would regard as one of the most central issues for philosophical theology today: *theologians who want to approach theological methodology from an anti-authoritarian and postfoundationalist viewpoint, precisely in our scientific age, will have to select from the manifold of interpreted religious experience those elements that plausibly claim to yield some form of knowledge of God.* The theologian must therefore not only have access to religious experience and what is revealed through interpreted experience, but should also formulate criteria for the proper means of distinguishing valid and reliable knowledge claims for theology. Drawing on the rich history of spiritual discernment in the works of Jonathan Edwards, Ignatius Loyola, and the Anabaptist tradition, Nancey Murphy takes up this challenge and develops her thoroughly postmodern idea of communal discernment as perhaps the most typical of Christian epistemic practices. Against this background, Murphy claims that the most pressing requirement in a search for suitable data for theology would be to find ways to distinguish data that have a bearing on the nature of God, and those that bear only on the psychology or history of religion (cf. 1990:130). For Murphy, suitable data for theology would eventually be the results of Christian discernment, i.e., specific communal judgments regarding the involvement of God in assorted events in the life of the church, and would therefore focus on moral and devotional practices. Christian communal discernment therefore determines suitable data for theology, and the participants' descriptions of the results of such communal discernment can in fact provide data for theology *that already contain reference to God* (cf. Murphy 1990:163). Crucial data for theology could eventually, however, also be scriptural texts, historical facts, sociological and anthropological data, and perhaps even facts from the natural sciences (1990:130). Murphy seems to be suggesting that, in both theology and science, the surest way to get from observations or hypotheses to theories that explain them is to begin with observations that are already expressed in language suggestive of the causes, or of a deeper explanatory commitment (Murphy 1990:164). Murphy thus proposes that the results of Christian discernment, i.e., judgments regarding the involvement of God in assorted events in the life of the church, be viewed as candidates for data in theology.

Murphy also stresses that the categories of appropriate data must be determined by the content of the research program itself, especially by its positive heuristic and by auxiliary hypotheses of a methodological nature. On this view, facts of the devotional and moral life of the church can now also function as data for theological reflection, and, as such, provide the data that serve to confirm theological doctrines. This leads to the basic question: How is one to distinguish in general between religious experiences that represent encounters with God, and those that do not? For Murphy the Christian church, in a long history of communal decisions and judgments, provides a rich treasury of answers to just these questions (1990:132). It is within this context that she proposes that the crucial data for theology are the results of Christian discernment. On the basis of the practice of communal discernment, participants in a wide assortment of Christian communities select certain observable events in ordinary church life and then designate them as acts (or words) of God. It is these discernments, resulting from Christian communal consensus, that form an important and often overlooked category of data for theology. It is also this practice of making knowledge claims about God's activity in human life on the basis of discernment, that Murphy calls a Christian epistemic practice (1990:159). An adequate set of criteria for discernment in the Christian church includes the following: (1) agreement with the apostolic witness; (2) production of a Christlike character in those affected, viz., freedom from sin and manifestation of the fruits of the Spirit; and (3) unity in the community based on prayerful discussion (Murphy 1990:152). When these criteria are met, the authentic work of the Spirit can be recognized with reasonable certainty and theologians can then proceed to claim it as data for theological research programs.

The following critical question, however, has to be put to Murphy: Are these criteria indeed appropriate to their explicitly stated purpose? If her goal is to meet the challenge of probable, nonfoundationalist reasoning, then not only her Lakatosian methodology, but also the data, and the epistemic status of the data that feed into it, must conform to certain scientific epistemic standards.[2] And precisely on this point Murphy's model for a nonfoundationalist theology seems to be suspect. In the light of Hume's and Stout's challenges, precisely the status and authority of the apostolic witness in Scripture, and the authority of Christ, is seriously in doubt in our complex and pluralized postmodern culture. Murphy would therefore not be justified in making Scripture a criterion for judgment in a cross-disciplinary conversation between theology and the sciences, since she gives no reasons why it should have even a formal authority, or what that authority may mean today (cf. van Huyssteen 1987:30f.). This is not to say that the authority of Scripture cannot be warranted on the basis of probable reasoning, but only that Murphy does not do it — at least not in the kind of interdisciplinary discussion that would go beyond the mere analogy to Lakatosian, scientific methodology, and also beyond the esoteric communal discernment of a very specific Christian community. This leads one to suspect that these criteria have their epistemic foundation in a deeper and prior commitment to a very specific confessional and theorized version of the Christian faith, carefully insulated and protected in the "hard core" of this theological program. This obviously raises the specter of an epistemological fideism that would not at all be commensurable with Murphy's nonfoundationalist attempt at probable reasoning. It furthermore raises the critical question whether a model from the natural sciences

2. I am indebted to James A. Moos for his insightful contributions on this specific issue.

94

(in this case that of Imre Lakatos) can successfully be appropriated to determine the rationality of theological reflection. Using the methodological framework of Lakatos's model as a protective strategy to safely locate and then isolate theist assumptions, as well as assumptions about the authority of Scripture and the Spirit within the unassailable hard core of a theological program, certainly does not guarantee probable reasoning. It leaves us wondering, instead, why in such an explicitly nonfoundationalist context, a (Lakatosian) model appropriated from (and for) the *natural* sciences should be so epistemically privileged as to shape theological reflection. What is more, in contradiction to Murphy's explicit goal, it demonstrates that theology is not at all indistinguishable from the sciences in its methodology (Murphy 1990:198), but could in fact turn out to be very different from the sciences. But if this were true, theologians would ultimately have to concede that theological rationality could indeed turn out to be radically different from current conceptions of scientific rationality. A crucial question for theology can now be phrased as follows: If, in the light of the Christian faith's traditional realist assumptions, we were to agree that faith in God is neither an epistemic virtue nor an epistemic vice, and therefore does not make the object of religious faith more or less probable (cf. Clayton 1989:143), how will it be possible to get out of the vicious cycle of fideism to gain access to cross-disciplinary, intersubjective criteria that may help us to determine Christian theology's location in the current interdisciplinary conversation?

For Murphy the answer to this question is to be found in the believing community's discerning evaluation of religious experience as the data for theological reflection. This may make theological reflection sound remarkably like scientific reasoning, but as such tells us nothing yet about the cross-disciplinary obligations and possibilities of theological reflection and other strategies of reasoning. In spite of the fact that Murphy attempts to construct a nonfoundationalist theology by seeing religious experience as the primary data for theological research programs, her model lacks a well-developed theory of experience. Such a theory might have enabled her not only to focus on religious experience as data for theological reflection, but also to move beyond fideist assumptions by highlighting the explanatory role of interpreted religious experience. This would include also, and maybe especially, those experiences that are inextricably interwoven with some of our most basic or "hard core" religious beliefs and convictions. And because of the meaning-giving role of experience, and the analogous role of experiential claims in science, precisely the explanatory role of interpreted experience can become an important and decisive link in the theology and science dialogue.

From this it will later become clear that, within a holist, postfoundationalist epistemology, any theory of experience will always be a further refinement of one's theory of rationality. In our quest for theological intelligibility, religious experience therefore not only guides us in finding ultimate meaning in our lives, but also ultimately connects the religious quest for understanding with our more general quest for understanding our world rationally. For the interdisciplinary dialogue of theology with the sciences, an adequate theory of experience thus becomes a crucial issue. Murphy, citing William Alston, correctly states that somehow what goes on in the experience of leading the Christian life indeed provides some ground for Christian belief and makes some contribution to its rationality (1990:159). Because we are convinced that somehow God is acting in our lives, we are more justified than we would have been otherwise. Thus, Murphy does claim that the results of Christian discernment can serve as data for theology despite the fact that such data always and inevitably involve a long and complex history of interpretation. A serious challenge to this view, however, involves not only the reliability of these communal discernments, but — as we have just seen — the need to justify conceptualizing experience in theistic terms in the first place. Murphy, however, not only argues for the need for communal discernment and the need to make more frequent and determined use of this practice (1990:166), she also argues for a degree of objectivity in these communal judgments. "Objectivity" for her simply means that others under similar circumstances, and with the same experiences, will see the same thing.

Thus, the process of Christian discernment not only satisfies the requirement of providing suitable data for theology, but actually turns out to be a replicable process. As such it can not only be repeated, just as scientists repeat experiments, but can also produce novel facts. Murphy, therefore, would conclude that theological facts do not differ all that much from scientific facts in this regard (1990:168). The replicable process of Christian discernment or community consensus can, however, hardly be compared so directly to the disciplined control of the scientific experimental context. At most, it demonstrates that both scientific and theological data are theory-laden, that they function within the context of traditioned experience, and that degrees of objectivity exist and are always context-bound. It does not, however, tell us anything about the epistemological problem of trying to formulate transcommunal criteria for some of the truth claims and realist assumptions in theological reflection.

Murphy does state (1990:173) that, although the results of Christian discernment meet all the standard requirements of scientific data, they will not be of the same quality (reliability, replicability) as those of the natural sciences. She qualifies this by stating that, as such, they may more justly be compared to those of the human sciences; but unfortunately, she does not expand on this. Thus, by evaluating the data of theological reflection, she argues for her view that Lakatos's model gives us a workable criterion for choosing between competing scientific programs. But because theological programs have been shown to function not at all like scientific research programs in Murphy's model, Lakatos's criterion of relative empirical progress could hardly be used to adjudicate between competing theological theories or schools. If what is acceptable to a specific theological community is always directly and contextually tied in with what that community has already, and in advance, decided to protect as the "hard core" of their beliefs, how would an epistemically rather insulated community like this be able to access transcommunal criteria so as to "empirically" discern which theological program(s) may be the more progressive one(s)? In addition, we are left with no idea how one of Murphy's most startling claims could ever be justified: that the more acceptable (and progressive) theological program(s) may in the end actually claim to provide (superior?) knowledge of God and of God's relation to the world (Murphy 1990:174).

Murphy's nonfoundationalist attempt at a Lakatosian theological methodology finally runs into its most serious problems when she proposes a convention for postmodern philosophical theology and radically opposes modern thought and postmodernism. For Murphy, postmodern theologians are those whose presuppositions are postmodern rather than modern and who have removed themselves decisively from the modern conceptual space (1990:201; cf. also 1989). Against the background of a discussion of Thiemann's and Lindbeck's work, she defines the typically postmodern change as (1) a change from foundationalism to holism in epistemology; (2) a change from the modern emphasis on reference and representation to an emphasis on language as action, and meaning as use; and (3) a change from individualism to the irreducible importance of communal thinking and consensus. Whether Murphy's version of postmodern nonfoundationalism can manage by itself to move beyond postliberal, neoconservatism toward a postfoundational framework with room for an interdisciplinary conversation along transcommunal criteria now seems rather problematical. By radically opposing postmodernism to modern thought (instead of distinguishing between affirmative and skeptical forms of postmodernism, and exploring the ongoing critical relationship between postmodernism and modernity), Murphy cuts herself off from perhaps the most distinctive trait of postmodernism — its ongoing, relentless criticism of modernist, foundationalist assumptions. Theology in this mode inevitably becomes, epistemologically at least, truly nonfoundationalist and therefore completely insulated, with no possibility of true intersubjective communication, in spite of its Lakatosian guise. Without any plausible intersubjectivity, however, one of the most salient features of the Lakatosian program falls away: the ability to make a choice, and to progress by critically choosing between competing research programs.

If we were to see rationality just minimally as a quest for intelligibility, or even just follow Lakatos in his notion of competing research programs, it becomes inevitable that we should move beyond contextualism and compare the rationality of our judgments and explanations in various and different contexts — including, therefore, the diverse contexts of theology and the sciences and the differences between them. This, again, touches the heart of Murphy's crucial notion of communal discernment — not only because of the troublesome question of how reliable these communal discernments in the history of the Christian church(es) are (even if, as Murphy claims, they are replicable by the same religious or faith group), but also because of their limited and severely restricted epistemic scope. For a viable form of explanatory progress in the life of the church and in theological reflection, Murphy appeals to communal consensus. Consensus, as a form of interpersonal agreement that may help us attain a uniformity of belief and action, has of course throughout history been a strong desideratum. Nicholas Rescher, however, has argued very persuasively (as we will see in more detail later) against the extremely restricted epistemic scope of communal consensus and has emphasized instead legitimate diversity and the epistemic importance of dissensus. The fact that different people may have different experiences in even the same situations makes it normal, natural, and rational that they should proceed differently in cognitive, evaluative, and practical matters (cf. Rescher 1993:3ff.).

The belief that communal consensus plays a leading role in matters of rational inquiry, decision, and practice is one of the oldest and most pervasive ideas in philosophy, and explains why communal consensus has so often functioned as the "touchstone of truth" (cf. Rescher 1993:6) and the guarantor of correctness in matters of belief, decision, and action. The fact of the matter is, however, that dissensus and diversity can often play a highly constructive role in human affairs. As to the question whether those of us who belong to the same community should not ultimately be able to reach agreement on meaningful issues, the answer is: not necessarily. As we will see in the next chapter, rationality consists in effecting an appropriate alignment between our beliefs and the persuasive reasons we have for hanging on to them. Rescher correctly argues that different individuals will, therefore, very often confront different bodies of evidence, identify different reasons as good reasons, and therefore evaluate them differently. Rationality and rational procedures, as we will see, do not necessarily have to lead to community consensus. It is, rather, rational to do what is *optimal,* as best as we can determine it, and to do the best we can manage to do in the actually prevailing conditions (1993:8f.). In this sense consensus is revealed as, at most, an ideal, but not always as a realizable fact of life. Because of important differences between our experiences, our epistemic situations, and our cognitive values, the diversity of our traditions will not only yield different communities, but also make for a difference in beliefs, judgments, and actions within one and the same community. In the postfoundationalist notion of rationality that I want to propose, the move beyond the extremes of foundationalism/nonfoundationalism will not first of all aim at consensus, because communal consensus is neither a requisite for nor a consequence of rationality.

What theology needs in its discussion with a secularized scientific culture, however, is to show that what really challenges the shaping of rationality in postmodern theology is its ability to represent an authentic Christian voice in precisely a radically pluralist context. In the end a postfoundationalist, holist epistemology should imply more than just communal discernment and nonfoundationalist consensus for contemporary theological reflection. It also demands a broader intersubjective coherence that goes beyond the limited parameters of the experience and reflection of a specific believing community. If Nancey Murphy's proposed convention for a postmodern theology cannot demonstrate this, the serious problem of how a Lakatosian theology would deal with the problem of fideism remains unresolved.

Closely linked to this is the question whether the Lakatosian model — even if it is well-suited to determining empirical progress in the natural sciences — can adequately cope with the broader and complex problem of meaning as highlighted by the social and human sciences, and by theological reflection. Murphy correctly and very efficiently disarms all forms of modernist foundationalism in her central argument. But when she designates the presupposed existence of God as "hard core" for a theological research program (à la Lakatos), and then adds that this hard core will always typically contain reference to God (1990:194), not only is the important hermeneutical problem of the metaphorical and epistemic function of religious language raised; also the very distinction between "hard core beliefs" and others that could be regarded as "less" hard core, or as auxiliary hypotheses, invariably raises the specter of at least a weak form of epistemological foundationalism.

Our discussion of these difficult but important issues does, however, benefit directly from the stimulating input of Nancey Murphy's recent work in the theology and science dialogue. She is certainly right in asserting that theology can constitute a kind of knowledge that does not conflict with, but actually is on a par with the epistemic status of scientific knowledge. That this possibility is embedded in the fact that theological reflection may actually share all-important rational resources with scientific and other modes of cognition, is finally, however, left unexplored in Murphy's Lakatosian model for a nonfoundationalist theology. We will see how important it is to realize that a postfoundationalist theology can properly aim for justified beliefs and for a tentative and provisional knowledge of what Christians have come to call God. Earlier we saw how Ronald Thiemann's work exemplifies a nonfoundationalist theology that insists on the unique logical integrity of theological reflection, an integrity which is understood as faithfulness to the central beliefs of the Christian narrative. In her brand of nonfoundationalist Lakatosian theology, Nancey Murphy has certainly managed to move beyond the restrictions of an esoteric theology that wants to assure its own logical integrity only and exclusively through the contextuality of its own disciplinary reasoning. For this reason she could conclude that a nonfoundationalist approach to theology should be guided by current philosophy of science, and that therefore "forms of reasoning common to all kinds of science" can be used as a basis for persuading those outside of the Christian community of the rationality and intelligibility of its claims (cf. Murphy 1990:206). Murphy's model thus certainly reveals both the seriousness of her commitment to Christian theology's interdisciplinary status and its ongoing debate with the sciences, and also her tolerance for the cognitive pluralism that necessarily flows from the fact that in theology too we relate to our world epistemically only though the complexity of interpreted experience.

Murphy's latest work certainly portrays a very distinct awareness of the "relativist worries" that come with much of nonfoundationalist theology. Her recent *Beyond Liberalism and Fundamentalism* represents a huge step toward interdisciplinary awareness as she raises the important question of whether the beliefs and epistemological standards of a convictional community are always simply up to the community itself (cf. Murphy 1996b:98). Her answer to this is now a definitive move beyond the idea that standards of rationality are always and only context dependent. For Murphy the justification of our beliefs now involves two sorts of questions: First, is a particular belief justifiable within the particular web to which it belongs? Second, is a specific web of belief, a paradigm, or research tradition, justifiable over against its competitors? This second question clearly and radically focuses a concern for the interdisciplinary status of theological reflection.

In *On the Moral Nature of the Universe*, Nancey Murphy collaborates with physicist George Ellis and they now boldly proceed to relocate theology within a broader, interdisciplinary context (1996). The specific aim of this book's central argument is to develop a unified worldview that will relate the natural and social sciences in a hierarchy of disciplines, all held together by theology at the very top of this hierarchy. Murphy and Ellis, however, are not just attempting an interdisciplinary link between theology and the sciences, but are also aiming at providing an objective grounding for ethics and the social sciences. To reach this goal they propose a branching hierarchy of disciplines: at the "bottom" the fundamental disciplines of physics, chemistry, and biology, followed by the "higher" disciplines which then branch into the natural sciences (ecology, astrophysics, and cosmology) and into the human sciences (psychology and the social sciences, with ethics as a science at the top of the hierarchy of the social sciences).

The purpose of this book is to argue that when we take into account the full range of human experience, as described by such a hierarchical ordering, the generally accepted body of scientific knowledge (as exemplified by the natural and human sciences together) is in fact incomplete. Murphy and Ellis therefore argue that in both cosmology and ethics (respectively at the "top" of the natural and human sciences) boundary questions arise which ultimately are unanswerable by each discipline: science cannot explain why the universe exists, nor can it provide a compelling explanation for its fine-tuning and propensity for intelligent human life, while the human sciences cannot give a complete account of reality without taking into consideration the importance and pervasiveness of a sense of moral obligation. This can be done only by ethics, and only by an ethics that has been metaphysically grounded in theology. Murphy and Ellis then finally argue for a *theological* account of ultimate reality, and place theology at the "top" in order to complete the hierarchy of the sciences (cf. 1996:15-87).

Murphy and Ellis thus aim to provide a structure or model for understanding the relations among the natural and social sciences, ethics and theology, that sees them as hierarchically ordered but also as intrinsically connected. On this view there are aspects of reality at every level that can be explained reductively, in terms of lower levels. There are also, however, boundary questions that can only be answered by turning to a higher level: scientific cosmology raises boundary questions that can only be answered theologically; and the social sciences raise questions that can only be answered by turning to ethics. Ethical systems, in turn, ultimately raise theological questions also (cf. Murphy and Ellis 1996:250). As the natural sciences give rise to questions of the overall structure and scope of the natural world, thereby making the discipline of cosmology necessary, so the human sciences, focused on questions of human intentionality and organization, give rise to moral questions, thus necessitating the discipline of ethics. The highest disciplines of each branch, i.e., ethics and cosmology, finally give rise to the kind of boundary questions that require grounding in the "highest" discipline of theology. Theology, and the theological worldview it shapes for us, thus literally becomes the most coherent and comprehensive in explanatory power. However, not just any theology or any ethic is compatible with the findings of science. Only a theology that incorporates a "kenotic ethic" is capable of fully providing an explanation both for the fine-tuning and indeterminacy of the universe, as well as for the most adequate social organizations and structures of our human community. The self-renunciation implied in the moral nature of God and God's will for human life, is then ultimately revealed as at the very "hard core" of this theological program, and is, for Murphy and Ellis, uniquely fitted to the universe as we now understand it (cf. 1996:220).

Unlike Joseph Rouse, who developed a much more extremely nonfoundationalist model for postmodern science, Murphy and Ellis maintain a very distinct place for epistemology and refuse to subsume the sciences into cultural or social practices.[3] They try to do this by making use of three theories of rationality: Carl Hempel's hypothetico-deductive method, Imre Lakatos's notion of research programs, and Alasdair MacIntyre's theory of tradition. It is clear at this stage, however, that Murphy's earlier use of Lakatos's views on the way natural science empirically functions in terms of research programs, has now been extended significantly: on *each* level of the hierarchy of the sciences, now elaborated to include both ethics and theology, the epistemological structure is that of a research program (cf. Murphy and Ellis 1996:222). This does raise the serious concern as to whether this tacit admission to the superior nature of natural scientific rationality is even compatible with the appropriation of MacIntyre's notion of the epistemic and hermeneutical importance of traditions. In Murphy's interdisciplinary work we do therefore find a rather strange mixture of nonfoundationalist theology (now with Anabaptist principles like the central role of ethics in religious life, and a commitment to self-sacrifice and nonviolence added to its "hard core"), connected to other reasoning strategies via a normative model of rationality that clearly still privileges the natural sciences. This could mean, of course, that Murphy may just be convinced that, although natural scientific

---

3. I am grateful to Kimlyn Bender for significantly contributing to this point in discussion.

rationality is not a superior form of human rationality, it may still qualify as our clearest example of human rationality at work, although this is never really explained. The choice for a Lakatosian methodology does of course, as we saw earlier, enable Murphy (in a typically nonfoundationalist way) to epistemologically justify the transference of the notion of a research program with a "hard core" to theology, and to use it there as a protective strategy for not really challenging the most basic beliefs and principles protected in that hard core.

This still leaves us, however, with some serious questions. Murphy has recently written that we can now begin to see the emergence of a consistent postmodern worldview involving science, philosophy of language, epistemology, and ethics (cf. 1996a:152). Of course, we have seen in the preceding chapter that there are many and varied notions of postmodernism alive today. Even so, it is not at all clear how exactly the epistemic move from a postmodern nonfoundationalism to an ambitious interdisciplinary project (carefully structured as a hierarchy of the sciences, with theology emerging as the queen of the sciences, "back in her rightful place" [cf. Murphy 1996a:109]) has taken place. How does the epistemic sovereignty that theology now enjoys, *not* become a brand new modernist metanarrative that totalizes and subsumes all disciplines under a unifying worldview that can ultimately never really be challenged thanks to its privileged, protected position in the program's "hard core"? And does the fact that all sciences, including now ethics and theology, ultimately share the structural similarity of a rather normative Lakatosian concept of rationality really qualify as true interdisciplinary reflection?

The comprehensive interdisciplinary program as envisioned by Murphy and Ellis does seem to leave unexplored important questions as to the nature of rationality, and to what extent diverse and often very different reasoning strategies may share in the rich resources of rationality without being totalized into one, unifying worldview. Already with Joseph Rouse we saw how postmodernism has exploded rigid distinctions between hermeneutics and epistemology, and even challenged the boundaries between the natural and human sciences in ways that were not thought to be possible before. I will argue that a postfoundationalist clue to interdisciplinary reflection will be found when in widely divergent reasoning strategies we discover the same interpretive procedures at work through our sharing of the rich resources of rationality. Rouse has opened the door for a revisioned look at a more holistic form of interdisciplinary reflection. The hierarchical model proposed by Murphy and Ellis may actually share this kind of holism if the hierarchy of emerging complexity does not claim to be more than just a descriptive model, if boundary questions between all disciplines can be discussed in an open, democratic epistemological space, and if theology (as "queen of the sciences") does not usurp her power to freeze the interdisciplinary endeavor by again totalizing it into a grand and royal new metanarrative.

In Conclusion

In Thiemann's model for a narrativist form of postmodern, nonfoundationalist theology, it quickly became clear how a fideist construal of the way we hang on to our beliefs can isolate and push theology to the brink of complete epistemic relativism. At the same time, both Thiemann and Murphy have argued successfully that foundationalist accounts of knowledge have never worked well for theologians. Nancey Murphy takes this one step further and, while rejecting foundationalism, also strongly denies the claim that nonfoundationalist, holist theories of knowledge need be the cause of relativism and nihilism. In Murphy's view relativism arises for foundationalists only when no single set of indubitable foundations can be found. The history of modern epistemology and philosophy of science shows, however, that these purported foundations either turn out to depend on nonfoundational knowledge for acceptance, or turn out not to be indubitable, or, if indubitable turn out to be useless, since there is no reliable way to argue from them to any interesting conclusions (cf. Murphy 1994:268f.). So it is this epistemic predicament, along with the assumption that there must be foundations, that finally produces skepticism and relativism. In Murphy's own words: to foundationalists, holists sound like relativists because they admit there are no foundations (Murphy 1994:269). I am suggesting, however, that nonfoundationalists not only sound like relativists because they admit that there are no foundations, but that nonfoundationalism can actually collapse into relativism when a retreat to commitment becomes a protective strategy for a theology already fideistically insulated from other modes of reflection.

Murphy's claim, that the absence of foundations entails relativism only if foundationalism is true (cf. 1994:269), also seems to be vulnerable to another line of criticism that John Thiel recently pointed to. Those who share nonfoundationalists' criticism of foundationalism but who are nonetheless wary of nonfoundationalism's apparent epistemic relativism, are tempted to seize the opportunity to argue that such relativism is in any case self-defeating: nonfoundationalism may condemn a particular notion of foundations for knowledge, but the strong commitment to meaning, action, or faith must require *some* foundational presupposition (cf. Thiel 1994:81). And it is indeed tempting to read Murphy's views on the crucial epistemic role of hard core beliefs and communal discernment in much the same way as Stanley Hauerwas would have us believe that "in a world without foundations all we have is the church" (cf. Hauerwas 1994:145). Is Murphy's appeal to the believing community — and Hauerwas's appeal to the church — a new form of crypto-foundationalism, where it finally becomes clear that nonfoundationalists cannot avoid an appeal to some authoritative givenness that always functions as an epistemic assumption in their understanding of the way we justify our belief? My answer to this would be: only if the conceptual set of beliefs in which we hold this commitment is first and carefully isolated in a protective strategy, from where it can then anew start functioning as an uncritical, fideistic foundation for the rest of our knowledge. Nancey Murphy's model for a nonfoundationalist Lakatosian theology clearly does not fall into this trap: her claim is not that we can transcend our assumptions or strong convictions in interdisciplinary discussion, or in the construction of theories in theology, but only that no privileged assumption possesses the ability to ground the edifice of our knowledge (cf. Thiel 1994:28). To protect herself from similar accusations, Murphy may have to spell out more carefully what the epistemic role of rational judgment is in identifying the already highly theorized and multi-interpreted hard core of her theological program. This of course would make the conceptual network of beliefs in which such a hard core of Christian beliefs is held, much more vulnerable to criticism, but it would also protect Murphy from the misunderstanding that epistemically legitimate assumptions and commitments might in fact conceal deeper theoretical "foundations." There is indeed a sense, as we will soon see, in which our background beliefs can be regarded as a *post*foundationalist context for our acts of knowing.

John Thiel has also very successfully argued that nonfounda-tionalists are often reluctant to acknowledge the metaphorical char-acter of the "foundationlessness" of postmodern rationality. As con-sistent as the nonfoundational argument may be against the logical viability of foundations for knowledge, there remains a temptation in nonfoundational discourse to regard the counter-metaphor of "foundationlessness" as oddly immune to or unaffected by the very relativity it expresses, and so as no metaphor at all (cf. Thiel 1994:85). Nonfoundationalist discourse, however, is in itself an ex-pression of the utter contextuality and fallibilist nature of human knowledge, and when nonfoundationalist theologians use the meta-phors of "foundations" and "foundationlessness" in particular ways, it is always to specifically reflect value judgments about what is re-garded as theologically appropriate or inappropriate in a particular situation or context. "Foundationlessness" in the work of theolo-gians like Thiemann refers to the Christian faith as it has been nor-matively expressed, practiced, and experienced through the ages. In Nancey Murphy's theology, this "foundationlessness" also names the web of practiced Christian belief, faithful to the norms shaped by communal discernment and supported philosophically by the nonfoundationalist work of Quine and Lakatos. As a metaphor "foundationlessness" has, as John Thiel has shown, not only episte-mic, but also very specific contextual limitations: for this reason nonfoundational philosophers like Quine and Rorty (and, I would add, even Lakatos) would hardly accept the specific theological con-ception of "foundationlessness" delineated in the work of Thie-mann, Hauerwas, and Murphy. Indeed, for these philosophers, any appeal to a self-authenticating revelation in Scripture or tradition would qualify as a claim to an immediately justified belief, and as such would constitute a form of foundationalism. The fact that phi-losophers like Quine and Rorty have been unwilling to raise their critical voices against such specific theological claims cannot be at-tributed to their high regard for the foundationlessness of Christian contextualist rationality, but rather to their judgment that authorita-tive claims of faith such as these are examples of a foundationalism too obvious to refute (cf. Thiel 1994:87).

This now poses tremendous problems for a theology that wants to move beyond the constraints of both foundationalism and non-foundationalism in a serious attempt to construct a postfoundationalist rationality for theological reflection: Do the ultimate faith commitments and strong convictions of the Christian faith mean that nonfoundational theology in the end really is a contradiction in terms, or does a "foundationlessness" theology only stress how contextually bound definitions of nonfoundationalism (and the foundationalism against which it defines itself) really are? Even more challenging questions can be added here: What is the epistemic status and shaping role of our ultimate religious commitments? Are strong and personal religious convictions radically opposed to and different from other forms of knowledge, and would this again imply a radical difference between theological and scientific rationality? Nonfoundationalism may offer valuable insights into the contextuality of knowledge, but if that contextuality were to extend to rationality itself, how would intellectual reflection and criticism be able to transcend a circular and fideist reiteration and restatement of reasoning's background beliefs (cf. Thiel 1994:93)?

A postfoundationalist notion of rationality should in fact be able to claim the exact opposite: as theologians we should be able to enter the pluralist, cross-disciplinary conversation with our full personal convictions, while at the same time being theoretically empowered to step beyond the limitations and boundaries of our own local, disciplinary contexts. I will argue that, even with widely divergent personal, disciplinary, or even religious viewpoints, we still do share (even in a fragmented, postmodern culture) the rich resources of human rationality. And because of these shared resources of rationality, we also share an epistemological overlap of beliefs and reasoning strategies that may finally provide a safe space or a common ground for a cross-disciplinary conversation between theology and the other sciences to begin. As a response to the postmodern challenge, fideism therefore remains maybe the most important pitfall for postfoundationalist theology to avoid. We now know, however, that the strong religious convictions and ultimate commitments presupposed by theological reflection by no means necessarily lead to this religious version of foundationalism.

Finally, it is clear that the postmodern challenge to both theology and the sciences leaves us with serious problems as well as exciting challenges. Both in postmodern science and in nonfoundationalist theologies the powerful step beyond modernity was taken by a radical return to local, interpretative contexts. What is first required here is a trusting attitude toward local contexts of practice, toward scientific and theological traditions, respectively, where these are understood, not as representing an authoritative consensus, but rather a field of concerns within which both consensus and dissent acquire a local intelligibility. We have also seen, however, that both Nancey Murphy and Joseph Rouse have attempted to step beyond the new tribalism and new conventionalism of a nonfoundationalist rationality (cf. Haack 1996:222). Murphy's attempt was defined by her significant extension of the notion of a Lakatosian research program: on each level of the hierarchy of the sciences, now elaborated to include both ethics and theology, the epistemological structure of the specific reasoning strategy is that of a research program. This, as we saw, however, still leaves us with the question of how a nonfoundationalist theology can be interdisciplinarily connected to other reasoning strategies via a normative model of rationality that still so clearly privileges the natural sciences. Joseph Rouse also realized that the local, narrative reconstruction of postmodern science as social practice could easily slide into an incommensurability of disparate and isolated language games, and a relativism of localized, disciplinary rationalities. Rouse's way to avoid this was to introduce the notion of "standardization," which helped him to extend local scientific knowledge to other locations where science is being practiced. It remained unclear, however, how exactly his postmodern notion for "a cultural studies of science" would allow for the broader issue of interdisciplinary reflection, and how that may or may not involve a distinct cultural domain such as religion, and theology as a critical reflection on religious experience. Ultimately, however, it has been *the notion of rationality* itself that has been seriously and fundamentally challenged by postmodernism. It is to the problem of the nature of human rationality, and its standards and rich resources, that we have to now turn.

Chapter Three

Rationality and Postfoundationalism

"The fact of the matter is that postmodernism has been unable to come to terms with the issue of rationality from a more positive perspective."

Calvin O. Schrag, *The Resources of Rationality*
(Bloomington: Indiana University Press, 1992:155)

It has now become quite clear that the postmodern challenge to the theology and science dialogue very specifically demands that we reflect critically on the epistemic and nonepistemic values that shape the rationality of our reflection. Especially in theology, this implies, first of all, a challenge to transcend the intellectual coma of fideism and foundationalism. This challenge will also bring us face to face with the issue of the truth claims of our religious and theological statements. Religious beliefs are normally — and often passionately — held to be true and not just merely useful, and their assertions about reality are indeed universal in intent. From an epistemological point of view this obviously raises very difficult questions: What exactly do our religious beliefs explain, what is the epistemic status of these explanations, and how do the nature and status of these explanations compare to the theories that scientists use to explain our world? And as far as the truth of our religious and theological convictions goes: Since religion and theo-

111

logical truth claims are almost always inextricably linked to communities, is there a way beyond communal consensus to justify the cognitive claims of religious beliefs, or should these beliefs always be seen as merely expressing our own deepest personal convictions?

Those of us who work in philosophical theology really do find ourselves at the crossroads of an even broader range of rather bewildering sets of questions: How, and why, do some of us hang on to some form of religious faith in our very fragmented and confusing postmodern age, an age that often and ambiguously seems also to be shaped by the imperialist claims of natural scientific rationality? What happens to the problem of the certainty of faith, to passionate commitments and deep convictions, in a postmodern cultural context that after the jettisoning of all forms of foundationalism now seems to be celebrating cultural and religious pluralism with such abandon? In the light of this pervasive pluralism, does it even make sense to still aim for some unified form of knowledge where all our diverse and disparate epistemic claims can somehow be integrated with one another? Can Christian theology, as a disciplined reflection on religious experience, ever really claim to be part of a public, interdisciplinary conversation, and if so, will it be able to do that without retreating to the esoteric world of private, insular knowledge claims?

At the heart of this contemporary form of the problem of interdisciplinary reflection obviously lies the deeper problem of how the epistemic and nonepistemic values that shape the rationality of theological reflection will be similar to or different from those that shape the rationality of other modes of reflection — especially the rationality of the natural sciences, which have acquired such a normative and paradigmatic status in our culture. This special status of science, even if it is to be questioned and toned down, still is the reason why I argue that contemporary philosophy of science, with its enduring focus on the problem of rationality, has indeed earned a place as perhaps the most important link in the ongoing interdisciplinary debate about the nature and status of theological knowledge. Not only in philosophy of science, however, but also in theology, alternative interpretations and constructive appropriations of postmodern themes have now become viable options. This positive appropriation of a constructive form of postmodernism is crucial for what I am calling *postfoundationalist theology*.[1]

---

1. Cf. J. Wentzel van Huyssteen, *Essays in Postfoundationalist Theology* (1997a).

Postmodernism, as a complex and pervasive cultural attitude (as we saw in the first chapter), first of all and very pointedly rejects all forms of epistemological foundationalism, as well as those ubiquitous, accompanying metanarratives that so readily claim to sanction and legitimize all our knowledge, our judgments, our decisions, and our actions. Over against the alleged objectivism of foundationalism and the extreme relativism of most forms of nonfoundationalism, I will pursue the argument that a postfoundationalist theology will enable us to fully acknowledge the role of context, the epistemically crucial role of interpreted experience, and the way that tradition shapes the epistemic and nonepistemic values that inform our reflection about God and what some of us believe to be God's presence in this world. At the same time, a postfoundationalist notion of rationality in theological reflection claims to point creatively beyond the confines of the local community, group, or culture, toward a plausible form of cross-contextual and interdisciplinary conversation. Postfoundationalism in theology should therefore emerge as a viable third option beyond the extremes of epistemological foundationalism and nonfoundationalism (cf. van Huyssteen 1997a:1-8). It should free us to approach our cross-disciplinary conversations with our strong beliefs and even prejudices intact, and while acknowledging these strong commitments, to identify at the same time the shared resources of human rationality in different modes of reflection. When we have achieved this, we will be able to reach beyond the boundaries of our own epistemic communities in cross-contextual, cross-cultural, and cross-disciplinary conversation.

As the epistemological fallout of the postmodern challenge to theology and the sciences has already made clear, the truly post-foundationalist move beyond the objectivism of foundationalism and the relativism of nonfoundationalism will only be found when, first of all, we rediscover the embeddedness of our rational reflection in the context of living, evolving, and developing traditions. However, this distinctly communal character of a refigured postfoundationalist rationality will have to be fused, as we will soon see, with a cross-contextual obligation to reach beyond one's own immediate local context in interdisciplinary conversation and deliberation. In this sense, the appropriation of a postfoundationalist notion of rationality will enable us to explore some positive epistemic resources for interdisciplinary dialogue and communication. In this chapter I will argue that human rationality, while so often expressing intelligibility, optimal understanding, and the skill of good judgment, also enables us to discern and hang on to the best reasons for our acting, believing, and choosing. And because rationality will emerge here as always embedded in our social, communal practices, it will necessarily always also express a specific community's implicit values and commitments. Only in this sense will a choice — in theology as well as in the sciences — be considered rational, as a judgment made in the light of the best possible reasons, and as validated by the expertise of a community that shares the same values. The question, however, remains: How is this interdisciplinary rationality to be credibly achieved, especially for the epistemic community that constitutes theology? Furthermore, what kind of epistemological link might this open up to other reasoning strategies? Finally, what are the shared resources of rationality that would have to be identified for theology and other forms of inquiry, so that theology can speak intelligibly — and with authentic Christian conviction — in a postmodern, pluralist situation?

But how do we grasp hold of a phenomenon as protean and elusive as human rationality? As a first step, and in the most general sense of the word, the nature of human rationality is to be found in the way that we use our intelligence to pursue particular epistemic goals and values, of which *intelligibility* may be the most important. The ubiquitous quest for understanding our world and ourselves optimally can certainly be seen as the most typical of our human intellectual endeavors. In its own ongoing attempt to provide us with an optimal understanding of faith, and of what believers commit themselves to in religious faith, theology obviously shares this quest for intelligibility with all other reasoning strategies, whatever other differences or similarities there may be. For theology this quest for ultimate meaning and optimal intelligibility will mean, as it does in the sciences, that rationality will always be very specifically determined by certain epistemic goals and criteria. But most typically rationality can be seen as the means by which we aim for optimal understanding in our various and diverse reasoning strategies (cf. McMullin 1988:25). And since, as soon will become clear, we pursue this kind of intelligibility by making what seems to be the best or the most progressive theory choices to attain the most comprehensive understanding available to us (cf. Laudan 1977:121ff.), intelligibility itself can certainly be seen as the crucial epistemic value that exemplifies our human quest for understanding. What we regard as our very own "rationality" thus turns out to be this human quest for intelligibility: our ongoing attempts at optimal understanding as a way of coping with ourselves and with our world. This quest for intelligibility, however, is not at all about modernity's zeal for secure foundations, nor is it about the hope for indubitable certainty. Rather, a postfoundationalist notion of rationality is about moving beyond the search for foundations, and about filling the void left by the deconstructive postmodern displacement of modernity's epistemological paradigm (cf. Schrag 1992:57). In theology this degree of intelligibility will be achieved, not through foundationalist notions of revelation, tradition, or inspired texts, but through responsible judgments about the explanatory role of those beliefs that are part of our interpreted religious experience. In both theology and in the sciences we should therefore beware of an overly narrow and "rationalistic" conception of rationality; rationality will turn out to have many faces, and it is indeed as complex, as many-sided, extensive, and wide-ranging as the domain of intelligence itself.

In both theology and the sciences — whatever their other differences may turn out to be — the most characteristic epistemic goal or value that shapes the rationality of these reasoning strategies is, therefore, intelligibility, and our never-ending quest for optimal understanding. For theology, what is at stake here is obviously not only the general epistemic status of religious beliefs, but especially the implications this will have for theology's ability to take part in interdisciplinary conversation and public discussion with some measure of rational integrity. Of course, the high degree of personal involvement and commitment in religious faith will present a very special challenge to any theory of rationality in theology. Because of this, and because of the radical contextuality of religious experience as well as the cognitive claims that necessarily arise from this, I shall argue for a theory of rationality that encompasses both *experiential* and *theoretical adequacy* in theological reflection. From this it will become clear, I hope, that religious experience and the explanatory commitments implied by this specific kind of experience are not only closely interrelated but are also crucial epistemic factors which very much determine the values that shape rationality in theological reflection. Clearly, important analogies to the philosophical problem of rationality in general, and the rationality of science in particular, emerge here; and it leaves the philosophical theologian with little or no choice but to reflect on contemporary epistemological issues.

Furthermore, what proved to be true for postmodern science is certainly true for theology too: since theology always first of all is an intellectual activity of a very specific community of inquirers, there can be no way of refiguring rationality for that activity without also looking at its actual practice, and thus the local context within which the theologian reflects on specific forms of religious experience. Delwin Brown takes this an important step further by arguing that the manner in which theology is to be rooted in the vital affections of communal practice can never be governed by fixed rules of method or practice, but only by the fluid and debatable judgments of common sense (cf. D. Brown 1994:146). This clearly will reveal the resources of rationality as deeply embedded in common sense, and — as we will see — rationality itself as person- and domain-specific. The back and forth between the epistemic skills of responsible judgment and interpreted experience will therefore turn out to be at the heart of a postfoundationalist notion of rationality. It will also, as I will argue, yield the only meaningful way to talk about the *experiential adequacy* of theological reflection today, and reveals, on this point at least, a significant epistemic consonance with Joseph Rouse's proposal for seeing science nonfoundationally as local, social practice. On this postfoundationalist view both theology and the sciences will be empowered to each identify the rational integrity of their own disciplines by offering their own resources of critique, articulation, and justification, and thereby fulfill one of postmodernism's most important challenges: neither theology nor the sciences require universal epistemological guarantees anymore.

As we saw, however, a nonfoundationalist view of rationality can have its own disturbing consequences when it leads to the epistemological relativism of all forms of thought. A well-defined theory of experience could, therefore, help theology move beyond both the relativism of nonfoundationalism and the absolutism of foundationalism, and clear a postfoundationalist space for interdisciplinary reflection. To accomplish this we will first of all need to realize that, although we cannot think and act except through engaging with our local contexts and traditions, our task is always to stand in a critical relation to tradition precisely by stepping beyond its epistemic boundaries in cross-contextual conversation. This chapter will begin to take up this difficult challenge and initiate the effort to retrieve the enduring accomplishments of modernism precisely by appropriating a constructive form of postmodern critique. This kind of attempt to honor the deeply contextual nature of human rationality while at the same time securing skills for reaching beyond the boundaries of our domains, has aptly been called a *splitting of the difference between modernism and postmodernism* by Calvin Schrag (cf. 1992:7, 166). A postfoundationalist notion of rationality will exactly aim to carefully capture the intellectual to-and-fro movement between the modern and the postmodern, because it is indeed rationality, and rationality as it figures in the philosophical discourse of modernity, that has been challenged and problematized by postmodernism (cf. Schrag 1992:166). But this does not mean that it will be an easy task to construct a model of rationality that will be both theoretically and experientially adequate for interdisciplinary reflection. Not only is the concept of rationality truly protean in its various and complex meanings (cf. Echeverria 1986:372), but the lasting influence of the positivist or classical model of rationality in securing the prestige of the natural sciences presents direct challenges for our attempts to reconstruct a postfoundationalist concept of rationality.

At the same time, as we saw with Joseph Rouse's proposal for postmodern science, much of post-Kuhnian philosophy of science has now convincingly argued that there can in fact be no sharp line of demarcation between scientific rationality and other forms of rationality (cf. also van Huyssteen 1989:63ff.). In fact, even scientific rationality relates directly to the preanalytic reasonableness of a broader kind of "common sense rationality" that informs all our everyday goal-directed actions. It is exactly within this broader reflective context that theology should seek the best and most plausible form of knowledge that it can achieve, a knowledge that will allow us to understand optimally what we are committing ourselves to, and where possible, to construct theories as better explanations of what is experienced in the life of faith. In the end this epistemic goal of theological reflection, more than anything, will determine the shaping of rationality in theology, as well as its relationship to the rationality of science. And if in both theology and the sciences — in spite of important differences — we strive to *explain* better in order to *understand* better, then surely the problem of the nature of rationality will be the one issue that should be our prime focus in trying to relate theology and the sciences to one another in a meaningful way today.

Our very human quest for optimal understanding is of course fundamentally shaped by our value judgments, i.e., by the way we see ourselves, one another, and the world we share. Our value judgments often function as prejudgments in our communication with one another and our world. These prejudgments display our embeddedness in linguistic communities and our involvement and participation in a world of dynamic social practices. Calvin Schrag has called the understanding that flows from the embeddedness of our discourses and actions in our concrete life-worlds a quintessentially *pragmatic* form of rational understanding (1992:65), and rationality itself a refigured form of praxis. What this will mean for theology in its relation to other reasoning strategies and practices is the complete impossibility to think of rationality in abstract, highly theoretical terms; rationality is present and operative in and through the dynamics of our words and deeds, and it is alive and well in our discourses and action. At the same time, there is no form of individual or communal discernment, no form of judgment or rational choice possible without the shaping role of our prejudgments. It is therefore by virtue of the values that we adopt, by nature or nurture, that we are installed in the world in such a manner that we are already oriented toward an understanding of it. None of our various forms of knowledge, however diverse the different modes of inquiry, are therefore possible without this background of contextualized prejudgments, habits, and skills that inform our participation in a communal world. The problem of the shaping of rationality in theology and the sciences therefore will center to a great extent on identifying the role that value judgments play in our decisions to commit ourselves — for what we see as the best possible reasons — to specific viewpoints, theories, and doctrines in these very different forms of knowledge.

I shall argue that in our ongoing quest for understanding the experience of faith, rationality in theology — as in other reasoning strategies like the various sciences — ultimately consists of discerning and arguing for those theories, models, or research traditions that are judged to be the most progressive and comprehensive, and thus the most effective problem-solvers within the concrete context of theological reflection. This will require, however, a careful analysis of exactly what is meant by "progress" in different reasoning strategies. The difficult question of how to justify our commitments (often passionate ones), our choices for only certain research traditions, certain theories, or doctrines, in a way that would really make them *rational* choices, will therefore inevitably lead to another problem: Would it be rational, whether in the sciences or in theology, to expect these choices to imply some form of gradual or sudden *improvement* in our knowledge, a degree of advancement or intellectual growth that involves some form of progress in our different modes of inquiry? Or would the notion of making good, better, or best choices, and the epistemic progress this seems to imply, be available only to the sciences but not to theology? Furthermore, is not the notion of progress in and of itself already enough to take us back to a modernist notion of rationality that would not at all be consonant with a postmodern critique of rational reflection? Obviously these questions force us to address difficult epistemological issues such as what degree of truth and objectivity (if any) we may reasonably claim for our statements in theology and in the sciences. The relationship between explanatory power and truth has of course always been a central issue in the understanding of science, and is today as problematical as ever (cf. McMullin 1986:52). Post-Kuhnian philosophers of science have also consistently pointed out that there can be no monolithic notions of truth, objectivity, explanation, or even of rationality today: the objects of our interests not only dictate different strategies, but also different contextually determined views on each of these crucial issues.

This central question, however, remains: *Does theology exhibit a rationality that is comparable to the rationality of science, overlaps with, or is informed by the rationality of science, and should the rationality of science still be seen as normative and paradigmatic for other forms of rationality today?* For those of us who are theologians, it will be important to realize that the epistemological questions raised by reflecting on religious faith and theological reflection might not always be the same as those raised by reflecting on science. However, as I have suggested before, accepting that different reasoning strategies — as diverse forms of intellectual inquiry — are involved in theology and the sciences does not mean that they do not also share the same resources of human rationality and, along with that, overlapping epistemic goals and similar interpretative procedures. Moreover, as is well known, various theologies and the sciences have a long history of at least indirectly informing the cultural context within which each respectively constructs its theories (cf. Barker 1981:276). In spite of important differences, theology and the sciences may therefore turn out to share the same resources of rationality, as well as some crucial epistemic values and value judgments that shape the way rationality is operative in each of these respective fields.

Problems with the Classical Model of Rationality

A postfoundationalist rationality should be developed beyond the extremes of modernist universalism and postmodern, historicist relativism, and as such will imply a refiguring of the dynamics of critique as we assess and discern how our discourses and networks of belief are intellectually shaped by our social contexts. In reflecting on the values that shape rationality in theology and the sciences, we will have to move beyond the modernist, standard (cf. van Huyssteen 1989), or classical model of rationality (cf. H. Brown 1990). The classical model of rationality is amazingly pervasive in Western thought, and although not always explicitly formulated, has played a major role in establishing foundationalist epistemologies in areas as diverse as theology and the sciences. According to this standard or classical model of scientific rationality, a decision, a judgment, or a belief becomes rational only when it is based on an evaluation of relevant scientific evidence through the application of appropriate rules (cf. H. Brown 1990:vii). The classical or modernist model of rationality thus determines that for our beliefs to claim rational status, they would have to meet at least three conditions: they must show universal validity, exhibit necessary relations between the different components of arguments, and be determined by specific logical rules (cf. also van Niekerk 1990:179). The particular thesis that rational results must be universally evident in terms of empirical facts and the rules of logic, and must necessarily flow from the information given, became a guiding principle and was exemplified in the logical positivist movement in the first half of this century (cf. van Huyssteen 1989:3-23). The demand for this kind of universality is in fact so deeply embedded in our current understanding of rationality that to question the universality of a discipline's foundations would amount to questioning the rationality of that whole enterprise.

On the classical model of rationality, then, a belief, act, choice, or decision is rational only if it conforms to a set of logical and factual criteria that are applicable in every context. This model insists that rationality will look the same in different and diverse contexts, because of a reluctance to move to principles that are domain-specific. In Harold Brown's words, according to this model "anyone who arrives at a different solution must either have made a mistake, which can be found and corrected, or failed to arrive at a solution in a rational manner" (1990:14). In the classical model of rationality this kind of universality thus becomes very closely aligned with necessity. This close connection between rationality and necessity in foundationalist epistemology is perhaps best illustrated by the sharp and unfortunate distinction often drawn between accepting results on a *rational* basis and accepting results on the basis of *experience* alone. Implied in this distinction is the conviction that conclusions accepted on the basis of experience do not have the universality or necessity that characterizes reasonable results (cf. H. Brown 1990:15). The elevation by some theologians of supernaturalist and self-authenticating concepts of revelation above and beyond the domain of religious experience can certainly be traced to this unfortunate distinction.

The classical model of rationality's claims to universality and necessity is very closely connected to a commitment to "appropriate, objective rules." "Rules" is indeed the key concept in the classical model of rationality: if we have universally applicable rules, we are free from the arbitrariness of nonrational decisions and irrational, subjective judgments. The rationality of any conclusion is therefore determined by whether or not it conforms to the appropriate objective rules (cf. H. Brown 1990:17). In both theology and science it would be easy to point to the power of rule-governed procedures. In science it is the "objective" rules of scientific methodology that determine which tests and verification procedures are relevant, and whether a body of empirical results is sufficient for accepting or rejecting a new proposal. In theology the rules will be determined by a strong precommitment to a specific doctrinal, confessional, or philosophical methodology and hermeneutics. On this view a "rational decision," then, is one that is guided by the appropriate objective rules, which as such yield the knowledge that will form the epistemological foundation for all further judgments and decisions. Rules in this sense are at the heart of the classical model of rationality: we often strive for the security and certainty afforded by universally accepted and applicable rules, so that all who begin from the same information must necessarily arrive at the same conclusion. In this standard modernist notion of rationality, it has clearly been the natural sciences, and natural scientific knowledge, that have emerged as a superior form of human rationality. Science on this view has always been equated with true objectivity, because the controlled collecting of experiential data makes it possible to arrive at certain empirical generalizations or laws by way of inductive generalizations. And when hypotheses are successfully tested or verified, a new scientific law has been discovered and can now be integrated accumulatively with the overall objective growth of scientific knowledge (cf. van Huyssteen 1989:7f.).

This modernist notion of rationality also provides the basis for the classic distinction between the *context of discovery* and the *context of justification*.[2] The whole point of this distinction was that discovery, understood as the process by which individuals came up with new ideas, is distinct from the procedures by which such ideas are objectively tested and evaluated. On this view, rational reconstruction, and therefore also the question of the justification of scientific concepts and theories, is done in the so-called context of justification. How scientists actually creatively arrive at new theories belongs to the context of discovery, and should be seen not as a *scientific* problem, but rather as a psychological, sociological, and historical problem. Only within this context is it appropriate to ask how scientific discoveries also relate to such issues as intuition, creativity, cultural, political, and ethical values, and, of course, the influence of religion and religious issues. On a classical, foundationalist view questions of rationality, however, typically arise only in the context of justification (cf. van Huyssteen 1989:7ff.; H. Brown 1990:30). Thomas S. Kuhn, and with him all post-Kuhnian philosophy of science, would understandably (and predictably) break down the sharp distinctions between these two epistemological contexts. Kuhn aligned himself with Karl Popper and highlighted precisely the historical development of scientific theories. In doing this Kuhn famously maintained that not only the choice of our scientific theories but also the very nature of the whole scientific enterprise should be explained in sociohistorical terms. With this Kuhn not only rejected the classical idea that science essentially implies a growth of knowledge toward truth, but

2. A distinction originally made by Hans Reichenbach, in *Experience and Prediction* (1938:6ff.).

also the rigid distinction between one class of problems that relates to the *origins of our knowledge* (the context of discovery) and another class of knowledge that relates only to *the rational evaluation and justification of knowledge* (the context of justification). As we all know today, this would dramatically refigure the notion of scientific rationality and place notions like intuition and creativity at the very heart of scientific knowledge (cf. Kuhn 1970:171).

It is therefore significant to note that amidst his own attempts to move beyond foundationalism in epistemology, Harold Brown still sees the virtue of the classical model of rationality in the fact that it provided us with an answer to the question "Why be rational?" Why in fact should we make rational decisions, adopt rational beliefs, rather than choosing on the basis of impulse, emotion, or even at random? Part of the answer to this question derives directly from the fact that when we are trying to answer any kind of question, one of our aims normally is to get *reliable* results. Rational procedures thus allow us to arrive at nonarbitrary answers to our questions (H. Brown 1990:35). What is needed to be rational, then, are good reasons, valid arguments, and (in science) reliable, empirical evidence.

At this point it is also clear why in our modernist Western culture the contrast between reason and faith has been so pervasive and influential. Being asked to accept a religious claim "on faith alone" normally means that we are asked to accept it without any reasons at all (cf. H. Brown 1990:36). In theology this is complicated even more when we are asked to accept the apparently dogmatic authority (cf. Hoering 1980:133) of a seemingly irrational revelation which normally seems to be accessible and intelligible only to a very specific community. Within the context of modernity, theology has always suffered from the absence of the kind of objectivity provided by universal or necessary rules, a problem that has often left theologians unable to determine how to justify their actions, beliefs, or theory choices in ways that would be clear and publicly convincing for everyone. As we saw earlier, this situation is even more aggravated today by the fragmentation and pluralism of postmodern thought. In his discussion of the classical model of rationality, Harold Brown is therefore correct in linking this model's claims to universality, necessity, and appropriate rules, directly to epistemological foundationalism (1990:38f.). Clearly the classical model, as our most familiar

123

model of rationality, embodies a set of powerful and plausible ideas. This model, however, faces serious problems when challenged on two accounts: first, on what basis do we select information from which to begin (facts)?; and second, on what basis do we select our rules (logic)? If a belief is to be rational according to the classical model, it has to be rational on both these counts. In the classical model the answer to both these questions is found in epistemological foundationalism: finding a set of propositions that are rationally justified without that justification being dependent on other propositions (H. Brown 1990:40).

Whether in theology or the sciences, the classical model of rationality clearly always requires some form of foundationalism. Foundationalism, as we have seen, requires that foundationalist propositions must be self-evident and indubitable. Since, however, there are no grounds for believing that there exists a body of self-evident or given propositions that will allow us to justify our beliefs, foundationalism ultimately fails (cf. H. Brown 1990:58). If the classical model of rationality therefore requires a foundationalist epistemology, and if this foundationalism fails, then the classical or modernist model of rationality fails too: without self-evident foundationalist propositions, we seem to be (at least in terms of the rules of this model) powerless to arrive at any rational beliefs. In Brown's own words: "The failure of foundationalism is an epistemic failure; it underlines a point about the limits of our knowledge of the truth of our premises and the adequacy of our rules" (1990:107).

Mainly as a result of the pervasive influence of the classical model of rationality in our culture, and in spite of this epistemic failure of foundationalism, the natural sciences — especially the physical sciences — are still regarded by many as the paradigm for rationality today. Postmodern philosophy of science has, as we saw earlier, not only challenged all foundationalist epistemology, but has also severely challenged this special status and epistemic sovereignty of the natural sciences. In his important work on the nature of rationality, Harold Brown has persuasively argued, however, that an adequate post-classical model of rationality should indeed be exemplified by those disciplines that we take to be paradigm cases of rational endeavor (cf. 1990:79ff.). In a very special sense then, in spite of the breakdown of the classical model of rationality, science may still provide a crucially important test case for rationality since it currently still seems to stand as our clearest example of a cognitive, rational enterprise. Brown points to serious conflicts between the classical model and scientific practice, and introduces an alternative view of science which rejects the idea that science is governed by the kinds of methodological rules that philosophers have consistently sought in terms of the classical model of rationality (cf. H. Brown 1990:80ff.). It is of course well known today that Thomas Kuhn's introduction of his influential paradigm theory (cf. Kuhn 1970) caused a major shift in current postclassical views on scientific rationality (cf. van Huyssteen 1989:44-70). Not merely his controversial notion of *revolutionary science,* but more importantly Kuhn's notion of *normal science* gives us a crucial key to understanding scientific rationality: most scientists spend their professional lives solving problems within the framework of an accepted theory (such as special relativity, quantum theory, or evolutionary biology). They use these theories or paradigms as a basis for their work, and do not consider themselves to be under a methodological injunction to test or even to attempt to falsify these basic theories (cf. H. Brown 1990:99).

Both Imre Lakatos and Larry Laudan have tried to improve on Kuhn's view of scientific rationality and have suggested alternative proposals. According to Lakatos, as we saw in our discussion of Nancey Murphy's work, the guiding principles that organize scientific research are provided by a "research program," i.e., by a set of hypotheses that guides research in a specific discipline much the way that a Kuhnian paradigm does (cf. Lakatos 1970). The research program's hypotheses are in fact explicit propositions that are divided into sets that do different jobs (cf. also H. Brown 1990:99). One of these sets is called the "hard core" of the program, which as such encompasses a set of claims about nature that forms the heart of the program. Other less central claims, involved in the development of the research program, function as "auxiliary hypotheses" that can be sacrificed without abandoning the central characteristics of the program. As such they form a "protective belt" that can be modified. Also, the research program provides a "positive heuristic," as a set of suggestions on how to proceed in deploying the program as a way to understand nature, and a "negative heuristic," as a set of injunctions that protects the hard core of the program by telling us how not to proceed in developing the program (cf. H. Brown 1990:100). Kuhn and Lakatos therefore agreed that much of scientific research is organized around substantive claims about some aspects of nature that function, for a time, as methodological principles not open to empirical refutation.

Like Lakatos, Larry Laudan (1977) has argued that scientific research is typically guided by a set of principles that transcends the particular theories of a particular discipline. Laudan has called these "research traditions," but has also argued that they are less specific, and more capable of change, than a Lakatosian research program. For Laudan a research tradition is a set of ontological and methodological do's and don'ts (cf. Laudan 1977:80), but at the same time "research traditions" lack the unchanging hard core that Lakatos attributed to "research programs." So, instead of dramatic paradigm shifts or necessarily moving to a new research tradition, Laudan proposes that many features of a research program may be altered, but enough will remain unchanged for us to claim some form of continuity. At the same time, Laudan does allow for considerable competition between research traditions, as well as for the possibility that a research tradition could indeed be abandoned and replaced. In fact, it is precisely these scientific "revolutions" that go directly against the foundationalist classic model of rationality: if the history of science provided us with a steady accumulation of truths, with no major revolutions, then we would have strong grounds for believing that we have in fact stumbled onto a foundationalist starting point for scientific epistemology. It is thus the occurrence of revolutions that shows most clearly that, even in the natural sciences, we have not achieved the kind of universal basis for mediating disputes that the classical model requires (cf. H. Brown 1990:107). Clearly we are required not only to reconsider the rationality of science, but also on a deeper level to refigure the modernist/classical model of rationality itself.

Today, in a postmodern age, we know that the rules according to which scientific decisions are made are neither universal nor necessary, but in fact change as science itself develops. Precisely the fact that the rules change shows that they do not meet the conditions of universality and necessity imposed by the classical model of rationality. The historicist or postmodern turn in philosophy of science, initiated by Kuhn, has thoroughly replaced the foundationalism of the classical model, opening the way (as we saw with Joseph Rouse) to various attempts at non- or antifoundationalist models of rationality in philosophy of science. What we saw earlier in postmodern views of both science and theology is now confirmed: in a strong reaction against a modernist notion of rationality that stresses universality and necessity, nonfoundationalism highlights the fact that every group and every context may in fact have its own rationality. If nonfoundationalist views were to be true, then any social or human activity could indeed function as a test case for rationality.

This notion leaves us, however, with an extreme relativism of rationalities: a relativism that not only forms the opposite of the classical model's objectivism, but which in fact turns out to be a response, *within the framework of the classical model of rationality itself,* to the failure of foundationalism. Ironically, extreme nonfoundationalist relativism here turns out to be a direct continuation of the classical model of rationality. If we finally acknowledge that there are no foundations, no universal basis for our knowledge claims, but at the same time are not prepared to reject the classical model of rationality itself as unintelligible, then a natural move is to hang on to (at least a weakened form of) this rule-governed rationality and maintain that different groups use different sets of rules, and that each set of rules specifies a different form of rationality (cf. H. Brown 1990:131f.). Proponents of this nonfoundationalist kind of relativism would hold that the rules which govern science are internal to science in the same way that other human activities (cf. religion, business, magic, etc.) are governed by their own internal rules. As we have already seen, in the relativism that flows from this nonfoundationalism it is maintained that each area of human activity has criteria internal to a specific culture or social group, and each therefore has its own criteria of rationality. There is no epistemological framework here for deciding whether one approach may be more rational than another, since rationality can only and exclusively be understood as relative to a specific conceptual scheme, theoretical framework, paradigm, form of life, society, or culture. On this "many rationalities" view, the relativist denies that there can be any overarching framework or single metalanguage by which we can rationally evaluate competing claims, and therefore truly believes in the nonreducible plurality of conceptual schemes (cf. Bernstein 1983: 8ff.). On this view, even science can be seen as merely one more feature of contemporary Western society among others. In fact, all cultures or societies build cognitive structures that explain the world around them, and science is an example of one such cognitive structure. On this view, it obviously would have to be denied that the

127

body of beliefs developed by science could be in any way cognitively superior to other beliefs. Ironically, then, the classical model of rationality, in both its foundationalist proposals and nonfoundationalist responses, makes interdisciplinary reflection hazardous, if not impossible.

Toward a Postfoundationalist Model of Rationality

A first helpful step toward getting beyond the rather stark choice between epistemological foundationalism or the extreme relativism of nonfoundationalism, is found when we move beyond narrow theoretical, cognitivist definitions of rationality, and, following the lead of Nicholas Rescher (cf. 1988; also 1992), identify at least three broader dimensions of rationality that are crucially relevant for all modes of knowledge: the *cognitive,* the *evaluative,* and the *pragmatic* (cf. van Huyssteen 1997a:246f.). These different dimensions of human rationality will help us recognize the many faces of rationality as performatively present in different modes of knowledge and in the different domains of our lives. Extremely significant for theology, however, is that in a postmodernist, postfoundationalist context, theology — as a reflection on religious experience — not only can no longer be excluded from the broader epistemological endeavor, but epistemology itself will have to be creatively refigured. What this concretely means for theological reflection is that in our quest for theological intelligibility, theologians too are challenged to sound rational judgment: giving good reasons for hanging on to certain beliefs, good reasons for making certain theoretical and moral choices, and good reasons for acting in certain ways. Within a comprehensive, postfoundationalist epistemology, the cognitive, pragmatic, and evaluative dimensions of rationality go together as a seamless whole; they ultimately merge in the common task of finding optimal understanding by uniting the best reasons for our beliefs, evaluations, and actions. We therefore act rationally in matters of belief, action, and evaluation when our reasons "hang together," i.e., when they are cogent. In theology too, rationality always should imply the capacity, the willingness, and ability to "give an account," to provide a rationale for the way one thinks, chooses, acts, believes, and commits. In both theology and the sciences, therefore, theory-acceptance (that epistemic practice in which we judge certain theories and opinions as worthy of our belief) will obviously have a profound cognitive dimension. When we ask, however, what else (other than theoretical belief) is involved in theory-acceptance, the rich pragmatic and evaluative dimensions of theory-acceptance are also revealed (cf. van Fraassen 1989:3ff.).

In both theology and the sciences, then, rationality and the quest for intelligibility pivot on the deployment of good reasons: believing, doing, judging, and choosing the right thing for the right reasons. Being rational is therefore not just a matter of having some reasons for what one believes in and argues for, but having the best or strongest reasons available to support the comparative rationality (cf. Hoering 1980:126f.) of one's beliefs within a concrete sociohistorical context. The hazy intersection between the diverse fields of theology and the other sciences is therefore not in the first place to be determined by just exploring methodological parallels, similarities, or even degrees of possible consonance between theology and the sciences. What should be explored first is what exactly happens when we make the choices we regard as our *rational* choices in both theology and science. This will focus the problem of rationality on the question of the nature and status of rational judgment, and on the scope or range of the epistemological "overlaps" shared by these two forms of rational inquiry. This process of reflection on the nature of rationality, by refocusing on the crucial role of individual judgment and its all-important link to a process of ongoing collective assessment, will move us beyond abstract, generic, and universalist notions of rationality, precisely by rediscovering the radically experiential and interpretative nature of the contexts in which we live and think as rational agents.

This fact alone should make us wary of some of the dangerous epistemological short cuts we inherited from modernity: rationality should indeed never again be reduced to mean scientific rationality only, and scientific rationality should never be reduced to natural scientific rationality. In committing itself to certain specific beliefs, certain specific moral choices, and certain specific actions, theology in particular — in its attempt to obtain optimum intelligibility in its own field — makes claims ultimately related to and based on the interpreted religious experience of a broad, complex, and pluralist Christian tradition. And as in science, this experience (although different from the kind on which scientific statements are based) should be understood as arising out of a context of shared assumptions and commitments, a field of mutual concerns. In both science and theology cognitive claims are made within a very specific context of inquiry, but this kind of contextuality need not imply a relativist position at all. In both theology and science this embeddedness in social, historical, and cultural contexts implies that it is rather claims to experiential/empirical and theoretical adequacy — and not to justified, foundationalist certainty — that make a belief a responsible belief, and a judgment a rational judgment. A model of rationality that is rich enough to accommodate this pragmatic embeddedness in context and tradition may already be on its way to justifying its interdisciplinary claims to epistemological adequacy.

The postfoundationalist model of rationality I am arguing for will clearly be consonant with an interactionist model of knowledge that enables us to move beyond objectivism and relativism, i.e., a third option *vis-à-vis* the stark alternatives of foundationalism and nonfoundationalism. What is presupposed here is not only that there is an interaction between the object of our investigation and the theoretical or cognitive instrumentalities by means of which we focus on it, but also that reality, as we grope to understand it, seems to reflect the workings of the human mind. As such our inquiring minds make formative contributions not only to our understanding of what we call "reality," but even to the resulting character we attribute to it (cf. Rescher 1992:xiii). The epistemological basis for this will be found in what Jerome Stone has called the transactional character of all interpreted experience: experience is always a complex interaction between the self and the world, between the environment and lived feelings (cf. Stone 1992:128). As we will see in the next chapter, this certainly means that we have no access to any points of "pure" experience that might have been used as epistemological anchors or sure foundations to solve our philosophical problems in theology and science. It also means, however, that we are not out of touch with our world, or what we normally call "reality": we are not wholly adrift in a linguistic sea, and it is not "language all the way down" (cf. Stone 1992:128). On this view, our interpreted experience will emerge as a transaction, and as such will become a crucial part of a postfoundationalist epistemology. Although we now have to learn to live without secure epistemological foundations, we still have reasons to believe that we may trust some of our fallible judgments for making responsible and trustworthy contex-

130

tual, as well as cross-contextual, choices. The resources for this trust are found in a broader notion of postfoundationalist rationality, and in the cognitive, evaluative, and pragmatic resources that will always be presupposed in this relational or interactionist view of knowledge. Presupposed in this relationality is an epistemic humility, a fallibilism that accepts that the theorizing through which we come to understand our world is always going to be tentative and imperfect.

As was argued earlier, the nature of rationality — in the most general sense of the word — consists of the intelligent pursuit of certain epistemic values, of which intelligibility is the most important. This also reveals a close connection between intelligibility, as the epistemic goal of both theology and science, and human intelligence. Various philosophers have argued that it should not at all surprise us that as human beings we could have acquired intelligence, enabling us to secure information and survive in our world. As Nicholas Rescher correctly points out, intelligence naturally arises through evolutionary processes because it provides one very effective means of survival. Rationality, in this broadest sense of the word, can therefore be seen as conducive to human survival, and the explanation for our cognitive resources as fundamentally Darwinian (cf. Rescher 1992:3f.). Rescher's observation here is sharp and to the point: the imperative to understand is something altogether basic for *homo sapiens*. In fact we cannot function, let alone thrive, without reliable information regarding what goes on about us. Intelligence is therefore our peculiar human instrumentality, a matter of our specific evolutionary heritage. In our quest for intelligibility, then, rationality primarily consists in the intelligent use of our ability for rational judgment to determine the choices we make, for the best possible reasons. Therefore, optimizing our judgments regarding what we think, do, and value, indeed forms the crux of human rationality (cf. Rescher 1992:5).

Rationality thus emerges as not only a protean, complex notion, but also as inextricably linked to having good reasons for making the most responsible choices in concrete situations. The problem of rationality is therefore all about the way we form our beliefs and how and why we hold on to them in the various domains of our lives. Mikael Stenmark has recently argued that this kind of focus on the problem of rationality reveals how much the ways we form and hold on to our beliefs in various areas of our lives actually have in common. We are also challenged, however, to find out exactly what it is that the various intellectual domains of our lives have in common (cf. Stenmark 1995:3). Even on an everyday, preanalytic level, our judgments and beliefs are regarded as rational if we can appeal to good reasons for having them, and if we can provide those reasons on request (cf. H. Brown 1990:183). In fact, our everyday life is the one area where we have most of our beliefs: beliefs about other people, about our relationships with them, and about how to cope with our world. Stenmark correctly argues that on this level, in contrast to the domains of science and religion, we have no real option whether or not we participate in it. In this sense everyday beliefs are also paradigm cases of rationality in action. In religion too, believers form beliefs about God or the divine and how that relates to our concrete situations, while religious convictions typically result from experiences of suffering or joy, meaning or meaninglessness, guilt or liberation (cf. Stenmark 1995:3f.). In the Christian religion, it is by means of theological reflection that we take up the task to reflect on the acceptance or rejection of beliefs and networks of belief, and should pointedly ask the question if any belief of this sort is rationally acceptable. Finally, science, of course, is often regarded to be the paradigm example of rationality at work, as scientists theoretically form beliefs about how many natural and cultural phenomena in our world interact with one another.

Any proper theory of rationality will indeed have to deal carefully with the way rationality performs in all the various domains of our lives. And on all levels the fact that we need plausible reasons to hang on to our beliefs will have a crucial effect on how we understand human rationality. Having good reasons will lead to proper discernment and responsible judgments, and will also form the basis for distinguishing between rational and nonrational beliefs, i.e., beliefs not properly grounded in good reasons. Good reasons are also what we normally regard as "appropriate evidence": to be rational we have to believe on the basis of some form of appropriate and carefully considered evidence, which thus makes our beliefs more rational than nonrational or irrational beliefs. Rationality therefore involves this capacity to give an account, to provide a rationale for what we believe, do, and choose, and as such has an inescapable rhetorical dimension: through our persuasive discourse and action we try to demonstrate *to others* the reasonableness of our thinking, judgments, choices, values, and actions.

Precisely in this sense rationality and rhetoric will thus always be inextricably bound together, because it is through persuasive discourse and action that we communicate with others in our attempts to convince them of the good reasons we have for our beliefs and actions. Rhetoric, as a crucially important dimension of rationality, is also seen by Calvin Schrag as directly relevant for bridging action and discourse: not only does rhetoric lie across and bind together the spoken and written word, as the two modalities or forms of discourse, but it also binds this discourse with action (cf. Schrag 1992:116). In this sense one could say that rhetoric links our discourses with our deeds and actions, and rhetoric thus emerges as the crucially important dimension of rationality that weaves together the cognitive, evaluative, and pragmatic aspects of rationality. Rhetoric also, of course, is directly relevant for our place in the community and the demand for communication from individuals and the community as such. Rhetoric, as persuasive discourse and action, is thus the interweaving of discernment, judgment, deliberation, and action, and thus emerges as at the heart of human rationality. As one of the most important facets of rationality, it actually illustrates the rationality of our judgments and fitting responses by giving an account of the reasons why we hold certain beliefs and indulge in certain actions. As such, moving across the many and varied expressions of human rationality, rhetoric provides an integrating force and function in our interpersonal communication and interdisciplinary reflections.

Calvin Schrag has therefore correctly identified rhetoric as a most important dimension of rationality, and as a ubiquitous binding force that moves across the multiple expressions of rationality in our daily lives (cf. Schrag 1992:116ff.). And as a crucial facet of our rationality, rhetoric in this sense can be seen as the interweaving of rational discernment, of responsible judgment, assessment, and action. A belief, action, or choice is therefore rational if we can convince others that it was a sensible thing to arrive at in the specific circumstances of a specific social context. A human being therefore becomes a truly rational agent when he or she does what he or she does for good reasons, and good reasons are those whose rhetorical plausibility and guidance optimally serve our best interests in specific matters at hand. And the best reasons are those that rhetorically achieve the most by focusing our judgment in appropriate directions (cf. Rescher 1992:7), and by bridging the gap between discourse and action. In this sense the rhetorical character of postfoundationalist rationality can be seen as a truly rational way of coming to terms with the provisionality of human reason, in a world where we have lost the false security of foundationalist knowledge.

A broader notion of rationality now emerges which not only implies rational accountability, but which also necessarily focuses on historical and social context, on praxis, and on the crucial epistemic role of interpreted experience. This move poses an exciting and significant challenge to both theology and science in a postmodern context. But what are the epistemic and other values that shape the rationality of theology and of science, and how are they different or similar? At this point an interesting possibility emerges: if rationality is not just a matter of having some reasons for what one does, but of aligning one's beliefs, actions, and evaluations with the best available reasons within specific contexts, then all domains or levels of rationality are held together in the common or shared quest of finding the best available reasons to attain the highest form of intelligibility. This reveals a common or shared dimension in all human rationality, and a way to integrate the performative presence of rationality in various domains of our lives without again totalizing it into a modernist, rationalistic vision where different modes of knowledge are united in a seamless unity (cf. Schrag 1992:125, 149). This is also what is implied by Nicholas Rescher's reference to human rationality as inherently universalistic in its intent (cf. Rescher 1992:11), and will be crucial to any notion of postfoundationalist rationality. As human beings, then, we are indeed rational agents, and the claim to rationality is a profoundly crucial, perhaps even the most important aspect of our human self-image.

The discussion of the rich resources of human rationality has lately been greatly enriched by Calvin Schrag's important work on the postmodern challenge to rationality. Schrag has pointed out how common it has become to ascribe antireason and "end of philosophy"–talk to what is broadly referred to as *postmodernism:* although, as we saw, there is no unified voice of postmodernism, it has always been clear that the problematization of rationality has been one of its recurring themes. Indeed, the postmodern celebration of pluralism, multiplicity, heterogeneity, and incommensurability makes the task of finding a valid place for the "claims of reason" (1994:61) a particularly demanding one. Schrag's recent work, however, can be seen as exactly a response to the postmodern challenge to the resources of rationality.

134

Schrag's attempt to move beyond both the totalizing meta-narratives of modernity and the unrestrained pluralism and self-isolating relativism of extreme forms of postmodernism, is found in his proposal for a notion of *transversal rationality* (cf. Schrag 1992; 1994). Schrag is proposing to use this metaphor in a new way and takes his cue from mathematicians (who take up the vocabulary of transversality when speaking of the transversality of a line as it intersects a system of other lines or surfaces), but also from physicists and physiologists: in the interdisciplinary and varied use of this concept a shared meaning emerges, having to do principally with the related senses of extending over, lying across, and intersecting (cf. Schrag 1994:64). Schrag goes even further and follows Sartre in using the notion of transversality to indicate how human consciousness and self-awareness are unified by a play of intentionalities which includes concrete retentions of past consciousness. In this sense consciousness is unified by our experiences of self-awareness, emerging over time from a remembering consciousness in which diverse past experiences are transversally integrated. In using the notion of transversal rationality in this way, Schrag eventually wants to justify and urge an acknowledgment of multiple patterns of interpretation as one moves across the borders and boundaries of the different disciplinary matrices (cf. 1994:65).

In making this move Schrag acknowledges that he shares the postmodern suspicion about various subject-grounded and consciousness-centered approaches to rationality within modernity. But, importantly and correctly, for him this does not automatically lead to the jettisoning of the vocabulary of subjectivity *per se* (cf. 1994:66). Therefore, precisely in splitting the difference between modernity and postmodernity, not every notion of self, and not every notion of rationality should be jettisoned. On exactly this point I will take my cue and argue also that the vocabulary of *epistemology* should not just be jettisoned too easily and completely in a revisioning of rationality as transversal or postfoundationalist rationality. On a postfoundationalist view, talk about the human subject is indeed now revisioned and moves from seeing the self as a pure epistemological point, to resituating the human subject in the space of communicative praxis. Thus the notion of transversal rationality opens up the possibility to focus on patterns of discourse and action as they happen in our communicative practices, rather than focusing only on the structure of the self, ego, or subject (cf. 1994:67). Transversal rationality is not, however, just a "passage of consciousness" across a wide spectrum of experiences and held together by our memory. It is, rather, a lying across, an extending over, a linking together, and an intersecting of various forms of discourse, modes of thought, and action. Transversal rationality thus emerges as a place in time and space where our multiple beliefs and practices, our habits of thought and attitudes, our prejudices and assessments, converge. The texture of this transversality thus resides in the domain of our social, communal, and institutional practices. In this postfoundationalist move we can never again enjoy the epistemological or metaphysical security of originating or first, foundationalist principles, and rationality is revisioned as socially and historically qualified, performatively present in all the various domains of our lives.

On this postfoundationalist view a new and promising understanding of interdisciplinary dialogue now emerges: in interdisciplinary conversation the degree of transversality achieved will ultimately depend on the effectiveness of our dialogue across the boundaries of different domains, and on the (often fragile) understanding we achieve in our interaction with one another. What is at stake in this notion of a transversal rationality is to discover, or reveal, the shared resources of human rationality precisely in our very pluralist, diverse assemblages of beliefs or practices, and then to locate the claims of reason in the overlaps of rationality between groups, discourses, or reasoning strategies. This is exactly what Calvin Schrag means when he argues that reason is operative in the transversal play of thought and action in the guise of three interrelated moments/phases of communicative praxis, which he names as *evaluative critique, engaged articulation,* and *incursive disclosure* (cf. 1994:69ff.). For Schrag the adjective "praxial" qualifies all three of these moments, and distinguishes the operation of rationality as critique, articulation, and disclosure from the theory-grounded, subject-centered paradigm of modernity. This clearly involves a radical shift from a focus on thought and experience as a-contextual systems of belief, to an acknowledgment of the relocation of thought, experience, and belief systems in our assemblages of social practices (cf. 1994:69). In this move the concepts of theory and practices are themselves refigured: theory is here no longer viewed as a system of a priori rules and principles, and practice is liberated from its subordination as a mere application of theory. What now emerges is a third option, the third dimension of *praxis,* which indicates a fusion of thought and action that displays its own discernment, insight, and disclosure, no longer needing a transcendental ego or a system of universal rules to swoop down from on high.

At this point it may be helpful to take a closer look at the three interrelated moments of this communicative praxis, namely (praxial) evaluative critique, (praxial) engaged articulation, and (praxial) incursive disclosure, which Calvin Schrag has distinguished as the most important dimensions of a refigured transversal rationality:

1. *Evaluative critique* highlights the performance of critical discernment, where discernment is seen as a separating, sorting out, distinguishing, contrasting, weighing, and assessing of our different options (1994:69). Transversal rationality is revealed in the performance of critique as judgment or discernment when we either (a) link some of our practices up with other practices by accommodation or simple adoption, thus revealing lines of continuity between different domains; or, (b) when our discourses and practices impinge on other practices and discourses in such a way that they may actually be modified or transformed; or, (c) when our practices and discourses contrast or conflict in such a way that we find ourselves facing dissensus or even incommensurability (cf. Schrag 1994:70). Just the rational ability to discern which of these three options may be the viable one in a concrete, specific (interdisciplinary) conversation, already reveals transversal rationality at work.

2. *Engaged articulation* is another important moment in the dynamics of evaluative, praxial critique. This moment of articulation associates rationality directly with discourse, with rendering an account, giving the best possible reasons, and with articulating sense or meaning. Schrag rightly sees meaning here as a social practice, a communicative achievement rather than a mental act issuing from a subject-centered reason (cf. 1994:71). Rationality as articulation thus proceeds in tandem with a refigured notion of meaning where the weight of especially tradition is necessarily to be seen as considerable. Each domain or configuration of our praxis has its own specific and inherited characteristics which shape the identity of our discourses. In this sense articulation is *recollective*. Articulation is also, however, *anticipative* and runs

forward in the sense that it marks out new possibilities for new forms of discourse and new forms of action. This articulation of meaning as possibility not only enables new forms of discourse and praxis against which past and present forms can be judged and reevaluated, but also rescues our critique from being simply a strategy of negation and deconstruction. Exactly on this point a postfoundationalist notion of rationality goes beyond extreme forms of postmodernism by not only countering what is not feasible, not desirable, not workable, but by actually projecting the positivity of the possible (cf. Schrag 1994:72)

3. A third moment of transversal rationality is the moment of *(incursive) disclosure.* This moment is tied very closely to that of articulation and can be explained as a postulate of reference, a claim for reality that brings us out of the "closure" of the isolated subject. In Schrag's own words: it is disclosure that keeps articulation from circling back on itself to a space where there is nothing outside of language, nothing beyond the text (1994:72). Disclosure in this sense is the achievement of reference that ultimately leads us beyond language and textuality. This revisioning of epistemological reference does not fall back onto a modernist truth theory of correspondence, and it does not objectify. Disclosure in this sense brings us face to face with the fact that we relate to our world(s) only through interpreted experience, and that the world as a phenomenon shows itself precisely in the manifold of human experience. The performance of reference thus supplies that which our articulatory gestures of discourse and action *are about* (Schrag 1994:73). But what do we mean when we talk about disclosure as *incursive?* The feature of incursivity points to the resistance, the encounter with otherness, that is implied by referential disclosure, and as such it is an effect of the transversal lines of force that issue from that which is other (cf. Schrag 1994:74).

This discussion certainly gives new depth to the important notion of *transversality,* and thereby greatly enhances our emerging notion of postfoundationalist rationality. The modern epistemological paradigm, as we saw, was typified by claims for universality. The postmodern challenge typically calls into question any search for universals: instead of a "God's-eye view" perspective from the other side of history, we are offered only a fragmented vision from this side of history that typically leaves us with a complete relativization of all forms of thought and all contents of culture. Schrag's response to this has been the pursuit of a third option, i.e., the "splitting of the difference" between modernity and postmodernity, and of thinking *with* the postmoderns while thinking *against* them (cf. 1992:129). In this move the postmodern problematization of the classical, modern claims for universality is embraced, but then postmodernism is used against itself by showing how the figure of transversality can more productively address the issues at hand. On this view, therefore, transversality replaces universality (cf. Schrag 1994:75). On this view, again, the knowing subject is not just jettisoned, but is refigured in a praxial performance of critique, articulation, and disclosure. By discovering the resources of reason in transversal/postfoundationalist rationality, modernist epistemology finally has to make room for a fusion of a refigured epistemology and hermeneutics in postfoundationalist rationality. Transversal/postfoundationalist rationality thus enables us to shuttle in the space between modernity and postmodernity: the space of interpreted experience and communicative praxis which enables praxial critique, articulation, and disclosure. Here, finally, transcontextual, even transhistorical judgments and assessments can be made without gravitating into an empty universalization on the one hand, or a pluralism of culture-spheres, particularized language games, and relativized moral claims on the other hand (cf. Schrag 1994:75). A postfoundationalist notion of rationality thus creates a safe space where our different discourses and actions are seen at times to link up with one another, and at times to contrast or conflict with one another. It is precisely in the hard struggle for interpersonal and interdisciplinary communication that the many faces of human rationality are revealed.

Schrag's work on the resources of rationality thus manages to avoid the extremes of the modernist nostalgia for one, unified form of knowledge, as well as the relativism of extreme forms of postmodernism. As such it greatly enhances the notion of postfoundationalist rationality that I am developing here. Over against the objectivism of foundationalism and the extreme relativism of most forms of nonfoundationalism, what is emerging here is a refigured postfoundationalist model of rationality that is thoroughly contextual, but at the same time will facilitate an interdisciplinary reach beyond one's own local group or culture. In splitting the difference between modernity and postmodernity, this view of rationality aims to capture those features of science that theoretically make it a paradigmatically rational enterprise without, however, falling back onto the totalizing foundationalism of the classical view of rationality. It is only within the framework of this kind of a post-classical view of rationality that Harold Brown can persuasively argue for positive reasons for believing that, although science did indeed develop in the Western world, there still are powerful grounds for maintaining that science has a significance that transcends the particular culture in which it first appeared (cf. H. Brown 1990:114). Brown certainly does not argue for the superiority of natural scientific rationality, nor does he specifically argue that only science has trans-social or cross-contextual significance. He does, however, leave open the question of whether or not other human endeavors may also have this significance.

Whatever else a postfoundationalist model of rationality might imply, it certainly means at least the following: while we always operate in terms of concepts and criteria that appeared in a particular culture, we are nonetheless able to transcend our specific contexts and reach out to more intersubjective levels of discussion, without necessarily falling back into any of modernity's typically totalizing meta-narratives. Brown goes further and correctly argues that a universal social relativism, one that denies any cross-contextual mode of cognition, cannot be coherently defended: if we cannot consider claims whose import goes beyond the confines of our own group, we cannot begin to explore the role that context, culture, and language play in determining beliefs (cf. H. Brown 1990:130). Brown's own model of rationality precisely wants to show that science can indeed be a potential source of knowledge that transcends the culture in which the various sciences first appeared, although in no way any longer exemplifying any claims to superior or normative rationality.

This finally brings us closer to the important question: What would a postfoundationalist notion of rational accountability look like? Earlier we briefly discussed the cognitive, pragmatic, and evaluative dimensions of rationality. In his own move to an alternative post-classical model of rationality — a move that anticipates Calvin Schrag's important notion of *evaluative critique* — Harold Brown emphasizes the evaluative resources of rationality by highlighting the important and often neglected role of assessment or *judgment* in human cognition. I believe that focusing on the relevance and significance of the role of judgment will not only reveal a crucially important dimension of scientific rationality, but will also finally reveal the true nature of the rational resources shared by scientific and other reasoning strategies. Even if the natural sciences may differ significantly from the human sciences (and because of differences in epistemological focus and experiential scope, also from theology), the shaping role of values and of our value judgments may not be all that different in these various modes of inquiry. Because of this, rational accountability and the way this is exemplified by *the rational role of responsible judgment* will be crucially important for defining what we mean by a postfoundationalist model of rationality.

Within the rule-governed context of the classical model of rationality, scientific statements are seen as rational because they are normally judged to be objective, impartial, and based on empirical evidence alone. Values and value judgments, however, are viewed very differently in this model. These are normally seen as nonscientific, and therefore subjective, partial, the expressions of individual feeling, religious belief, or social convention, and as such necessarily nonrational because there is no way in which they could ever be justified. In an insightful paper on the question of the rationality or nonrationality of values, Bruce B. Wavel has argued that this view implies not only a gross misrepresentation of what values are, but also of what science is (cf. 1980:43-56). Not only can scientific knowledge and a strictly scientific rationality not be opposed to values and value judgments in this way, but science — and therefore all scientific knowledge — is in fact always based on value judgments. In science the acceptance and rejection of hypotheses, and finally also theory choice, are indeed based on evaluation and deliberation. This places the making of certain kinds of value judgments at the heart of the scientific method itself. This also means that the human rational agent, and therefore the context of our personal decisions, forms a crucial part of the rhetorical strategies of present-day science (cf. also Hoering 1980:127). And because science, and the discipline of scientific thinking, so obviously exemplifies cognitive rationality, its unavoidable dependence on values and value judgments implies that these too must be part of what it means to be rational. In fact, not only could it be argued that decisions by individual scientists to work on one problem rather than another already involve obvious value judgments, but *the decision to have science at all* implies value judgments as to the superiority of knowledge to ignorance, intelligibility to nonintelligibility, truth to error, etc. (cf. Wavel 1980:43f.).

Those who want to deny that these value judgments are rational do so largely because they still assume that science, as the alleged "superior" paradigm of human rationality, somehow excludes these obviously very personal and subjective value judgments. Both Harold Brown (1990) and Bruce B. Wavel (1980) have argued persuasively, however, that science not only employs value judgments at crucial epistemic junctures, but also that their role in science is so basic that the common sense procedures of evaluation and deliberation, which are based on value judgments, are in fact essential to scientific rationality. And if procedures of evaluation, assessment, and deliberation are rational, then value judgments are essentially part of the process of scientific reflection, and should thus also be regarded as rational. The crucial role of value judgments in rational reflection therefore also points to the fact that theory appraisal and ultimately theory choice in science implies a complex and sophisticated form of value judgment. Theory choice, on this view, can no longer be seen as the result of rule-following, as in the classical model of rationality, but instead reveals the influence of pragmatic, empirical, and extra-empirical factors. Included in these extra-empirical influences that shape the rationality of science are epistemic values such as predictive accuracy, coherence, simplicity, etc., as well as a host of nonepistemic values that could be held by scientists, such as values profoundly shaped by a commitment to either naturalism, realism, or various forms of empiricism, pragmatism, feminism, etc. (cf. Jones 1994:184ff.). The variety of empirical and extra-empirical factors, epistemic and nonepistemic values that shape the process of scientific reflection are, however, not a chaotic collage of random beliefs or values, but on the contrary are normally fairly coherent and as such reflect our fundamental commitments to specific research traditions and worldviews. Clearly, these research traditions and broader worldviews are for the most part tacitly assumed and rarely produced through rational reflection. As such they actually show science and scientific reflection to be very specific social, cultural, and human phenomena (cf. Jones 1994).

Because of the breakdown of the stark opposition between scientific and other forms of rationality in a postfoundationalism, it can now also be argued that there is no essential difference between the epistemic function of values and value judgments in science and their function in other modes of rational inquiry like the humanities, ethics, and theology. If the use of value judgments in science is therefore rational, so is the use of value judgments in the humanities, ethics, and in theology. Moreover, if value judgments in ethics or theology sometimes appear to be more subjective than in science, this says nothing about how a judgment in each of these fields of inquiry would be more or less rational; it merely reveals a different epistemological focus and a broader experiential scope. A disregard of subjective factors in the making of our judgments — whether scientific, ethical, or theological — would therefore make any evaluation nonrational (cf. Wavel 1980:94). The shaping role of human judgment and the procedure of deliberation by which we consider reasons for or against a position, a commitment, or a viewpoint, a theory, doctrine, or a specific action are therefore equally valid for moral and nonmoral value judgments in theology, in science, and in all other forms of intellectual inquiry. Once again the cognitive, evaluative, and pragmatic dimensions of rationality are revealed, as well as the fact that theology and the sciences, along with all other modes of intellectual inquiry, share these common rational resources and should therefore all be capable of rational value judgments.

The way in which personal value judgments and rational reflection have now been inextricably linked finally gets us beyond the modernist dilemma of polarizing theology and science, subjectivity and objectivity, contextuality and rationality (cf. Bell 1996:179f.). Rational reflection and personal value judgments thus merge in a postfoundational notion of rationality, where rationality and context are not only compatible, but also in fact inseparable (cf. also Clayton and Knapp 1993:151). Rational judgment in this broader epistemic sense is the ability to evaluate a situation, to assess evidence and then come to a responsible and reasonable decision without following any preset, modernist rules (H. Brown 1990:137). On a postfoundationalist view of rationality, the notion of responsible rational judgment therefore plays a crucial role, and it would be hard to understand the broad domain of human knowledge fully without recognizing the role that judgment plays at key epistemic junctures. Rationality, as we saw, is about intelligibility and rational accountability, and we need to make responsible judgments precisely in those situations where we lack sufficient foundations or rules to determine our decisions and actions. Although judgment in this postfoundationalist context is never rule-governed, it also is not arbitrary, but is always based on quite specific information from very particular shared contexts.

Responsible rational judgment, in spite of its focus on the particular and its subjective enactment, is, therefore, a communicative project, irretrievably intersubjective (cf. Schrag 1992:57), never reducible to just the expression of private feelings, and as such exemplifies the contextual as well as the communal nature of human rationality. The main deficiency of the classical model of rationality has been exactly its inability to recognize the rational status of these judgments in spite of their fallibility (cf. van Niekerk 1990:184). Rational judgments are therefore made by individuals who are in command of an appropriate body of information relevant to the judgment in question. Harold Brown develops this idea further by seeing rational judgment as an epistemic skill that should be performed by a community of "experts" through a process of intersubjective deliberation and collective assessment. It is important to note, however, that there is nothing mysteriously intuitive about epistemic judgment, and for Brown it can therefore be included in a thoroughly naturalistic view of human cognition (cf. H. Brown 1990:137).

Learning to make the right or appropriate decisions, or to solve certain problems, therefore involves the development of intellectual skills that are, in many ways, analogous to physical skills (cf. H. Brown 1990:143). Brown's notion of the role of judgment in rational decision-making is exciting because in the end it frees us from the idea that only infallibility or perfectibility count in epistemic matters, and thus opens up the way to the kind of epistemic humility that goes with all fallibilism. When at any point in time we make a strong and particular decision for something in the light of the best reasons available to us, there need be no incompatibility between accepting that set of fallible claims for a substantial period of time, and also being prepared to reconsider them when we have good reasons for doing so. This will turn out to be important for theological reflection in situations where no fixed or absolute rules are available. Therefore responsible judgments are called for in theology, and may turn up even more frequently than in the hard sciences. On this view the development of responsible judgment as a cognitive skill is indeed closely analogous to the development of physical skills. The conscious, explicit rule-following that has long been taken as the paradigm of intelligent mental life indeed captures only a small portion of our cognitive resources (cf. H. Brown 1990:177). Harold Brown has, to my mind, successfully shown how the classical model of rationality selected only certain theoretical features of our preanalytic or common sense concept of rationality (especially the cognitive dimension of rationality) and then left out others, and that the motivation for these choices lies in the classical model's inherent foundationalism (cf. H. Brown 1990:182ff.). Precisely because of the failure of foundationalism, however, we are empowered to argue for those aspects of rationality that have been neglected or ignored, in order to point to the much richer resources of human rationality.

We also saw earlier that perhaps the most important element of our common sense or preanalytic notion of rationality is that we normally have good reasons for holding what we regard as our rational beliefs. Precisely because our judgments and rational beliefs are rhetorically based on the persuasive power of good reasons, we also regard them as more rational than nonrational or irrational beliefs. In addition to *rational beliefs,* however, we also need to identify *rational persons,* i.e., persons who can exercise good sense and good judgment in difficult and complex circumstances. We expect a rational person to be open to new ideas, and — as Harold Brown puts it — to function well in the context of discovery (1990:183). Three important steps, which should highlight the epistemic skill of responsible, intersubjective judgment and dovetail neatly with Calvin Schrag's notion of *praxial critique,* can now be proposed:

First, moving out of the constraints of the modernist aura of universal rationality, a new self emerges: a praxis-oriented self, defined by its communicative practices, oriented toward an understanding of itself in its discourses and action, and in being with others (cf. Schrag 1997:9). The focus is now on the very personal and contextual situation of those of us who want to cope meaningfully with ourselves and with the world as we have learned to experience it. For this reason the notion of the human self as *rational agent,* and not just rational beliefs as such, should be taken as fundamentally important, and notions like *rational belief* should be seen as derivative, at least in the sense that a rational belief will be one that is arrived at by a rational agent (cf. H. Brown 1990:185). The classical notion of rationality stressed the idea that a belief's rationality is connected with the way we arrive at that belief, i.e., by way of a body of appropriate evidence, which then makes it a rational belief. This evidentialist aspect of the classical model of rationality is now included in Harold Brown's own (post-classical) model, but it is developed very differently. In the classical model the central emphasis is placed on the logical relations between the evidence and the belief, while the role of the agent is minimized. In Harold Brown's move to an alternative model, which has already been identified as pointing the way to a postfoundationalist rationality, the human agent is taken to be basic, and the way that an agent deals with sufficient reasons or evidence in arriving at a belief will be determinative of the rationality of that belief for him or her (1990:185).

Second, the ability to discern, and to make responsible value judgments in those situations where we lack sufficient rules or foundations to determine our decisions, can now be seen as the most characteristic feature of a rational agent. As in Nicholas Rescher's notion of rationality, the evaluative dimension and the accompanying ability to execute *responsible judgments* are therefore central to a postfoundationalist model of rationality. It also entails, of course, that our ability to act as rational agents is limited by our expertise (H. Brown 1990:185). This does not mean that only experts can be rational, however, but it does mean that in cases where we may lack expertise, there may be only one rational decision open to us: to seek expert advice.

The third step required for a postfoundationalist model of rationality is precisely the retrieval of a *radical awareness of our social and communal embeddedness*. For a belief based on judgment to be a rational one, it must be submitted to the relevant epistemic community, a community of those who share the relevant expertise. Both our rational decision-making and what we judge to be our expertise are therefore very much a socially mediated rather than a rule-governed process (cf. H. Brown 1990:187). This demand that our rational beliefs be critically subjected to collective assessment, to intersubjective evaluation and criticism, is in conformity with our common sense understanding of rationality, where we accept that our all-too-human judgments are always fallible, and that the best chance of eliminating error is to expose our judgments to the expert deliberation of other people. Postfoundationalist rationality thus emerges as a quintessentially social phenomenon. On this view postfoundationalism therefore clearly

146

appropriates a constructive postmodern awareness that all our reasoning strategies are practices within specific contexts and for particular purposes. Rationality indeed requires other people, and not just any people, but people with the skills needed to exercise judgment and deliberate on particular issues within specific contexts.

This idea of responsible judgment and critical discernment is enhanced by Calvin Schrag's notion of the *fitting response* in fleshing out the profile of the human self in community. Although he primarily talks about an "ethic of the fitting response" (cf. 1997:98), I believe that my own notion of *responsible judgment* should be seen as an attempt at defining the rich epistemological resources of this notion, which Schrag primarily uses to indicate our response to the discourse and action of others in our community. This notion of the *fitting response* is reminiscent of Harold Brown's idea of *rational judgment:* a fitting response, as a proper rational judgment, is not to be confused with simple accommodation, but rather involves discernment, evaluation, and critical judgment (Schrag's notion of *praxial critique*). This notion of judgment clearly places a premium on context and on the contingency of local and historically specific social practices, but does not, however, lead to complete moral or epistemic relativism. We escape this relativism because our criteria, as resources for critical evaluation and grounds for critique, are *conditioned* by historically specific contexts, but they are not completely *determined* by such contexts (cf. Schrag 1997:107). In the making of moral and epistemological judgments the distinction between "context-conditioned" and "context-determined" is therefore crucial. Although conditioned by its context, human thought is nonetheless able to transcend the particularities of its social and historical contexts. Thus it is that we can critique our traditions while standing in them: and this refusal to be determined by a particular tradition, a particular conceptual system, or a particular form of behavior, enables a standpoint of critique that delivers us from the kind of relativism in which all interpretations and perspectives are granted an equal claim to thrive (cf. Schrag 1997:108).

Whereas the relativist embraces contextuality and contingency, the absolutist simply reflects the obverse side of the same mistake: by assuming that contextuality entails determinism, the absolutist appeals to a priori and context-free conditions and yearns for a foundationalist universality to ground a transcending critique that is wholly contextless (cf. Schrag 1997:108). It is exactly the *bogus dichoto-*

mies of the absolute versus the relative, the universal versus the particular, the necessary versus the contingent, that need to be exposed for what they are — namely, conceptual constructs of a theoretical position-taking that has been revealed as no longer compelling at all (cf. Schrag 1997:108). Truth claims and effective critique thus retain a central place in postfoundationalism, but the space for this is now communicative praxis, transversally textured, where personal judgment and communal feedback guide a fitting response that is neither a-historically absolutist nor historically relativist. The rational self is therefore a self in community, a self situated in the space of communicative praxis, historically embedded, existing with others: others that always include predecessors, contemporaries, and successors. In this way the rational self is *in* history, but not just *of* history (cf. Schrag 1997:109).

This emerging postfoundationalist notion of rationality differs significantly from Thomas Kuhn's views and what is often referred to as his "consensus" model of rationality. For Kuhn the sociohistorical dimension of our rational behavior replaces positivist rules as the basis for scientific research and decision-making, rational decisions are those made by the scientific community, and in normal science theses become embodied in communally approved and transmitted practices (Kuhn 1970:175, 238). Kuhn thus holds to the position that when the majority of a relevant scientific community reaches agreement, we have a rational decision. Harold Brown, however, differs from Kuhn precisely at this point: agreement with the majority does not automatically make a belief rational at all. For Kuhn the conclusion of the community is the only one that can be rationally accepted. On Harold Brown's view, however, what is required is only that individuals submit their judgments for evaluation and assessment by their peers, and that they take this evaluation seriously. This is also much closer to real-life situations where, as academics and even as Christian theologians, we often hardly agree at all. Closely related to Nicholas Rescher's criticism of any claim that sees consensus as the "highway to rationality," and therefore as a rational or moral imperative, Harold Brown also argues that rationality never requires that each member of a community has to agree with the majority, or that only this kind of consensus will yield true rationality. In fact, agreement with the majority view is neither necessary nor sufficient for rationality (cf. H. Brown 1990:192). Scientific practice clearly demonstrates that rational disagreement is certainly an important and pervasive feature of science. The mere fact of agreement with the majority does not make a belief rational at all, and while a postfoundationalist model of rationality requires that our beliefs be based on individual judgment, exactly this judgment is shaped by strong personal values and convictions, and it still requires deliberation and rational accountability, i.e., some form of assessment by both the individual rational agent as well as the community or communities he or she belongs to (cf. Wavel 1980:52ff.).

In this postfoundationalist model of rationality, therefore, the predicate "rational" first of all characterizes an individual's decisions and beliefs, not propositions or communities. Even if a community of experts is necessary for an individual to arrive at a rational belief, it still is the individual's belief that is rational, and not the community (H. Brown 1990:193). In a postfoundationalist notion of rationality, those agents who exercise responsible judgments are therefore central to rational procedures, and it is the fallibility of these agents' judgments that leads to the requirement of ongoing critical evaluation by others. As we saw, it is precisely this resituation of critique and communal judgment within the spaces of our communicative practices that Calvin Schrag has called *praxial critique* (Schrag 1992:57f.). In a postfoundationalist theology it is precisely the much neglected role of personal, responsible judgment and discernment in rational decision-making that will be retrieved as crucially important, but always within the larger context of the community. Because of the way we exercise our value judgments, as well as choose and construct our theories, the mediating role of our interpreted experience is now revealed as crucial for the process that leads to rational judgment, even if we cannot always capture the complexity of interpreted human experience in exact propositions.

At this point, however, we need to consider an important question in more detail one more time: How does a postfoundationalist model of rationality, so strongly connected to the individual rational agent and the evaluation of individual judgment by communities of experts, get us beyond the social relativism of nonfoundationalism? If rationality involves nothing more than judgment and critical evaluation by the members of an appropriate community, then we may obviously find rational belief and decision-making in communities that we may normally even characterize as irrational. For Harold Brown theologians are a case in point: various groups of theologians who belong to different religions may indeed all be engaged in a fully rational endeavor, and the same may hold for, say, Azande witch doctors (cf. H. Brown 1990:194). Brown is fully aware of the fact that this possibility follows from his model of rationality, and therefore argues along the following lines: first, to claim that a belief is rational is not the same as to claim that a belief is true; second, while rational acceptance of a claim indeed depends on the assessment of evidence, some forms of evidence provide a stronger warrant for belief than other forms of evidence. In his own words:

> Thus while questions of denominational theology may be capable of a rational solution, it does not follow that we have no basis at all for choosing between, say, a scientific and a theological worldview at those points at which the two views conflict. (1990:195)

Because of the shared resources of human rationality, plausible rational choices across the boundaries of epistemic communities, in terms of the good, better, or best reasons available to us, now indeed become an intersubjective, interdisciplinary, and even interparadigmatic possibility.

This important dimension of a postfoundationalist notion of rationality is further enhanced when we realize that rationality not only involves evaluation against the standards of a community of inquiry, but also assures that the personal voice of the individual rational agent is not silenced in this ongoing process of collective assessment (cf. Gregersen and van Huyssteen 1998:29ff.). In an important paper, Philip Clayton and Steven Knapp (1993) identified what the epistemological ramifications of relating strong individual, personal convictions to the broader standards of a community of inquiry would be. Clayton and Knapp also confirm that rationality in general, and properly understood, always involves evaluation against the standards of a community of inquiry (cf. 1993:151). Of course, the standards for what we see as good or bad reasons are never independent of our specific social and cultural contexts. This contextual view of rational agency is furthermore enhanced by the fact that in a postfoundationalist epistemology the modernist distinction between "objective" empirical (read: scientific) reasons and more "subjective" ethical, religious, or aesthetic reasons is revealed as nonsensical. In all our reasoning strategies — and therefore in theology and the sciences too — this interactionist epistemology will imply that we need to move beyond the forced separation of so-called "purely objective" factual issues and "purely subjective" religious or theological issues. The responsible judgments that we hope to make, and the strong personal convictions that will flow from this, should substantiate the claim that some of our convictions are binding to us as rational agents *precisely* as a consequence of our commitment to rationality. This again confirms that rationality and context are more than just compatible; they are in fact inseparable (cf. Clayton and Knapp 1993:151f.). When we try to make a responsible judgment, the rationality of a given claim indeed lies in its relation to an ongoing process of collective assessment. On this view, a necessary condition for my claim that a judgment or belief is rational is that it has been subjected to — or is genuinely open to — criticism by the "experts," i.e., those whom I take to be the relevant community of inquiry.

But what of the individual who sees beyond the available community, the gifted visionary or prophet who may be severely misunderstood by the community's ongoing collective assessment of his or her judgments, beliefs, and strong convictions? In an innovative twist Clayton and Knapp here open the door to another possibility: the rationality of a given claim is indeed to be found in an ongoing process of collective assessment, but at the same time there is no reason to hold that *any* presently existing community fully represents a rational agent's sense of what a community is or should be (cf. Clayton and Knapp 1993:152). What is forcefully revealed here is the very specific limits of communal rationality, when — for instance — a visionary, a genius, or a prophet relies almost exclusively on the standards of an as-yet-nonexistent communal rationality. This also again reveals the richness of the resources of human rationality, as the cognitive, pragmatic, and evaluative dimensions of rationality merge in the rational agent's own reasons for believing, acting, and judging. This means that our good reasons for making certain judgments, which will lead to certain strong convictions which will and should be critically evaluated in our epistemic community's ongoing process of collective assessment, are first of all evaluated against the standards implicit in each rational agent's *self-conception* (cf. Clayton and Knapp 1993:152). By recognizing how a rational agent's personal judgments, beliefs, and actions are shaped by his or her self-conception, we have truly moved beyond any modernist attempts to argue for a universal, rule-governed, general account of human rationality. As human beings we are characterized by self-awareness, and our individual, personal motivations or reasons for believing, acting, and choosing are not only closely tied in with some sense of who this "I" is, but are indeed epistemically shaping the value judgments we make in terms of this self-conception.

For Clayton and Knapp the notion of an individual's self-conception provides the indispensable starting point for an account of ethics (cf. 1993:152). I want to claim the same for our reflection on human rationality: the rational agent's self-conception and self-awareness is not only intrinsically connected to rationality, it is indeed an indispensable starting point for any account of the values that shape human rationality (cf. van Huyssteen 1998b:30f.). In the absence of the availability of modernist rules, metanarratives, or transcendental standards for rationality, each of us is left with only one viable option: in assessing what rationality is, I must assess it as I see it, from where I stand. As a human being with a distinct self-awareness, and a very specific quest for intelligibility, I can step into the reality of communicative praxis only from where I stand, and begin any intersubjective conversation only by appealing to *my* rationality (cf. Rescher 1993:110). Thus not only rationality and context, but also rationality and strong personal commitments inextricably go together. And as long as I participate in a rationally conscientious way in the back and forth of the feedback process that makes up our communal discourse, I am rationally justified in holding on to my commitments and strong convictions.

As a rational agent I can enter any conversation only from my own perspective on what the rational explanation of experience is. It does *not* follow from this, as we have seen, that for my standards to be rational, they should ultimately also be in agreement with those of others who are differently situated (cf. Rescher 1993:110). Rationality therefore does not presuppose consensus. The epistemic tolerance that emerges from this pluralism flows from the experiential and contextual nature of rationality, but it should never lead to relativistic indifference. Precisely on this point Nicholas Rescher has argued persuasively that when it comes to making good rational choices for the right reasons, all perspectives that are taken to be normative are *not* going to be equally acceptable. If the experiential bases and the values that shape our judgments are at issue, then the pattern of our own on-going, contextualized experience is going to be altogether decisive — for us at any rate — in communal discourse. And because rationality requires that we attune our beliefs and judgments to our own self-conception and self-awareness, rationality also requires that we attune our beliefs, convictions, and evaluations to the overall pattern of our experience. On this view, it should be clear that a postfoundationalist notion of rationality could never be some kind of superimposed metanarrative, but itself develops as an emerging pattern that unifies our interpreted experience without totalizing it (cf. Schrag 1992: 154ff.). In this sense the claim that rationality is always embedded in the rational agent's self-awareness also implies that one's own experience is always going to be rationally compelling (Rescher 1993:119).

Rationality cannot be adequately understood if we do not completely accept the ramifications of the fact that every person has some form of self-awareness, some image of the kind of self he or she has been, or wants to become. This self-conception always shapes what we regard as the most plausible reasons for the choices we make, the beliefs we commit ourselves to, and the actions we take. But this trust in our personal convictions must always be open to intersubjective assessment as we walk the fine line between our personal standards and the standards of what we regard as the ideal epistemic community. What is suggested here is a necessary "feedback relationship" between the self-aware individual and his or her social context (cf. Clayton and Knapp:153), an epistemic relationship where we learn with discernment to acquire rational beliefs, not just about our worlds, but also about ourselves. Both individual and communal rationality therefore have necessary limitations, but for a full picture of the richness of human rationality it is necessary to see how they enhance one another. Communal consensus by itself can therefore never adequately define the epistemic goal of rationality, but it also would not be rational for an individual to insist (without good reasons) on holding beliefs that conflict completely with the epistemic community's ongoing process of collective assessment. Rationality thus clearly entails an unavoidable investment in the interest of others. Because our epistemic communities never exist in complete isolation from one another, it will be important to realize that an adequately contextualized notion of rationality is necessary to facilitate intersubjective, cross-disciplinary conversation.

A postfoundationalist model of rationality therefore manages to move beyond the constraints of the classical model, and shows that rationality in the modernist sense is not at all enough when it comes to the cognitive assessment of our knowledge claims. It has also become clear, however, that a postfoundationalist notion of rationality also has to move beyond Harold Brown's post-classical model in broadening the scope of rationality to include not only natural science as an optimal form of rational practice, but also our other domains of reflection and action, and to give the important notion of the *rational agent* flesh and blood by identifying him or her as someone with an acute self-awareness, someone who is consciously embedded in the concrete, living traditions of our various cultural domains and diverse reasoning strategies.

In his own search for a metacriterion that could appropriately assess our different models of rationality, Mikael Stenmark has also critiqued what he calls Harold Brown's *social evidentialism* and the limitations of this model as a general model of rationality (cf. 1995: 142ff.). In Brown's work the strong argument for the *evidential principle* (a belief is rationally acceptable only if it is arrived at by a person who exercises informed judgment) and the *social principle* (a belief is rationally acceptable only if it has been exposed to or tested against the judgments of a community of relevant expertise) certainly is a definitive move beyond the formal evidentialism of the classical model of rationality. Each of these two principles by itself, however, is insufficient for claiming rationality: the evidential principle is not sufficient because it is not enough that a belief is arrived at by an exercise of informed judgment to qualify as rational. Because of this, our beliefs must always be submitted to critical evaluation by the informed members of a specific community. But (as we saw before) the mere fact that a belief has been accepted by the agreement or consensus of a community is not enough to automatically qualify it as rational.

Stenmark correctly wants to move beyond Brown's somewhat idealized model of rationality and its idealized rational agent: if rationality is always *agent-* or *person-related*, it should also be *agent-* or *person-relative* (cf. Stenmark 1995:195). Our turn to self-awareness and to the person as rational agent now also means that on a certain level rationality cannot be the same for all rational agents, and that we cannot deal with rationality without also asking whose rationality and rational beliefs it is that we are talking about. For a postfoundationalist model of rationality where we want to "split the difference" between modernity's universalism and postmodernism's radical relativism, the crucially important question now is: *What exactly is it about human rationality that is general or universal, and what about it is relative or changing* (cf. Stenmark 1995:227)? Although he bypasses completely the important issue of how the postmodern challenge has affected our various notions of rationality, Mikael Stenmark does suggest a helpful distinction on exactly this point: at the level of *the nature of rationality,* rationality is unrestrictedly universal in intent. As we saw earlier, rationality is so closely aligned with human intelligence and with the survival of our species, that the intellectual obligation to understand our worlds and ourselves at an optimal level is shared by all humans. Nicholas Rescher thus rightly argued that this imperative to understand and cope is altogether basic for *homo sapiens* (cf. 1992:3ff.). In our quest for intelligibility it is the intelligent use of the human ability for rational judgment that we all share in principle. On the level of the *standards of rationality,* however, rationality is person-relative (cf. Stenmark 1995:229f.), and as such directly shaped by the richness of the various contexts in which humans as rational agents find themselves embedded. This does not make rationality itself relative (and does not take us back to a nonfoundationalist "many rationalities" view), but it does mean that what is rational to believe, choose, and accept is always person- and situation-relative. It also explains why we need a feedback relationship between the self-aware individual and his or her social context, the kind of epistemic relationship where we learn with discernment how to acquire rational beliefs about our worlds, about ourselves, but also about other people, other contexts, and other reasoning strategies.

If we should still want to accept with Harold Brown that natural scientific rationality is still the *best* example we have of cognitive rationality at work and that belief-formation in the sciences is still an important control case for rationality in general, we should now also be willing to move beyond the limitations of a strictly scientific rationality, to the rich resources and different dimensions of rationality as it is performatively present on the various levels and in the diverse domains of our lives. On this point Stenmark makes a persuasive case by arguing that, if not the "best" we have, everyday believing (real life situations where we as rational agents are contextually situated) is in a sense a stronger paradigm case for rationality — not in the sense that it is the *best* we humans can do, but in the sense that it is the *most* we do (1995:200f.). Everyday beliefs are by far the largest domain of beliefs we have, and they are about one's own self-awareness, about other people, about how we relate to one another and live our lives, and ultimately also about how we find (ultimate) meaning in life. In this sense the everyday beliefs of our "pre-scientific" everyday lives indeed are a paradigm case for rationality and are in a way more fundamental than scientific beliefs because we cannot avoid believing them and at the same time function normally as human beings. The rich domain of human rationality therefore stretches wide, and includes our day-to-day lives, our art, our religion(s), science, and technology. An adequate model of rationality therefore needs to have the scope to include these diverse domains without again, however, totalizing rationality into an idealized and universalized metanarrative.

Rationality, Truth, and Progress

With the specific postfoundationalist focus on the individual rational agent and his or her intersubjective deliberating link to communities of expertise, we have not returned to the relativist or nonfoundationalist position according to which every group or language game is automatically rational according to its own internal set of rules. The postfoundationalist move to responsible judgment, which gives up access to clear or absolute rules, also involves tighter constraints, as we have seen, than just agreement on issues by experts in the field. But how important is the role of communal or interpersonal agreement in our various reasoning strategies, and particularly also in theology and the sciences? This is a particularly important question, since it inevitably raises the question of how rationality relates to truth.

As we saw when we discussed the importance of communal consensus in Nancey Murphy's thought, the belief that consensus or interpersonal agreement plays a leading role in matters of rational inquiry, and in the way we come to our decisions and judgments, is among the oldest and most pervasive ideas in philosophy. On precisely this point Nicholas Rescher has explained why it is that consensus is often seen as the "touchstone of truth" (cf. 1993:6), and that the question that now confronts us is whether or not rational persons must ultimately reach agreement on important issues. Rescher has convincingly argued that diversity and dissensus can often play a highly constructive role in our communal discourses, and that rationality thus does not necessarily have to lead to consensus. It is therefore rational to optimize our choices rhetorically by providing the best available reasons for our beliefs, actions, and choices. *Vis-à-vis* all our attempts to attain a uniformity of consensus as interpersonal agreement, Rescher has argued instead for a legitimate pluralism of diversity: the fact that different people have different experiential situations makes it normal, natural, and rational that they should proceed differently in cognitive, evaluative, and practical matters. In this sense consensus is revealed as (at most) an ideal, and not a realizable "fact of life" (cf. Rescher 1993:9). As rational agents we are embedded in, and live out of, concrete contexts and traditions, and the diversity of our traditions will yield a diversity of experiences, epistemic situations, cognitive values, and methodologies. Consensus is therefore not a prerequisite for, nor a necessary consequence of, rationality. It also never is the "highway to truth" (cf. Rescher 1993:52).

It does seem, however, that the notion of truth is so deeply embedded in our thinking about cognitive matters that we can barely get along without it (cf. Brown 1990:198). On the classical view of rationality there is, of course, a close tie between rationality and truth, and for this reason false propositions could never be rationally accepted. Contemporary nonfoundationalist and postmodern thought, on the other hand, emphasizes that people from different societies can accept radically different sets of claims as true, and that it is impossible to determine which of these claims are really "true." Both Kuhn (1970) and Laudan (1977) have also shown that human beings manage to function very successfully on the basis of convictions and beliefs that they may later reject as false. It is, however, extremely difficult to dispense with the notion of truth completely. Whatever we say or claim about truth, "truth" or "true premises" will do us little good unless we have reasons for believing that they are true. Harold Brown correctly points out that this is where rationality enters the picture, since rationality is concerned with assessing reasons and then making a judgment for believing one claim or another (1990:201). This of course makes the great attraction of the classical model and the search for foundations so understandable. The failure of foundationalism, however, has left us without any absolute truth claims; the only reasons we now have for hanging on to our cognitive claims are those that we judge to be the best ones available to us.

Harold Brown's point with this argument is that (as in the case of consensus and rationality) the notions of truth and rationality are distinct in the sense that achieving one of them in no way entails that the other has also been achieved (1990:202).[3] There is, however, a weaker but vital tie between rationality and truth, and on this point Brown's thinking again converges closely with that of Nicholas Rescher: we proceed rationally in attempting to "discover" truth, and we take those conclusions that are rationally acceptable as our best estimates of the truth. Brown argues persuasively that the search for truth is a long-term process and we need coherent procedures to carry out this pursuit for optimal intelligibility, which for him too is the ultimate function of rationality (cf. H. Brown 1990:202). His argument for a weak tie between truth and rationality finally turns out to be very helpful for any attempt to arrive at a plausible notion of progress too, first in science, but also in other modes of inquiry. Even if we are committed to the view that later theories are better theories, it does not have to imply a closer-to-the-truth position. In his argument against such a theory of verisimilitude, Nicholas Rescher (1992:48) has warned against the temptation to think of improvement in *warrant* (having better reasons) as implying improvement in *approximation* (moving closer to the truth). In fact, since we now accept that science often progresses through revolutions and radical shifts, there is no way that we can still think of science as developing by way of convergence as a mere linear accumulation of knowledge.

What is achieved in scientific inquiry is therefore not so much an *approximation* of truth, but an *estimation* of it. Scientists form, as best as they can, a reasoned judgment of where the truth of the matter lies. In this way we do not manage to get nearer to "the truth," but we do present our best estimates of what we believe the truth within a specific context might be. As far as scientific theorizing goes, our present world picture thus represents a better estimate than our past attempts only in the sense that it is, comparatively speaking, more warranted than they are because a wider range of data has been accommodated. This fallibilism is also strengthened by Rescher's con-

---

3. In his argument for a presumptionist model of rationality, Mikael Stenmark also disconnects *rationality* from *truth* (cf. 1995:221-25).

sistent and helpful distinction between a *better estimate* (one that has fewer deficits and may be based on fuller information) and a *closer estimate* (one that claims to be closer to the "real truth"): in scientific theorizing we must settle for a qualitative "better" because there is obviously no way of monitoring the issue of a measurable "closer" (cf. Rescher 1992:53). The fact that scientific knowledge also moves through radical changes and discontinuities thus invalidates any talk of successive approximation. In the epistemic humility that should flow from this kind of fallibilism, our accepted "truths" should be viewed as nothing more than the best possible estimates or judgments that we are able to make in the present moment. For pragmatic reasons, however, it might still make sense to talk about "pursuing truth" (cf. Rescher 1992:56). This conception of truth enhances and deepens the meaning of a postfoundationalist notion of rationality and will indeed pose an intriguing challenge to the rationality of theological reflection.

A postfoundationalist model of rationality can even manage to preserve the idea of progress, as well as the idea that rational beliefs are based on the best available evidence, although there now will be different sources of evidence for different kinds of claims. This becomes even clearer when we take a closer look at the way Harold Brown defines the concept of objectivity. Obviously we first need to disassociate ourselves from the positivist view of objectivity, which requires that we approach our subject without any preconceptions. Brown has argued that objectivity means at least this: the evidence or good arguments supporting an objective belief must derive from a source that is independent of that belief (H. Brown 1990:203). The example that Brown uses to illustrate this is taken from physics: a physicist, working within a certain historical and social context, might claim that all matter is constructed of electrons, neutrons, and protons. What is normally claimed here is that these are actually features of the physical world. Of course these claims, like all intellectual or specifically scientific claims, are made from within a certain historical and social context. Such claims are nonetheless not only claims about that context, culture, or language.

We saw earlier that within a postfoundationalist notion of rationality it is through the important dimension of disclosure that language permits us to make claims about items that exist apart from ourselves and our language. Once we have acknowledged the cultural, linguistic, or social context of a specific claim, the point remains that many claims make assertions about some state of affairs that is independent of those claims. In this sense it is hard to avoid the "primordial intuition" (cf. Bernstein 1983:4) that there is a world that is independent of our beliefs, a world that somehow constrains what we can think, say, or do. For Harold Brown this would imply some paradigm examples of the pursuit of objectivity (cf. Brown 1990:204), and is close to what Nicholas Rescher has called the pursuit of truth. It is important to remember, of course, that not all matters can be studied objectively in this *strictly natural scientific* sense of the word: some subjects may not deal with what Brown has called "items that have the required ontological status" (1990:205). We have, for example, no "objective basis" (in the strictly scientific sense of the word) for evaluating ethical claims, or theological claims, for that matter. This, however, does not by itself block the exercise of rationality in these fields, for there may be other considerations that can provide the basis for responsible rational judgment and deliberation in these other domains.

When Harold Brown argues for a plausible post-classical notion of objectivity, he is clearly not arguing for a monolithic notion of epistemological realism that stretches over all possible fields of inquiry. He is only arguing that we normally study items or issues that are relatively independent of the claims we make about them. In the case of theology, about which Brown says nothing, we need to carefully unpack the relationship between the fiduciary structure of the believer as rational agent, the epistemic influence of a faith commitment, religious texts, religious tradition, and religious experience. For theology the coherence of this context could possibly provide the best available reasons for believing, doing, judging, and choosing in specific ways, and thus reveal the values that shape the rationality of theological reflection. However, rationality and objectivity should always be carefully distinguished: rationality is possible (more often than not) in the absence of regular scientific objectivity.[4] However, a weak notion of objectivity is still epistemically important, because in the sciences it provides us with an especially powerful body of evi-

4. Mikael Stenmark makes a similar distinction between *questions of rationality* that deal with when a person (or group of persons) should be entitled to believe what he or she believes, and *questions of justification* that deal with when a belief should be generally acceptable or be considered a part of our body of knowledge (cf. 1995:221).

dence, or, as will be the case in theology, with persuasive reasons to be used in the judgment and rational assessment of our knowledge claims.

This discussion of the role and characteristics of truth, progress, and objectivity in science obviously reflects on the problem of the *status* of science, and on how much we can really hope to achieve through scientific knowledge. The key question here is: How far can the scientific enterprise advance toward achieving a definite and complete understanding of nature? The fallibilism implied in a postfoundationalist notion of scientific rationality necessarily leads to what has been called the imperfectibility of science (cf. Rescher 1992:77f.). A fallibilist epistemology necessarily implies that our knowledge — including our scientific knowledge — can never be complete or perfect. For Nicholas Rescher this *fait accompli* invites a description of the cognitive situation of the natural sciences in theological terms: expelled from the Garden of Eden, we are deprived of access to the God's-eye point of view. We yearn for absolutes but have to settle for plausibilities; we desire what is definitely correct but have to settle for conjectures and estimates (cf. 1992:85). The ideal of a perfected science, though unattainable, is nevertheless epistemically highly useful. Rescher calls this idea of a perfected science a *focus imaginarius* whose pursuit canalizes and thereby structures our scientific inquiry:

> As such it represents the ultimate telos of inquiry, the idealized destination of an incompletable journey, a grail of sorts that we can pursue but not possess. (Rescher 1992:94)

With this we return once again to one of our most important initial questions: If scientific knowledge itself is so imperfect and essentially fallibilist, why does it provide such an important test case for our reflection on models of rationality? Having now moved beyond the foundationalism of the classical model of rationality and its restrictive notions of justification and empirical evidence, it is still possible to claim the following: rationality (especially now a postfoundationalist notion of rationality) requires serious assessment of good reasons and available evidence, and we should therefore find our best examples of rationality in an area or field where the most reliable evidence is systematically gathered and deployed (cf. van Huyssteen 1997a:255f.). In

161

this sense "objective" procedures (now understood through a more nuanced, interactionist view of objectivity) still provide the richest and most reliable evidence, and one of the most important features of science is precisely its systematic pursuit of objective evidence (cf. H. Brown 1990:207).

In this sense, I think, the selection of science as our clearest example of the *cognitive/theoretical dimension* of rationality at work is indeed justified. What is not justified, however, is any claim for the superiority of scientific rationality, and any attempt to extend uncritically the nature of a strictly scientific rationality to the rationality of religious or any other reflection. The special position of science, however, as (in a qualified sense) still the clearest example of cognitive rationality at work is ultimately also the reason why philosophy of science forms such an important epistemological link in the current theology and science dialogue. Because of the nature and the comprehensive resources of human rationality, the rationality of science and the rationality of religious reflection — in spite of their important differences as reasoning strategies — do seem to overlap at some very crucial junctures. The theologian shares with the scientist the crucial role of being a rational agent, of making the best possible rational judgments within a specific context and for a specific community. The theologian also shares with the scientist the fallibilism implied by the contextuality of rational decision-making, and thus the experiential and interpretative dimension of all our knowledge. As we will see later, precisely the experiential and interpretative roots of religious knowing, however, are much more complex than the mostly empirical roots of natural scientific knowledge. Rationality in religion and in theological reflection is indeed a much broader and more complex affair than what here emerged as a strictly scientific rationality (cf. Moore 1994). The lingering imperialism of a modernist notion of scientific rationality should not close our eyes, however, to the shared rational resources, and the remarkable epistemic consonance between scientific and theological ways of thinking. This is especially true in the light of the fact that, as we saw before, some scientists and philosophers of science are now acknowledging the very specific limitations of scientific rationality (cf. D'Espagnat 1989; Davies 1992), are recovering the hermeneutical dimension of science in both the natural and the social sciences (cf. Bernstein 1983:171), and are thereby also opening the way to the acknowledgment of a richer notion of human rationality.

162

While a postfoundationalist model of rationality — which I have attempted to develop above in dialogue with Nicholas Rescher, Calvin Schrag, and Harold Brown — should exemplify epistemic humility by moving beyond all modernist, metanarrativist notions of necessary rules and objectivism to contextual decision-making and personal judgment, it should also, as we have seen, aim for plausible, intersubjective, rational accountability. Thanks to post-Kuhnian philosophy of science we now know that across pertinent shifts and revolutions in scientific reflection, we have rationality neither in the sense of a cumulative development with respect to phenomena expressed in a neutral observation language, nor in the sense of scientific development or progress being guided by a set of persistent or universal criteria of rationality (cf. Hoering 1980:123f.). Instead, scientific reflection has shown itself as a historically dynamic process in which there are conflicting and competing paradigm theories, research programs, and research traditions. Harold Brown, Nicholas Rescher, and Calvin Schrag have all managed to plausibly argue that, in order even to begin to understand what rationality in different modes of inquiry is about, it is necessary to see that even in natural science, as arguably our best example of the cognitive dimension of rationality at work, the arguments and value judgments employed by scientists are grounded in historical contexts and social practices, and that there is an essential openness even in the very criteria and norms that guide scientific inquiry (cf. also Bernstein 1983:171f.). Precisely because of the extent to which scientific theories are underdetermined by facts, we have to allow for alternative and competing theoretical explanations. So, on the one hand, a constructive form of postfoundationalist epistemology stresses the communal and pragmatic character of rationality, in which contextual judgment, deliberation, and interpretation play a central role. On the other hand, however, we never escape the intersubjective and cross-disciplinary obligation to support our rational judgments with the best available reasons and the best possible arguments. The weak notions of "objectivity" and of "estimated truth" that arise from this, however, seriously challenge any of our attempts to argue plausibly for some form of improvement, success, or progress in postfoundationalist rational reflection.

I would like to argue that a postfoundationalist understanding of rationality, precisely by "splitting the difference" between modernist and constructive postmodernist challenges to our notions of rationality, does not call into question scientific or other qualified forms of intellectual progress, or even the growth of our knowledge, but only critiques faulty modernist/classical doctrines which claim that intellectual progress can only be measured by an appeal to a permanent ahistorical matrix of universal rules (cf. Bernstein 1983:172). We saw earlier that Harold Brown, while certainly not claiming outright superiority for scientific knowledge, argued very persuasively that it really would not be possible to grapple plausibly with the nature of our knowledge while at the same time remaining blissfully ignorant of what is arguably our best existing example of theoretical knowledge, i.e., the natural sciences. This leaves us with some crucial questions that, while already difficult for the sciences, may be even more complex and confusing for theological reflection. Does science really progress? Are some of our beliefs about the world — and about ourselves — more rational than others? Does it make sense at all to claim some form of intellectual progress for theological reflection, and if so, how rational would these judgments be? These questions become really poignant when we realize that many of us draw the bulk of our beliefs about nature, and about ourselves, from the corpus of the natural sciences. The ramifications of this have been carefully spelled out by Larry Laudan: if science is indeed such a rational system of inquiry, then it is only right and proper that we should emulate its methods, accept its conclusions, and adopt its suppositions (cf. Laudan 1977: 2ff., 148ff.). If science, however, is predominantly irrational because choices between competing, incommensurable theories must be irrational, then there would hardly be any reason to take the knowledge claims of science seriously at all. The skepticism of such an argument has of course been reinforced by many of the claims of contemporary postmodern cultural pluralism and postmodern philosophy of science, where scientific knowledge is often seen as just one more set of beliefs among many others.

To move beyond this impasse, the notion of a postfoundationalist rationality must be broadened even further. To talk about the shaping of rationality is not only to talk about accountability, optimal understanding, and responsible judgment, but should also reveal the intellectual activity of judgment and decision-making as a progressive, problem-solving process. On this view, where responsible, rational judgment should be revealed as a form of effective problem-solving, the scope of human rationality again goes far beyond a strictly natural scientific rationality. And although scientific rationality shows itself as a very disciplined and manicured (cf. Puddefoot 1994:10) form of rationality, problem-solving (like rational judgment) reaches beyond the sciences and already forms part of the preanalytic or common sense reasonableness we live by every day.

To get a better grip on the epistemic links between rationality, judgment, and problem-solving, it will be worthwhile to take a careful look at the way that Larry Laudan has related rationality to progress in intellectual inquiry. In his *Progress and Its Problems* (1977) Laudan, *vis-à-vis* the classical model of rationality, proposes that the rationality and progressiveness of a scientific theory are not most closely linked with its confirmation by verification or falsification, but rather with its problem-solving effectiveness. Like Harold Brown, Laudan argues that there are important nonempirical and even "nonscientific" factors which have played a role in the rational development of science. More importantly, however, Laudan's proposal actually involves the blurring of the classical distinction between scientific progress and scientific rationality. Traditionally these were seen as very different concepts and insofar as they were linked at all, rationality has always taken priority over progress, to such a degree that progress (on this modernist view) was often seen as nothing more than the temporal, linear projection of a series of individual rational choices. To be intellectually progressive, on the classical view, would therefore imply an adherence to a series of increasingly rational beliefs. On this view progress was not only made to be parasitic on rationality, but something that normally can be more readily understood (progress) is explained in terms of something else (rationality) that may in fact be far more obscure (cf. Laudan 1977:6).

In an innovative twist Laudan inverts the presumed dependency of progress on rationality, claiming that we actually have a clearer model for scientific progress than we do for scientific rationality. Closely aligned to Harold Brown's linking of rationality to the making of the most responsible judgments for the best possible reasons, this view of rationality consists in making the most progressive theory choices, rather than progress consisting in accepting successively what is regarded as the most rational choices. Laudan wisely distinguishes between material, spiritual, or social progress, and what he labels as cognitive progress, i.e., progress with respect to the intellectual aspirations of science (cf. 1977:7). In fact, for Laudan science is essentially a problem-solving activity: it is impossible to talk about the rationality of science if we do not also focus on the fact that scientific theories are usually attempts to solve empirical or conceptual problems. And the solving of empirical or conceptual problems, in my view, is exactly what our rational judgments are about. Science is, of course, about much more than just problem-solving.[5] In our quest for intelligibility, problem-solving, as the epistemic goal of rational judgment, does, however, capture what is most characteristic about science.

It is as important, however, to realize that problem-solving as such does not set science apart from other modes of rational inquiry, for exactly the same reasons that scientific rationality cannot be defined in opposition to the rationality of other forms of intellectual inquiry. The latter, as we have seen, share the same resources of rationality with scientific inquiry. Laudan understands this well when he states that "scientific" problems are not fundamentally different from other kinds of problems, and that the views he is arguing for regarding rationality and progress could be applied to virtually all modes of intellectual inquiry (cf. Laudan 1977:171f.). This certainly affords a fresh look at the role of theories in both theology and the sciences: theories matter insofar as they provide adequate solutions to specific problems. If problems constitute the questions of science, it is therefore theories which constitute the answers. Theology, I think, has notoriously neglected this issue and has rarely questioned the intellectual and experiential adequacy of opinions, theories, and doctrines as answers to specific experiential or intellectual problems. Our responsible, rational judgments are closely linked to theory choice, while the function of theories is primarily to resolve ambiguities. I therefore agree with Laudan's persuasive thesis on the close link between progress and rationality, which also dovetails neatly with Rescher's and Brown's notions of weak objectivity and estimated truths. In appraising the merits of theories as answers to specific problems, it is more important to ask whether they constitute adequate solutions to significant problems than it is to ask whether they are "true," "corroborated," "well-confirmed," or otherwise justifiable within the framework of contemporary epistemology (cf. Laudan 1977:14ff.).

Laudan therefore correctly sees the counterpoint between chal-

5. Cf. Laudan 1977:7, on attempts to explain and control the natural world, and the seeking of trust, influence, and prestige by scientists.

lenging problems and the responsible judgment and a choice for adequate theories, as the basic dialectic, not only of science, but of all our reasoning strategies.[6] One of the hallmarks of intellectual progress is therefore the transformation of anomalous and unsolved problems into solved ones. For both theology and science this will pose demanding challenges, since our problems are determined and defined by historical and social context, and our criteria for acceptable problem-solving evolve through time. Now, if problems are what challenge us to responsible judgment and progressive theory choices, i.e., to problem-solving, what else could be said about the kinds of problems that evoke the kind of judgment that ultimately defines what rationality is about?

Again Larry Laudan's work is helpful because he distinguishes between two kinds of basic problems that, in one way or the other, play a role in all intellectual endeavors and in our quest for ultimate intelligibility in diverse fields of inquiry: *empirical problems* and *conceptual problems* (cf. Laudan 1977:15-66). Laudan defines empirical problems in the broadest post-positivist way possible: anything about the natural world that strikes us as odd or otherwise in need of explanation constitutes an empirical problem (Laudan 1977:15). He also calls empirical problems first order problems (1977:18). As such they are problems created by those objects of study that fall within the focus or domain of any given science or form of intellectual inquiry. Some empirical problems, recognized as such within specific contexts, can of course — for perfectly rational reasons — at any time cease to be problems, or can be transformed into, or cause even more complex, conceptual problems.

It would certainly be an enormous mistake, as well as clearly reductionist, to imagine that scientific progress and rationality consist only in the solving of empirical problems. Laudan therefore claims a second and special type of problem (i.e., conceptual problems), which has largely been ignored by historians and philosophers of science, and which has been at least as important for the development of science as empirical problem-solving (1977:48). By focusing our attention on the role of conceptual problems in scientific reflection, Laudan not only wants to move beyond any remaining positivist or

6. I am indebted to Andrei Chirine for numerous discussions on these and related issues.

empiricist epistemology in science, but also wants to argue for a richer notion of problem-solving than empiricists have traditionally allowed. At the same time, of course, the notions of conceptual problems and problem-solving invoke a broader notion of rationality that ultimately reveals the shared resources of human rationality in different and often very diverse forms of intellectual inquiry. This broader notion of problem-solving is highly consonant with the postfoundationalist notion of rationality that I have been arguing for above. Again we are put in a position to understand better what happens when different and competing theories or positions are equally supported by the data, and when — with no rules to go by — we have to make responsible judgments, in the light of the best available reasons, in concrete social and historical contexts.

But what are these conceptual problems really? Conceptual problems are created in the course of intellectual reflection and have no independent existence outside of the theories that exhibit them. If empirical problems are first order questions about the entities of some domain, then conceptual problems are higher order questions about the well-foundedness of the conceptual/theoretical structure which has been derived to answer first order questions (cf. Laudan 1977:48). What is most crucial, however, is that the increase — I would add, through judgment and intersubjective deliberation — in the conceptual clarity of a theory is one of the most important ways in which we may want to talk about progress in intellectual inquiry. To achieve some measure of this kind of progress regarding the solving of external conceptual problems — where two theories may be in tension, or where a theory may be in conflict with the methodological commitments of a specific community, or with any component of the prevalent worldview — may be even more harrowing in the human and social sciences, and in theology, than in the domain of the natural sciences. Even so, Laudan correctly argues for taking precisely the nonempirical dimensions of scientific deliberation very seriously: we now know enough about the nonempirical and even metaphysical factors in the evolution of science to say that any theory about the nature of science which does not acknowledge the role of conceptual problems forfeits any claim to being a theory about how science has actually evolved.

The responsible value judgment that should lead to plausible theory choice should now acknowledge the solved problem as the basic unit of scientific and other intellectual progress. The aim of science, in its quest for intelligibility, is to maximize the scope of solved empirical problems while minimizing the scope of anomalous conceptual problems. Laudan puts it as follows: if it counts in favor of a theory that it can generate solved empirical problems, then it should count against a theory if it generates anomalous conceptual problems (cf. 1977:67). Therefore, the soundness of our rational judgments, and thus the problem-solving effectiveness of a theory, depends on the balance it strikes between its solved problems and its unresolved problems. I believe that Larry Laudan thus presents us with a theory of progress that in itself qualifies as a postfoundationalist problem-solver. What we have here is not a modernist metanarrative, nor a set of fixed rules for rational progress, but rather a kind of progress that can occur only practically and contextually, and only if the succession of theories in any specific domain — as seen in retrospect — shows an increasing degree of problem-solving effectiveness. Again we see that good responsible judgments and progressive theory choices ultimately constitute the true nature of rational reflection. Moreover, both our rational beliefs and our notion of progress are thus rooted in specific locations, and in the context of living, changing, developing traditions: any time we modify a theory or replace it with another theory, that change is progressive if and only if the later version is a more progressive problem-solver than its predecessor (cf. Laudan 1977:68).

With this broader postfoundationalist view of rationality, and the shared resources and epistemological overlaps that are now possible and identifiable between often very diverse forms of intellectual inquiry, we can finally claim a remarkable consonance between the shaping of scientific and theological rationality. In spite of important differences between scientific knowledge and other forms of knowledge, we see that the character of rationality in the sciences — especially through the role of interpretative strategies in matters of judgment and theory choice — overlaps much more with the broader features of rationality than is often acknowledged (cf. also Bernstein 1983:47). In both scientific and theological reflection, as distinct but overlapping reasoning strategies, and in spite of often radical differences in focus and methodologies, the conscious judgment to make a choice, to act, or to believe something, not only evokes the cognitive, evaluative, and pragmatic resources of rationality, but is also closely linked to theory choice. Whether in theology or science, we aim for optimal intelligibility, and our theories are therefore always and inevitably involved in the solution of our empirical and conceptual problems.

Rational judgment as an ongoing process of problem-solving now leads us to yet another important issue: What are the *adequacy conditions* (cf. Laudan 1977:70) for determining when a theory provides an acceptable or plausible solution to the problems that confront us? I have argued that, since we have no necessary or final rules to go by, rational judgment, and the back and forth between personal conviction and intersubjective accountability, remains our only key to the evaluation of different theories, and different ways to act or believe. Therefore, those theories that we judge to be both experientially and theoretically adequate within specific domains will be the best theories to commit ourselves to within a given context. To understand this we have to keep in mind what theories are and how they function in a specific context. First, the evaluation of theories is always a comparative matter and as such precisely a truly intersubjective affair (cf. Laudan 1977:71ff.). Crucial in our evaluation and cognitive assessment of a theory will be how it fares with respect to other competing theories. The postfoundationalist notion of intellectual progress, outlined above, now makes it possible for us to ask: Within a specific context and in view of a distinct problem, is this theory better than that one, or is this doctrine the best — experientially and theoretically — among the available options? Reflecting on the adequacy conditions for progressive theory choice and problem-solving leads, secondly, to yet another careful distinction we should make when talking about theories. When reflecting on the role of judgment and problem-solving, we should distinguish between at least two different sorts of propositional networks: theories can refer to very *specific* sets of related doctrines, or to much more *general* sets of doctrines or assumptions. For instance, to speak about the "theory of evolution" is to refer not to a single theory, but to a whole spectrum of individual theories, an entire family of doctrines that are historically and conceptually related. Larry Laudan argues that modes of appraisal and evaluation between these two types of theories are different in important ways (cf. Laudan 1977:71f.), and he shares Kuhn's and Lakatos's conviction that it is these more general, global theories, rather than only the more specific ones, which are the primary tool for understanding and appraising scientific progress. These comprehensive or global frameworks of theories, which Kuhn has called paradigms, and Lakatos research programs, Laudan now calls *research traditions*. Research traditions are complex and comprehensive frameworks, which, when carefully analyzed, reveal a network of conceptual, theoretical, instrumental, and metaphysical commitments.

The resources of rationality that are shared by theology and the sciences as very distinct modes of inquiry have shown themselves thus far most prominently in epistemological overlaps exemplified by a quest for intelligibility, by rational judgment, deliberation, and by the way we come to responsible theory choice and theory commitment. The most important reasons for this are to be found in the nature and character of these research traditions, which as such shape the rationality of our scientific and nonscientific reflections, but which are also shaped, in turn, by our ongoing rational judgments and deliberations. Every intellectual discipline, of course, whether scientific or nonscientific, has a history replete with research traditions. Every research tradition, furthermore, not only consists of several specific theories which partially constitute it, but also exhibits certain metaphysical and methodological commitments which, as an ensemble, gives the research tradition its particular identity and thereby distinguishes it from others. Unlike specific theories, which are often short-lived, research traditions go through a number of different, detailed formulations and generally have a long intellectual history extending through a significant period of time.

A research tradition thus provides a set of guidelines for the development of specific theories, and as such exemplifies a set of ontological and methodological "do's" and "don'ts" (cf. Laudan 1977:80). A research tradition is therefore a set of general assumptions about the entities and processes in a domain of study, and about the appropriate methods to be used for evaluating and constructing theories in that domain. Unlike specific theories, research traditions are therefore not directly testable or justifiable. This does not mean, however, that they are outside the problem-solving process. On the contrary, the whole function of a research tradition is in a sense to provide us with the crucial tools, as Laudan puts it, for solving our empirical and conceptual problems (1977:82). A progressive or successful research tradition is therefore one that leads, through its component theories, to the adequate solution of an increasing range of empirical and conceptual problems. Again, this tells us nothing about the confirmation of truth

171

or falsity in a research tradition, because progress is exemplified in what was earlier revealed as our best estimates within certain concrete contexts. Our rational judgments, and the choices we make for the best reasons available to us, are the problem-solvers which — for the time being — may claim experiential and theoretical adequacy.

What now emerges as a criterion for rational judgment and theory choice is the following: we make what we believe to be a responsible judgment in favor of a theory, a viewpoint, or a research tradition, of which we are convinced — with good reasons — that it has the highest problem-solving ability for a specific problem within a specific context. On this view the rationale for the acceptance or rejection of any theory is fundamentally based on the idea of problem-solving progress within a broader research tradition. And again, this view of the role of rational judgment in all cognition is not only a distinctly pragmatic move, but also enables us to hang on to the process of collective assessment, to intersubjective rational appraisal, and to the idea of progress, in a clearly nonmodernist and postfoundationalist way. And even in the case of a strictly scientific form of theory choice, this broadened notion of postfoundationalist rationality reveals that the shaping influence of seemingly "nonscientific" factors on scientific decision-making is still an entirely rational process. In Laudan's own words:

> Far from viewing the introduction of philosophical, religious and moral issues into science as the triumph of prejudice, superstition and irrationality, this model claims that the presence of such elements may itself be entirely rational; further, that the suppression of such elements may itself be irrational and prejudicial. (Laudan 1977: 132)

Thus, once more, are revealed the shared resources of rationality and the epistemological overlaps between natural scientific and nonnatural scientific forms of intellectual inquiry, or, what Larry Laudan (1977:191) has called the *cognitive parity* between various and diverse fields of inquiry. The typically modernist identification of scientific rationality with experimental control and quantitative precision has stood in the way of a recognition of this cognitive parity of the sciences and other reasoning strategies. The recognition of the role of rational judgment in both scientific and nonscientific reflection, and the applicability of a problem-solving model to nonnatural scientific modes of inquiry, will have implications for their rational or cognitive status. Moving beyond stereotyped contrasts between natural science, the humanities, and theology, means moving beyond simplistic contrasts between rational and nonrational, progressive and nonprogressive, falsifiable and nonfalsifiable, commensurable and incommensurable. Larry Laudan has argued precisely on this point that disciplines as diverse as metaphysics, theology, and literary criticism exhibit all the features we require for making rational appraisals of, and judgments about, the relative merits of competing research traditions within them (cf. 1977:191). Diverse fields of inquiry therefore share the resources of human rationality, exhibit empirical and conceptual problems, and can develop standards of rationality, and therefore criteria for assessing the experiential and theoretical adequacy of solutions to specific problems.

Linking the role of rational judgment to theory choice and progressive problem-solving has made it clear that the adoption of theories or doctrines in nonnatural scientific fields of inquiry does not have to be more arbitrary or subjective than the use of rational judgment in scientific decision-making. Even the intersubjective, and often even interparadigmatic, choice between worldviews like realism and antirealism, capitalism and socialism, pragmatism or naturalism (or in theology between, e.g., postliberal neoconservatism and revisionism) could in fact be made by evaluating the relative problem-solving effectiveness, or relative progressiveness and rationality of competing research traditions. This is, of course, an argument against the idea that the acceptance or rejection of frameworks of thought can never be rationally justified, and is supported by Nicholas Rescher's warning (1992:48) to not confuse improvement in *warrant* (having the best possible reasons) with improvement in *approximation* (moving closer to the truth).

In Conclusion

In this chapter we took a closer look at the nature and character of rationality and discovered that human rationality is as complex, many-sided, and wide-ranging as the domain of intelligence itself. At the heart of the nature of rationality we found our never-ending quest for intelligibility: a quest for optimal understanding that as a survival strategy is a most important part of our evolutionary heritage. In our attempts to cope with our world on different levels, the universal intent of this quest for intelligibility is definitively expressed in our ability to solve problems through an ongoing process of personal judgment and intersubjective accountability. To arrive at a postfoundationalist notion of rationality, however, we had to rediscover the embeddedness of this process of rational reflection in the living context of our evolving, developing traditions. This distinctly pragmatic character of rationality was enhanced by ascertaining that rationality is always domain- and person-relative and thus shaped by the self-awareness of the rational agent, who as a person of flesh and blood has to figure out on many levels what it means to hold on to beliefs with strong convictions. Furthermore, this personal and communal character of rationality also has to be fused with the rational obligation to reach beyond one's own immediate context in interdisciplinary conversation and deliberation. While we always approach our cross-disciplinary conversations with a network of strong beliefs and convictions, a postfoundationalist notion of rationality enables us to at least epistemologically acknowledge these strong personal commitments, identify the shared resources of rationality in our different reasoning strategies, and then reach beyond the boundaries of our own epistemic communities in cross-contextual, cross-disciplinary conversation.

Over against the objectivism of foundationalism and the extreme relativism of most forms of nonfoundationalism, what has been developed in this chapter is a refigured model of rationality that encompasses radical contextuality as well as cross-contextual, interdisciplinary conversation. In splitting the difference between modernity and postmodernity, this postfoundationalist view of rationality aims to capture those features of scientific reflection that theoretically make it a paradigmatic rational enterprise without, however, falling back onto the totalizing foundationalism of the classical view of rationality. A crucial step beyond universalist and generic notions of rationality has been precisely the realization that the rational agent's self-conception and self-awareness is not only intrinsically connected to rationality, but is indeed an indispensable starting point for any account of the values that shape human rationality. But not only rationality and context, and rationality and strong personal convictions, but also rationality and cross-contextual obligations inextricably go together.

Finally, we saw that a postfoundationalist understanding of rationality does not call into question scientific or any other qualified forms of intellectual progress or the growth of our knowledge, but critiques only faulty, modernist doctrines of progressive knowledge that too easily conflate rationality with progress. The refigured, postfoundationalist notion of rationality outlined here clearly manages to move beyond the constraints of modernist notions of rationality, and demonstrates why rationality in the traditional, modernist sense is not enough when it comes to assessing the rationality of reasoning strategies as varied and diverse as theology and the natural sciences. As we have seen, it has been exactly the concept of rationality as it figures in the philosophical discourse of modernity that has been directly challenged by postmodernism. We saw in earlier chapters that postmodernism is not a period of history that comes "after" the modern, but that it is, rather, the radical refiguring of some of modernity's most crucial and profound themes. However, the typically postmodern challenge to rationality (at least in its negative and deconstructive form) also fails to grasp the richness of the resources of human rationality. Our attempt to explore a postfoundationalist space between modernity and postmodernity is therefore in itself a challenge to rethink carefully "high" postmodernism's farewell to reason, the overzealous jettisoning of any drive for rational unification, the easy toleration of incommensurability, and the celebration of rampant pluralism and ambiguity (cf. Schrag 1992:7). By attempting to split the difference between modernity and postmodernity, postfoundationalism proposes a third viable option between the classical overdetermination of theoretical reason and cognitive rationality, on the one hand, and the dissolution of the rational agent in much of deconstructive postmodern thinking, on the other hand.

Perhaps the most important result of our probing into postfoundationalist rationality will be the direct ramifications for the problem of interdisciplinarity, and to how theology ultimately relates to the sciences, as well as to other reasoning strategies. This strong contemporary sense for interdisciplinary reflection has been captured in the growing awareness that rationality is never housed within any one specific genre of discourse or reasoning strategy. That theology and the sciences share the rich resources of rationality has been re-

175

vealed precisely by a postfoundationalist perspective that perceives this rationality as operative between different modes of knowledge, as lying across diverse reasoning strategies, and linking different disciplines. As we saw earlier, Calvin Schrag has named this rich notion of rationality *transversal rationality* (cf. Schrag 1992:147), and Nicholas Rescher wrote eloquently of the *universal intent* of human rationality (cf. Rescher 1992:11). My intent, up to this point, has been to *fuse* as well as to refigure these profoundly important ideas into a postfoundationalist notion of rationality that will give us a window into the complex interdisciplinary problem of meaningfully relating theological reflection to the sciences. In our move beyond modernist foundationalism, we have not discovered a new kind of universal reason, and in our move beyond relativist nonfoundationalism we have not accepted isolated, sectarian, and multiple forms of rationality. Turning now to the problem of interdisciplinarity, we will take up the challenge of explaining exactly what it means to affirm that rationality, seen as inseparable from human self-awareness, as linked to social and historical context, always and again surfaces in diverse yet overlapping modes of knowledge.

But first we now have to turn to what it means that our self-awareness as rational agents lies at the heart of rationality, and what that may mean for the epistemic role of experience in rational reflection. We saw earlier in what sense the back and forth between the epistemic skills of responsible judgment and rhetoric, arising out of and weaving together our experiential understanding, turned out to be at the heart of a postfoundationalist notion of rationality. This idea will now be developed further as we ask whether it would be meaningful to talk about the *experiential adequacy* in reasoning strategies as different as theology and the sciences. If, on a postfoundationalist view, both theology and the sciences are empowered to each identify the rational integrity of their disciplines by offering their own resources and standards of critique, articulation, and justification, what will move us beyond the relativism of nonfoundationalism to clear a space for interdisciplinary reflection? The answer to this question will be found as we probe the experiential and contextual nature of rationality: if the experiential bases that shape our rational judgments are highlighted, then the pattern of our ongoing, contextualized experience is going to be altogether decisive for the way we cope rationally with our worlds. And precisely because rationality requires that we attune our beliefs

176

and judgments to our own self-awareness, rationality will also require that we attune our beliefs, convictions, and evaluations to the overall patterns of our experience. In a postfoundationalist notion of rationality, the narrative quality of one's own experience, therefore, is always going to be rationally compelling. And if this is taken seriously, the postfoundationalist notion of rationality itself could never be some sort of superimposed metanarrative, but will itself develop as an emerging pattern that unifies our experience without in any way totalizing it.

Chapter Four

Rationality and Experience

*"Knowledge is situated: shaped, limited, and specified by the lo-
cations of knowers, by their particular experiences, by what
works for them and what society permits to work for them, by
what matters to them and to other knowers with more (or less)
power, by what they trust and value and whether their objects of
trust and value carry any weight in their surroundings."*

Mary M. Solberg, *Compelling Knowledge:*
A Feminist Proposal for an Epistemology of the Cross
(Albany: State University of New York Press, 1997:9)

I n our quest for the values that shape the rationality of theological
and scientific reflection, a positive and constructive appropriation
of the postmodern critique of foundationalist assumptions in religious
and scientific epistemology has offered us two important insights.
First, when postmodernism is seen constructively as an ongoing and
relentless critical return to the questions raised by modernity, and not
only in radical opposition to modern thought, a postfoundationalist
notion of rationality emerges that creates a safe space for the multifac-
eted and interdisciplinary dimensions of our experience of knowing.
Second, based on the imperative always to return to our personal convictions and assumptions with critical and responsible judgment, it
would be highly implausible and certainly premature to claim that all
arguments about epistemology belong to the "preliminaries," which

179

as such — along with modernity — are now *passé* and thus, when jettisoned, will free us to finally "do" theology and science. It might look easier to go even further down this risky road and be convinced that those of us in the theology-and-science business should not restrict ourselves to conceptual analysis and thus remain in a limbo of philosophical and theological preliminaries: trying to "do" theology and science by directly engaging in specific content issues, where these two disciplines directly challenge one another, currently seems to be emerging as one of the major solutions for relating theological reflection to the sciences. However, we have seen that not only are the established categories by which we normally try to describe the way theology relates to science too broad to capture the many levels and nuances on which theological reflection relates to scientific inquiry, but also that the boundaries between these two modes of inquiry keep shifting because of the ever-changing and evolving models of rationality in our time. Especially the postmodern challenge to theology and the sciences has finally shattered easy attempts to establish generic categories for relating theological reflection to scientific reflection. The task of reflecting on the epistemic and nonepistemic values that shape the rationality of these two reasoning strategies is therefore never finished.

In the previous chapter we followed closely the emerging pattern of a postfoundationalist model of rationality. This has now given us important pointers to try to make intelligible the way in which theology might be located within the broader context of interdisciplinary reflection. My attempt to argue for such an epistemic location — where theology would emerge with both intellectual integrity and a public voice in interdisciplinary conversation — has already revealed remarkable overlaps between the respective quests for intelligible problem-solving in theology and science as often very diverse reasoning strategies. It has indeed become obvious that in their very different domains theologians and scientists share the cognitive, evaluative, and pragmatic resources of rationality and the need for the crucial epistemic skill of responsible judgment, as well as the goal of understanding the many dimensions of our world better through an ongoing process of progressive problem-solving. Locating theology within the context of interdisciplinary reflection will become increasingly possible because the focus here has been on relating the rationality of science to the rationality of *theological reflection,* and not just generically to "religion." Obviously the theology and science discussion is possible only because all religions, and certainly the Christian religion, presuppose views of the universe, of the nature of reality, of some form of "ultimate reality," of human beings, and of the nature of morality. Stanton Jones has rightly called this the *cognitive dimension* of religion, and as such it is indeed the dimension of religion most interesting for and relevant to the sciences (cf. Jones 1994:187). Obviously this does not mean that religion is only, or even primarily, a cognitive phenomenon, but this dimension of religion presents itself to us forcibly in theological reflection and as such remains the aspect of religion most relevant for an interdisciplinary conversation with other reasoning strategies.

The fact that the rich resources of human rationality are shared by and significantly overlap in scientific and theological rationality, as identified in the quest for optimal understanding, responsible judgment, and progressive problem-solving, has also revealed a significant breakdown of the traditional modernist demarcation between scientific and nonscientific rationality. Scientific knowing thus turns out to differ from other forms of human knowing, and therefore from theological knowing, only in degree and emphasis. In this sense one could say that theology and the various sciences all grapple with what we perceive as real aspects of our *experience*. Precisely for this reason, the ongoing discussion in contemporary philosophy of science has proved to be an all-important guide for all our reasoning strategies, and is turning out to be crucially important for making intelligible what the epistemological connection between theological and scientific reflection may be. This discussion, as became clear, not only opened up broader notions of rationality and an awareness of the various values that shape different forms of human knowing, but especially highlighted the crucial importance of experiential and pragmatic factors in a context where responsible, rational judgment is now demanded, but where we find ourselves without the rules of the classical model of rationality. Rationality thus emerged as a deeply social practice, always embedded in the narratives of our daily lives and contextualized by the radical interpretative nature of all our experiences. In this rich location of self-awareness and consciousness, rationality is then recognized as not only a socially embedded practice, but a practice that indeed involves the telling of our stories, laden with interpretation, but also containing all-important resources and strategies for critique. Not only the personal narratives of the way we experience ourselves and our worlds, however, but also the patterns, trends, narratives, and paradigms of our various disciplines thus emerge as deeply embedded in narrativity, interpretation, and critique (cf. Schrag 1989:87).

This interwovenness of responsible critique and narrativity within the texture of rationality will later be crucial when we pursue the richness of rationality's embeddedness with tradition. At this point it helps us to articulate certain failures within both modernity and postmodernity. Calvin Schrag puts it well: whereas modernity tended to gloss the role of narrativity in its preoccupation with subject-oriented critique, postmodernity tends to lose sight of the inescapable moment of evaluative criticism precisely through its enchantment with narrativity (cf. 1989:89). So, in refiguring this complementarity of critical judgment and the contextual nature of narrativity, we also get a new perspective on what it means to split the difference between modernity and postmodernity. The call to return to locality and context in a constructive form of postmodernity thus receives a rich texture. The narratives that bind our diverse communicative practices, also in theological and scientific reflection, are indeed at once performances of discernment, articulation, and critical judgment: through our story telling we articulate the sense of lived-through historical experience as we attempt to achieve both a self-understanding and an optimum understanding of our social and natural worlds.

In possibly the most crucial step beyond universalist and generic notions of rationality, and toward developing an adequate postfoundationalist model of rationality, we have also discovered the following: as rational agents situated in the rich, narrativical texture of our social practices, our self-awareness and our self-conceptions are not only intrinsically related to rationality, but are indeed indispensable starting points for any account of the values that shape human rationality. But if rationality and personal convictions go together and self-awareness thus lies at the heart of human rationality, what does that mean for *the epistemic role of experience* in rational reflection? If the experiential bases of our rational decisions and actions are highlighted, then the patterns of our ongoing experience are going to emerge as decisive for the way we rationally cope with our world. And precisely because rationality is so person-relative and thus requires that we attune our beliefs, decisions, and actions to our own self-awareness, rationality will also require that we attune our beliefs, decisions, and actions to the overall pattern of our experience. It is in this sense, then, that a postfoundationalist notion of rationality will highlight the fact that one's own experience is always going to be rationally compelling.

This postfoundationalist model of rationality, however, not only focuses on the experience of knowing, and thus on the experiential dimension of rationality itself, but — for both theology and the sciences — very specifically implies an *accountability to human experience* (cf. Jones 1994). Despite many important differences between these two reasoning strategies, I see this epistemic goal of experiential accountability playing out as only a gradual difference between *empirical adequacy* for science, and *experiential adequacy* for theological understanding, respectively. This will closely relate, as will soon become clear, to the differences between theology's and science's epistemological foci and experiential scope. We have already seen that the failure of foundationalism also was the failure of all forms of objectivist justification as handed down by the classic model of rationality. But both the extremes of an objectivist foundationalism and a relativist or subjectivist nonfoundationalism reflected the inability of our intellectual culture to unite personal experience and personal conviction with some form of rational justification.[1] I have, however, argued for retrieval of the experiential dimension of personal, responsible judgment as a truly postfoundationalist move to unite personal conviction with plausible, rational evaluation or justification through interpersonal expertise. This fallibilist alternative to the opposites of foundationalist and nonfoundationalist models of rationality, because of the shared resources of rationality between our various modes of human knowing, now again appears as a viable option for both theological and scientific reflection. And through the crucial epistemic role of judgment in the interpretation of our experience, the difficult question whether our personal convictions, opinions, and beliefs can be transformed to "genuine" knowledge may finally be answered positively.

1. Cf. Michael G. Harvey, *Personal Conviction and Rational Justification,* unpublished paper for a Ph.D. seminar on "Theology and Rationality" at Princeton Theological Seminary, April 1994.

Rationality and Interpreted Experience

Experiential accountability in theology and the sciences will reveal another important epistemological overlap between theological and scientific modes of inquiry: we relate to our world epistemically only through the mediation of interpreted experience, and in this sense it may be said that theology and the sciences offer alternative interpretations of our experience (cf. Rolston 1987:1-8). Alternative, however, not in the sense of competing or conflicting interpretations of experience, but of complementary interpretations of the manifold dimensions of our experience. Only in this sense could it be said that the epistemic communities of theology and the sciences make cognitive claims about the "same" world. And if these reasoning strategies reflect interpretations of our different experiences of the world — even if they are about different domains of the same world — we could never remain content with a nonfoundationalist pluralism of unrelated interpretations. The fact that we relate to our world epistemically only through the mediation of interpreted experience, now opens up a postfoundationalist (and nontotalizing) reading of Ian Barbour's statement: "If we seek a coherent interpretation of all experience, we cannot avoid the search for a unified worldview" (Barbour 1990:16). The location of theology in an interdisciplinary context will be one huge step toward achieving this coherent interpretation of our experience, and will finally be made possible by uncovering and retrieving the rich experiential resources of rationality as shared by our different and often diverse modes of human knowing.

I have argued before that all religious (and certainly all theological) language always reflects the structure of our interpreted experience (cf. van Huyssteen 1997a:40ff.). In science too our concepts and theories can be seen as products of an interaction in which nature and ourselves play a formative role. The personal dimension of this relational knowledge does not at all take away from its validity and objectivity, which is achieved through the back-and-forth between personal conviction and interpersonal expertise. Our search for knowledge always takes place within the social context of a community. Individuals who share a certain expertise make up this community, and help, challenge, critique, and confirm one another. Therefore, to talk abstractly about the intelligibility of nature, about the regularities of nature and the laws that express them, indeed remains incomplete until we can answer the more basic question: *Intelligible for whom?* This frees us to realize that the sciences and theology — like all our intellectual endeavors — are *our* sciences, and *our* theology. Thus the fact that human rationality is always person- and domain-relative obviously implies that nothing in our world can ever be described, explained, or presupposed in any absolute way, but is always known through investigator-relative results that will differ with the different modes of interactions between our world and us (cf. Rescher 1992:111).

Now, if in the sciences our concepts, theories, and models can be seen as products of an interaction between our world and ourselves, then clearly scientific knowledge too reflects the structure of our interpreted experience. Post-Kuhnian philosophy of science has explicitly taught us that when scientists observe, they do so selectively, and these selections are always determined by both theoretical and practical interests. Precisely for this reason scientific observation and theory testing are complicated activities, employing complex apparatus and relying on a host of auxiliary theories, prior determinations, and assumptions of other facts. There is, therefore, no such thing as the "direct" comparison of a scientific theory with observed facts. Closely following Thomas Kuhn, Joseph Rouse can therefore correctly state that we must always first describe what we observe, so that we can compare one statement with another, but we cannot describe what we observe without making use of the theoretical assumptions built into our concepts (cf. Rouse 1987:4). In exactly this sense scientific knowledge of our world is always epistemically mediated through interpreted experience: empirical scientific observation is theoretically selected and interpreted and functions only within the network of presupposed theories that constitute a specific reasoning strategy.

In our earlier discussion of Joseph Rouse's work we saw how much this "post-empiricist" shift in philosophy of science would not only affect our general notions of human rationality, but would actually affect directly the contextualized and local way that scientists now do their scientific work. Instead of comparing their theoretical representations with the observed, "uninterpreted" world, scientists now compare their theoretical representations with other theoretical representations. In a modernist world the objective natural sciences were carefully demarcated from those disciplines that study human beings, their artifacts, and their institutions, i.e., the human and social sciences. In a world challenged by postmodernism, stereotypical distinctions between the natural and human sciences fall away, especially when hermeneutics surfaces in the heart of the sciences and we discover that even the natural sciences study nature only as theoretically interpreted. Thus we could discover that, because of the shared resources of rationality, we use the same kinds of interpretative and evaluative procedures to understand nature, humans, and the social, historical, and religious aspects of our lives. The world as we encounter it is therefore already interpreted, and our theories play an important role in our received interpretations (cf. Rouse 1987:9). Because of this, as we saw earlier, the sciences cannot claim anymore linear "progress" as a story of accumulating, ever-increasing knowledge. However, some, like Larry Laudan (as we saw earlier), have convincingly argued that the sciences have exhibited a more refined and refigured notion of empirical and conceptual progress across their theoretical revolutions, even if the interpretations of what that progress consists of have changed.

Regardless of the extent to which the specific "reality" we focus on in theology and the sciences may be "mind-independent" or not (as in the realism/antirealism debate), our knowledge of this reality represents information only yielded in an interpretation of our experience. What is relevant for us therefore depends on how we go about experiencing our world, and how we interact with what we see as reality. For theology and the sciences the depth of the epistemological overlaps they share emerges only on this level. Furthermore, on a postfoundationalist view of rationality, epistemological fallibilism and rational accountability become viable options only when we realize that our only access to reality is via the construction of theories, models, or world-pictures, in which our intellectual resources have a crucially conditioning and shaping function, precisely because of their embeddedness in interpreted experience.

If we relate to our world epistemically through the mediation of interpreted experience, our attempt to locate theology in the ongoing and evolving interdisciplinary discussion now acquires new depth and meaning. It also brings us a few steps closer to answering Wayne Proudfoot's challenge to again reconstitute theology as genuine inquiry (cf. Proudfoot 1991:113). We may now identify not only important epistemological overlaps like our shared quest for intelligibility, the shaping role of personal judgment, the process of progressive problem-solving, and experiential accountability, but may also find the locus of important differences between reasoning strategies. These differences are revealed in the *epistemological focus,* the *experiential resources,* and the *heuristic structures* of different disciplines (cf. also Stoeger 1988:232ff.). What this means for theology and the sciences is that the differences between them are far more complex and refined than just differences in objects of study, language, or methodology: the differences revealed in interdisciplinary discussion are often radical differences in epistemological focus and experiential resources. William Stoeger has also argued for a necessary discussion of foci, experiential grounds, and interpretative scope, because it is here that the differences between reasoning strategies as ways of knowing are found. But what is meant by the focus and the experiential resources of a discipline? For Stoeger the focus of a discipline indicates the primary aspect of experienced reality to which a discipline gives attention and as such provides its primary point of reference (cf. 1988:233). The experiential resources of a discipline are the types of data, of phenomena, or of experience to which the discipline appeals, which it analyzes, and on which it reflects, in arriving at and justifying its conclusions, and in testing and modifying its models (cf. 1988:234).

It now becomes even clearer why mere differences in objects or aspects of reality will never be enough to specify important differences between disciplines: the object or aspect of reality which a discipline considers may often even overlap with other disciplines,[2] but the experiential resources to which each appeals in reflecting on that object of study will be quite different. Although in both the sciences and theology we relate epistemically to specific aspects of our world through the mediation of interpreted experience, and in both instances we should remain committed to some form of experiential accountability, the experiential resources and heuristic structures of the two modes of knowing will be significantly different from one another. This difference in foci, experiential resources, and heuristic structures obviously gives rise to the different languages, contexts, and methodologies of diverse reasoning strategies, and as such makes meaningful interdisciplinary communication and understanding very difficult. But this difficult and demanding process of entering the interdisciplinary context by attempting to survive with strong personal convictions in a com-

2. Cf. cosmology's focus on the origin of the universe and Christian theology's focus on the doctrine of creation.

plex, pluralist situation is just what a postfoundationalist model of rationality hopes to facilitate. Those of us who utilize diverse methodologies and techniques, who have very different foci while appealing to very different experiential resources and heuristic structures, are attempting in interdisciplinary discussion to understand and appreciate one another's viewpoints and commitments. As members of specific epistemic communities who would like to plausibly claim some form of expertise in our various fields of inquiry, we hope to discover in disciplines other than our own — and often in the hazy interfaces between disciplines — clues, indications, or some forms of persuasive evidence that will help us push forward the limits of our own disciplines (cf. Stoeger 1988:232). For theology to take part in this process of critical synthesis and creative communication, it first has to be taken seriously as a discipline with its own focus, experiential resources, and heuristic structures.

How do important differences and similarities between theology and the other sciences become more intelligible by focusing on their respective foci, experiential resources, and heuristic structures? In the natural sciences, broadly speaking, the focus is on detailed, reproducible behavior, on patterns of structure and behavior of physical, chemical, and biological systems, as given by systematic and controlled observation and experiment, and by precise measurement. Taking the next step, i.e., examining the limitations, horizons, and presuppositions of the natural sciences, already implies a move into the realm of philosophical reflection (cf. Stoeger 1988:236ff.). The focus of philosophy is essentially on the knower, on the experience of knowing, evaluating, and acting, and on the structure of what is known. In the broadest sense of the word this experiential scope of philosophical reflection touches on the limits of our experience, and at this point philosophy begins to open itself to the possibility of the focus and experiential scope of theological reflection. In both theology and the sciences we therefore indeed relate to our world epistemically through the mediation of interpreted experience, but for the Christian believer this interpreted experience will now often include *religious* experience, where the experiences of genuine love, faith, or permanent commitment may be deeply revelatory of what is believed to be beyond these experiences.

However different the foci, experiential resources, and heuristic structures of theology and the other sciences may be, a postfoundationalist model of rationality has already revealed remarkable epistemological overlaps between them because of the shared nature and resources of human rationality. In spite of important differences in foci and experiential resources, we now are on our way to recognizing some remarkable parallels in the interpretative strategies used in both theology and science. Ian Barbour has already revealed some powerful comparisons between the structures of scientific and religious/theological thought, and points to data and theory as possibly the two most basic components of scientific reflection (cf. Barbour 1990:31f.). Barbour is joined here by Nancey Murphy, who has very persuasively argued that data and theory play an equally important and crucial role in theological reflection (cf. Murphy 1990:130-73). The data of theological reflection that emerge here are judgments that result from communal discernment, religious experience, tradition, and Holy Scripture as the classical text of the Christian tradition (cf. also van Huyssteen 1997a:124ff.). The experiential resources of religious reflection especially point to religious experience, story, and ritual, and to the fact that religious beliefs and the commitments they constitute have explanatory functions similar to those of scientific theories.

The postfoundationalist acknowledgment that we relate to our world epistemically only through the mediation of interpreted experience at this point clearly surfaces in remarkable parallels between, on the one hand, the epistemic structure of science as revealed in the theory-ladenness of data and the fact that all scientific theories are therefore underdetermined by facts, and, on the other hand, our recognition that religious cognition is an equally unmistakable form of interpreted experience (cf. Rottschaeffer 1985:265-82). Just as all scientific observations are always theory-laden, so too are all religious experiences always interpretation-laden. For theology, as a reflection on interpreted religious experience and thus on the epistemic structure of religious cognition, this is the definitive move beyond foundationalism: if our beliefs are the results of our interpreted experiences, then the content of this belief (cf., for instance, the notion of divine revelation) can never be merely given — immediately or directly — in the experience itself. The possibility that religious cognition could in any way be directly experiential is therefore ruled out, not because in some reductionist way divine action is ruled out in principle, but because any claim to such direct experience presupposes an immediate givenness which, through the epistemic failure of foundationalism, has been shown to be totally absent.

The interpretation-laden character of religious experiences therefore leads to the conclusion that the structure of religious cognition is indeed shaped by interpreted experience (cf. Barbour 1974:122-26). In this sense one could also say that the models and metaphors of the basic religious language of a specific religious tradition are always used to construct creatively (but in continuity with the scope of the tradition) the conceptual web in which our religious beliefs are embedded. These religious beliefs in turn correlate with and point to certain experiences and, in a sense, explain them. And as in the scientific model, the religious model is drawn from the familiar realm of our experiences of our world, and by the way these experiences are held together by the narratives of our lives. In this sense it could be claimed that what gives *empirical* meaning to scientific theory are the scientific models and observations by which we interpreted data, and what gives *experiential* meaning to our religious beliefs are the religious models and the way they help to interpret experience (cf. Rottschaeffer 1985:271). It is thus the interpretation that provides the (valid) religious meaning. Religious cognition, as the basis of theological reflection, therefore indeed has the structure of interpreted experience. And just as theory-laden observations can still be used to test theories in science, so too interpretation-laden religious experiences may be plausibly used to support our religious beliefs.

For scientific modes of reflection the theory-ladenness of data not only means that theories always influence our observations in many ways, but that due to the focus and specific experiential/empirical resources of a discipline, even the object observed may be altered by the process of observation itself. This is particularly problematic in the microworld of quantum physics and the complex world of ecosystems, where we are never detached observers separate from observed objects, but participant observers who are part of an interactive system (cf. Barbour 1990:33f.). That we relate to our world epistemically through the mediation of interpreted experience thus reveals remarkable overlaps between theology and the sciences. In contemporary physics, for example, the role of the observer as participant becomes essential when we realize that quantum phenomena are given, never in themselves, but only in terms of a measurement made by an observer. What is thus given is never an object in itself, but an object in relationship, in interaction with the observer (cf. Stoeger 1988:237). Because we relate to our world epistemically only through the mediation of interpreted experience, the observer or the knower is always in a relationship to what is known, and thus always limited in perspective, in focus, and in experiential scope.

In this sense beliefs are both brought *to* experience as well as derived *from* it, and our interpreted experience thus becomes the matrix within which meaning and knowledge arise (cf. Gill 1981:19). Our world is thus experienced in direct relation to our active engagement with it, in terms of what phenomenologists have called "intentionality" (cf. Merleau-Ponty 1962:xviiff.). The religious dimension of our experience, however, comprehensively transcends other experiential dimensions by providing what Jerry Gill has called the "hinge" by means of which they are integrated, and through an ultimate commitment are endowed with deeper meaning (cf. Gill 1981:69). Because of this mediated structure of the religious dimension of our experience, other experiences provide the context for our religious awareness. All our knowledge therefore takes place in and is constituted by a relationship: every knower, from the theoretic scientist interacting with abstract symbols to the skillful athlete judging the angle and speed of a ball, acquires and employs his or her knowledge in relational participation with that which is known (cf. Gill 1981:91). Religious experience can therefore be thought of as arising out of and yet transcending the physical, social, moral, and aesthetic dimensions of reality. What is revealed here is the continuity between human awareness in general and religious awareness in particular, and thus also an experiential basis for the postfoundational epistemological overlaps already identified between theological and scientific modes of knowing. Religious experience thus depends on complex sets of beliefs, and although an insistence on the immediacy of religious experience may often be descriptively accurate, such a description will, because of the interpreted nature of religious cognition — by itself — always be theoretically inadequate (cf. Proudfoot 1985:3ff.).

Part of the problem of the shaping of rationality in theological reflection is precisely the fact that religious experience may often seem to be immediate and noninferential, while in reality it never is independent of concepts, beliefs, and practices. And if we always relate to our world epistemically through the mediation of interpreted experience, then our experience will always be theory-laden and tradition-specific. With this, the profound and comprehensive ramifications of a religious commitment become clear: the criteria for identifying a specific form of religious consciousness as such will always include not only a reference to a whole framework or network of concepts, but also to a specific belief about how the experience is to be explained (cf. Proudfoot 1985:14). This, however, will have important implications for any postfoundationalist critique of theological assumptions: precisely because all religious experience is intentional or transactional, it is always already interpreted in terms of the preexisting patterns of the belief systems to which we are committed. This then is the necessary tension we must hang on to: language gives us access to experience, while experience in turn predetermines linguistic expression. This is also the reason why the impact of a religious experience can best be accounted for by the fact that the criteria for identifying an experience as religious are always going to include reference to a very specific explanatory claim (cf. Proudfoot 1985:216). Thus, once more, is revealed why religious beliefs and faith commitments always already include in themselves important values and value judgments that shape the rationality of theological reflection.

From this, some crucially important conclusions have to be drawn. Religious beliefs and practices are interpretations of our experiences which in turn become objects of interpretation. As interpretations of our experiences, then, religious beliefs also assume explanatory roles (cf. Proudfoot 1985:41), which shows why even in theology, hermeneutics and epistemology will always go together very closely. To say, therefore, that there is no such thing as an uninterpreted experience is to say that all observation is theory-laden: this assumes a concept of interpretation that reaches deep into the pragmatic, cognitive, and evaluative dimensions of a postfoundationalist epistemology. Proudfoot says it well: our tacit theories and hypotheses have already played a constructive role in the perceptual judgments that make up our experience (1985:61). To say that experience is always interpreted is to say that all our experience presupposes particular concepts, beliefs, hypotheses, i.e., judgment skills about ourselves and the way we relate to our world through theological and scientific reflection. This, too, reveals the fiduciary rootedness of human rationality.

The distinguishing mark of religious experience in this sense would therefore be the individual's judgment that the experience, and the beliefs that constitute the experience, can only be accounted for in

192

religious terms. Why a person identifies an experience as "religious" could of course also be explained in many other ways, i.e., historically, psychologically, culturally, or epistemologically. But what is to be explained here is *why* we understand what happens to us in *religious* terms, and this requires the evaluation of the commitments and the tacit value judgments we bring to our experiences, as well as contextual conditions, and the network of concepts, theories, and beliefs that may support the plausibility of our judgments to identify our experiences in religious terms in the first place. It is our judgments about the causes of our respective experiences that account for the difference between one of us having a religious experience and the other not (cf. Proudfoot 1985: 231). In this sense an explanatory commitment is always embedded in the criteria we use to judge or identify an experience as religious. An interest in explanations and the value judgments we bring to them are therefore not alien epistemological elements illegitimately introduced into the hermeneutical study of religious experience: those of us who identify our experiences in religious terms are in fact seeking the best available explanations for what is happening to us.

Thus, once more, the rationality of the quest for intelligibility in theological reflection is revealed, and along with that the fact that through the crucial epistemic skill of responsible critical judgment, theological reflection too may claim that theory choice occurs through an ongoing process of progressive problem-solving. Locating theological reflection within the context of interdisciplinary reflection will be possible because theology and the sciences, in spite of important differences in focus, experiential resources, and interpretative scope (and the localized standards of rationality this will imply), do indeed share in the nature of human rationality and the richness of its resources. This explains why modes of critical thought that are at home in contemporary science, contemporary culture, and in common sense, should indeed have a bearing on our assessment of the plausibility or rationality of religious belief. Foundationalist as well as nonfoundationalist attempts to deal with the justification of theory choice in philosophical theology have typically resulted in, on the one hand, inferential procedures that completely lose the experiential basis of religious reflection or, on the other hand, in nonfoundationalist attempts to evade the issue of the justification of religious belief altogether. As we saw earlier, this fideist view that religious beliefs are commitments — which as such cannot and need not be accounted for — has become especially popular in some forms of contemporary postmodern and postliberal theologies.

Some philosophers of religion relate much of the current fideism in philosophy of religion and in philosophical theology directly to Wittgenstein's celebrated notion of language games, which as forms of life cannot and need never be justified (cf. Frankenberry 1987:11f.). Fideism, as a blind, uncritical commitment to a set of beliefs, could of course be at the heart of both foundationalist and nonfoundationalist models of rationality. What happens in the fideistic move, however, is that an ultimate faith commitment in (for instance) the Christian God is first isolated in a very definite protective strategy and then identified with a very specific set of foundational beliefs. As we saw earlier, however, fideism and nonfoundationalism often also collapse into one another when, for instance, religion, morality, theology, or science would claim to have criteria of rationality peculiar only to itself. No less than in foundationalism, any nonfoundationalist account of religious beliefs, practices, or experiences which is restricted to the perspective, world-view, beliefs, and judgments of the individual or the discerning community alone is thus equally revealed as a protective strategy (cf. Proudfoot 1985:197), i.e., as a fideist move where one's own experience and explanation is never contested, and the need for transcommunal or inter-subjective conversation is never taken seriously.

Several dubious and problematical assumptions, however, lie at the heart of all forms of theological and philosophical fideism. In her discussion of the problem of fideism, some of these assumptions were identified by Nancy Frankenberry (1987:11) and read as follows:

- forms of life, when considered as a whole, are not subject to criticism;
- each mode of discourse is in order as it is, for each has its own criteria and sets its own norms of intelligibility, reality, and rationality;
- there is no Archimedean point or common ground in terms of which a philosopher can relevantly criticize whole modes of discourse;
- commitment is prior to understanding, intracontextual criteria take precedence over extracontextual considerations, and confessional functions can substitute and finally supersede cognitive meaning.

194

In a postfoundationalist model of rationality this kind of isolation of religion and modes of religious cognition becomes completely unacceptable. If in both theology and the sciences we relate to our world epistemically through the mediation of interpreted experience, and if different reasoning strategies all share in the same rational resources and thus facilitate significant epistemological overlaps between different modes of cognition, then it becomes impossible to oppose the rationality of religion to that of the sciences in the way that theological fideism requires.

Furthermore, the fideist strategy is simply not capable of consistently evading the issue of truth or falsity of religious discourse once it recognizes that truth claims made by different theologies (and even more so, different religions) often conflict with one another. An uncritical retreat to a fideist commitment (cf. Bartley 1964), or to religious forms of life or narratives, therefore seriously challenges the epistemic status of theological reflection as a credible partner in the contemporary interdisciplinary discussion. On this point Roger Trigg was right to warn that fideism easily slides into conceptual relativism (cf. Trigg 1977:119ff.). Within a fideist context all commitment and religious faith therefore have to be blind or arbitrary (cf. Frankenberry 1987:12). What is more, it is clear that the notion that religious systems have their own autonomous principles and their own unique decision procedures not only denies the interdependence of religious cognition and other forms of human cognition, but also is fundamentally inconsistent with a postfoundationalist holist epistemology, which claims a network of interrelated intersubjective or transcommunal criteria for its statements.

Certainly the most serious limitation of any fideist epistemology, however, is its complete inability to explain why we choose some viewpoints, some language games or networks of belief over others, and why we believe that some in fact offer better and more plausible explanations than others. This not only brings us back to the crucial epistemic role of critical judgment in all human cognition, but also clearly suggests the need for some form of transcommunal or intersubjective criteria in theological reflection. There is obviously more to the matter of using religious language than just understanding and adopting the internal workings of some specialized linguistic system that is not answerable to anything or anybody outside itself (cf. Frankenberry 1987:13). There obviously also is more to the making of commitments than just being embedded in forms of life that can never be questioned. Religious language and theological theories are human conventions, and as such are closely interwoven with the way we relate epistemically to our world through the mediation of interpreted experience. As such they are the results of creative intellectual construction and should be examined and critiqued too along with the commitments they serve to express. If this does not happen, fideist epistemologies will be misused as ideological shelters and protective strategies for immunizing religious beliefs and theological theories from critical examination, refutation, or revision. Nancy Frankenberry goes even further and states that the work of some fideists is dominated by the same conservative attitudes that also characterize some fundamentalist forms of evangelical Christianity. In the end, both groups embed their arguments in assumptions that reinforce dogmatism and serve to insulate from criticism precisely those already established standards, frameworks, or activities that have come to be the most controversial in society (1987:13).

The fact that in contemporary religious epistemology theologians and philosophers of religion — in an attempt to move beyond the dilemma of having to choose between an absolutist foundationalism and a relativist nonfoundationalism or fideism — have increasingly come to depend on concepts like experience, and on what I have called experiential accountability, now shines through the work of various scholars, even those who normally would not call themselves empiricists. In her own work, Frankenberry has already creatively broadened the scope of what can be regarded as religious experience by arguing that sensing, perceiving, willing, doing, wondering, feeling, inferring, judging, and imagining are all modes of what we normally would call experience (cf. Frankenberry 1987:31f.). The work of both Frankenberry and Proudfoot has successfully also shown what kind of protective strategies are invoked when appeals are made to direct or immediate religious experiences. The fact that appeals to immediate religious experiences, and therefore also appeals to self-authenticating notions of divine revelation, have become almost universally suspect does not, however, take away from the serious challenge created by the claim that — as in science — so too in theology we have no access to uninterpreted experiences.

Experiential Accountability and Views of Life

In theology, then, all forms of fideist nonfoundationalism clearly (but ironically) turn out to be a continuation of the modernist dilemma, which so radically opposed a superior, universal scientific rationality to privatized, subjective religious beliefs. Instead of moving beyond this modernist dualism, religion and theological reflection on religious experience are again epistemically isolated, and in a sharp divide between faith and reason, placed outside the scope of possible interaction with scientific rationality. On this view, religious faith is isolated into something that could at most be reported or testified to, but that could never be reasonably justified, and as a result could never be brought into the public domain as part of a cross-contextual, interdisciplinary conversation. In a rejection of any claim to a publicly shared rationality (a loss that most certainly would be fatal for theological reflection), the network of beliefs in which we have and hold our religious experiences are therefore to be treated differently from our other beliefs in the public arena. The result of this kind of polarization is often found in the extreme opposition of scientism and theological fideism to one another. However, as Roger Trigg has convincingly argued:

> It may be tempting to imagine that we can have a sanitized form of reason for the public world while still making rational judgments within the cocoons of our private lives. That kind of schizophrenia is ultimately impossible without judgments being made to the detriment of our private beliefs. (Trigg 1998:20)

Fideistic interpretations of religious experiences (whether in philosophy of religion or in theology) thus turn out to be a complete capitulation to modernist notions of a superior and narrow view of scientific rationality.

But in even more benign views of the differences between religion and the sciences, what is often highlighted is not important epistemological differences in epistemic scope, experiential accountability, and heuristic structures, but views of religion and religious experience that make them seem the product of anything but human rationality. The fideist capitulation to the marginalization of religion and religious reflection in public life is often hidden behind the seemingly innocuous view that science and religion are complementary because they answer different questions: science tells us "how" and religion tells us "why." This distinction is only superficially plausible if it refers to important differences in epistemic focus and experiential resources between religion and the sciences (cf. Trigg 1998:70f.). Most of the time, however, it masks a radical privatization of religious experience where objective facts are assigned to the domain of the sciences, and religion is forcibly pushed out of the public sphere and assigned to the domain of subjective "values."

As we have seen before in our discussion of the problems caused by radical nonfoundationalism, both the sciences and religion — and by implication also theology — become impoverished if we lose the ability to sense that rationality is performatively present in all the different domains of our lives and in various ways links reasoning strategies as different as theology and the sciences to one another. How then can a *postfoundationalist notion of rationality,* and its crucial implications for the epistemic priority of interpreted experience in all our reasoning strategies, now be used to revision a legitimate, public place for religious convictions in interdisciplinary conversation? If theology and the sciences share the rich resources of human rationality, and if science is not just about what is "objective" and religion not just about the "subjective," i.e., the inner life of humans, and our fears, hopes, and aspirations, what will yield the quite specific epistemological overlaps between these very different reasoning strategies? I will argue that this link will only be uncovered if we probe deeper and explore further the rich dimensions of a postfoundationalist notion of rationality. Ultimately the argument that theology and the sciences share in the human quest for intelligibility, share the same interpretative procedures, and require similar epistemic judgment skills for making progressive theory choices, will very much hinge on recovering the different ways we justify our beliefs in various domains. This postfoundationalist move will be made when we carefully find a balance between the way our beliefs are anchored in interpreted experience, and the broader networks of beliefs our rationally compelling personal experiences are already embedded in.

Before we probe further the meaning for this kind of experiential adequacy for a notion of postfoundationalist rationality, it is important to look briefly at the particular nature and function of religious belief and practice, which so obviously provide theological reflection with their own epistemological scope and experiential resources. Like Roger Trigg (1998), Mikael Stenmark (1995) has also argued strongly for the public epistemological status of religious believing. As we saw earlier, Stenmark has plausibly argued that the nature of human rationality is comprehensively present across diverse reasoning strategies, but also in the various domains of our lives. In the previous chapter we followed closely Nicholas Rescher's analysis of the cognitive, evaluative, and pragmatic dimensions of rationality. This already implied that rationality is universal in intent, but also that a narrow view of rationality as a strictly epistemic or cognitive form of scientific rationality not only demeans the richness of natural scientific rationality, but also fails to recognize the crucial contextual, local nature of all domains of rationality. And a strong argument from nonfoundationalist forms of both postmodern science and theology was precisely the impossibility of talking about the rationality of either science or theology without looking at the actual practice that these reasoning strategies are about. Although any reference to postmodern views of science or religious reflection is strangely absent in his work, Stenmark does take up this idea of local practice and claims that we have to know the function and the content of a domain of beliefs before we can evaluate what standards of rationality would be appropriate to its use (cf. 1995:235). In precisely this sense, and because rationality is so person-relative and our own experiences are therefore always rationally compelling, rationality has rich pragmatic and social resources, or as Stenmark would say, it is always also *domain-* or *practice-relative*. What Rouse said about science as *social praxis* is now taken up in a broader context and plausibly revealed in its relevance for all reasoning strategies: the actual practice of anything, whether religion or the sciences, is relevant for settling the appropriate standards of rationality and explanatory interpretation in that domain (1995:236). In this definitive move away from an idealized rational agent and a modernist, generic rationality, Stenmark not only highlights the individual subject as an agent of rationality, but shows that for understanding rationality *the practices of rationality,* the kinds of beliefs that we as rational agents are accepting with good reasons and committing ourselves to, and the activities these commitments lead to, are crucially important.

What this will eventually mean for the rationality of theological reflection is that we do have to take a closer look at the character of religious believing, and also why the rationality of this domain is so essentially a public matter. For Stenmark religious believing not only helps humans deal with existential or ultimate questions, but rather profoundly fits into the broader category of *views of life* (1995:239ff.). These comprehensive systems of belief have more than a theoretical or explanatory function, and go beyond the intellectual dimension of our lives in shaping the way we live our lives on all possible levels. Religious views of life that do not have this active shaping or comprehensive regulative function are in fact dead.[3] For Stenmark the maintenance of a view of life is not in any way optional, and our only choices pertain to whether that view will be a form of secular or religious believing. In the broadest sense a religious view of life thus involves a consciousness of and a view of the sacred as something more real and transcendent than everyday life. Religion thus is characterized by some crucially important aspects; and this is certainly true for the Christian faith too: it fundamentally shapes one's picture of other human beings, it shapes values, regulates action, and expresses some consciousness of and trust in the sacred. Religion is thus constituted by those modes of thinking, speaking, feeling, and acting that express a consciousness of and a trust in what is seen as the sacred or the divine (cf. Stenmark 1995:246). But ultimately religious believing begins and ends with how religious views of life can manage to help us deal with the profoundly existential questions raised by our experience of our worlds.

Within the context of the Christian faith, theology (although Stenmark does not deal with the rationality of theological reflection) is a critical reflection on the rationality of all of the complex issues raised within the wider domain of everyday religious experience. The rationality of theological reflection therefore relates directly to the reasonableness of the choices that people make in living a life of faith in response to such existential questions. The acceptance of religion for a religious believer is ultimately, of course, an existential choice. However, this kind of comprehensive choice for a religious view of life is not at all similar to an irrational fideist retreat to specific sets of doctrines in which we may stubbornly believe. This is so because religious life-view beliefs are essentially answers to existential questions — not

---

3. I am grateful to Deirdre King Hainsworth for her valuable contributions on this particular issue.

just theoretical questions — and this implies, as such, a very specific cognitive choice and a responsible judgment for which we are rationally and experientially accountable. Choosing a religious view of life in this sense is therefore never just a matter of making up one's mind about whether certain beliefs are true, but implies a choice for how we actually should live our lives and be transformed by a comprehensive religious vision.

In theology, as a critical reflection on religious experience, we finally reflect critically on the cognitive content of our religious beliefs, and how they express more comprehensive networks of religious beliefs, often deeply embedded in tradition, that have helped us come to grips with our existential experiences of suffering, death, guilt, and meaninglessness, but also of peace, hope, and reconciliation. In the long history of theology we have developed a reasoning strategy that helps us to *rationally* make sense out of these experiences and the way we interpret them, to understand them optimally, and to choose theories for solving our religious problems in the best possible ways available to us. With this it is not at all denied that theology should always be seen contextually, as directly related to religious practice, and in that sense as developing and critically shaping its own *standards of rationality.* This does never, however, mean that the *nature of theological rationality* is unique and esoteric, or that the way in which we make what we regard as responsible theological judgments is in any way rationally distinct from the interpretative procedures we employ in other reasoning strategies. In the final chapter we will take a closer look at what the obvious theological pluralism, which logically flows from such a person-relative and domain-specific notion of rationality, will mean for interdisciplinary reflection. At this point it is becoming clear why we can maintain the universal intent of the nature of human rationality without again collapsing it into a totalizing, modernist metanarrative, and why we can also acknowledge that reasoning strategies (precisely because of their different experiential resources and heuristic structures) can develop their own rational standards without capitulating to nonfoundationalist relativism and isolationism.

At this point just the mere fact that we all have (religious or secular) views of life, and that theological reflection grows out of *religious* views of life that normally are totally comprehensive, belies the fact that the choice for religious belief, and for good, better, or best ways to choose theories to reflect on this kind of choice and its ramifications for what is believed, need never be seen as subjective or irrational again. The fact that theology and the sciences have different epistemic scopes, different experiential resources, and different heuristic structures does not mean that they also have different rationalities. At most it means that their standards of rationality, and what counts as good reasons in each of these reasoning strategies, will be context- and practice-dependent (cf. Stenmark 1995:272). This obviously means that no notion of scientific rationality can ever again claim to be superior or normative for theological (or any other) rationality: standards of rationality cannot be formulated properly without stating who the rational agent is, and what her or his concrete situation is. And because our experiences differ, it will be normal, natural, and rational to differ even when we argue within broadly the same views of life. But the fact that rationality lies across and links diverse reasoning strategies will also mean that we can step forth into cross-contextual discussion with personal convictions that we find rationally compelling, and at the same time be rationally compelled to open our strong convictions up to critical evaluation in interdisciplinary conversation.

A very sensitive attempt at exactly this kind of public conversation about the profound shaping force of religious experience is found in Jerome A. Stone's *A Minimalist Vision of Transcendence: A Naturalist Philosophy of Religion* (1992).[4] Stone advocates a carefully articulated form of radical empiricism, and the real test for his post-Christian views is exactly whether it can help us to step beyond the modernist dilemma which so radically privatized religion and theology, and open up some form of intersubjectively valid conversation on what it may mean for us to talk about the religious dimension of reality. What Stone wants to do in this book is precisely to clear a space for the renewed interest in the role of religious experience. In doing this he not only wants to reveal the weaknesses of foundationalism and fideism in religious epistemology, but especially wants to show how the problems of faith, theism, and realism look different when approached from a consciously chosen worldview of naturalism.

For the philosophical theologian this kind of focus on the role of religious experience opens up rather difficult but also exciting meth-

---

4. For an earlier and more detailed review article of Stone's views, see J. Wentzel van Huyssteen 1997a:91-102.

odological and epistemological challenges. The question of how our religious beliefs are related to the narrativical nature of our concrete experiences is central also to this form of radical empiricist naturalism. In the end, however, the focus of this challenge will be the crucial epistemological question: How do epistemic values like interpreted experience, personal commitment, and experienced tradition really shape the rationality of religious and theological reflection, and what is it about religious belief that will eventually make a public, interdisciplinary conversation possible? In his focus on religious experience, Stone is intensely aware of the pervasive presence of ambiguity in our daily existence, an ambiguity not only in what happens to us, but also in the way we respond to it. Stone is therefore skeptical of theological and metaphysical answers to the existential problems confronting us in religious experience, and in the end opts for (in Stenmark's terms) a *naturalist view of life* that learns from both the theologians, whom he admires, and the wary naturalists whose critical agnosticism he shares (cf. Gilkey 1992:ix). What is quite remarkable in this book is his accord with those who articulate a presence of transcendence in our everyday experience. This explains at least some of his appreciation for, and limited agreement with, some of the most important theological traditions of our century. But he consistently remains a strict minimalist: any theological or metaphysical explanation for the presence of this transcendence in our daily experience would be forbidden.

Stone calls his view a neonaturalistic philosophy of religion, combining a vision of this-worldly transcendence with an attitude of openness for public inquiry and interaction. Crucial to this view is his minimalist model of the divine, and Stone locates himself between believers and nonbelievers: not as confident as the humanists in their antitheism, but also not able to make the affirmations of most theologians. He also explicitly joins hands with the recent revival of radical empiricism in religious thought as a viable third option to the opposite extremes of foundationalism and nonfoundationalism. When lamenting the lack of the experience of transcendence in our Western culture, Stone eschews all traditional God-talk and focuses instead on the divine aspects of contemporary experience (1992:1ff.). This project is therefore about retrieving experiences of transcendence in secular life and about developing a theory of this-worldly transcendence, a theory that might uncover transcendent resources of renewal and judgment that would be available to us within secular life itself. For his theory of this-worldly transcendence Stone develops a minimalist model of the divine, a tentative conceptualization of what might be affirmed of God, since we cannot make a full ontological affirmation of an ultimate reality anymore. He does this, furthermore, with remarkable epistemological honesty and acknowledges that the ontological reticence underlying his naturalism is a metaphysical position, or *view of life,* that needs whatever justification a metaphysical position can get (1992:7). Stone's faith in naturalism as an adequate explanation for religious experience will eventually have to be challenged precisely at this point.

Jerome Stone's model therefore is a naturalist attempt to assert some notion of religious transcendence without ultimacy. What is affirmed here is that there are real creative processes transcendent in a significant sense to our ordinary experience, and that there are ideals which we may call transcendent. This model therefore is a long way from affirming or attributing an intelligent purposiveness to a transcendent creator, since purposiveness presupposes a unity of individuality, i.e., a personal God capable of entertaining such a purpose in the first place. Stone does say that the three elements of his model, i.e., transcendence, the real, and the ideal, correspond to the three most basic characteristics of religious experience: transcendence, blessing, and challenge (1992:13). His minimalist vision is thus transformed into a philosophical reconception of the object of religious experience. For Stone, situationally transcendent resources — for example, moments of unexpected healing — can only be explained in resolutely naturalistic terms. Within this minimalist context transcendent resources are therefore seen not as signs of the divine, but simply as part of whatever there is of the divine that we can know. Thus moments of extremity and of profound existential despair, as moments of real transcendence, are no bearers of grace but are gracious themselves (1992:15).

Closely aligned with the real aspect of transcendence is its ideal aspect. Defined minimally — and experientially — the latter is a set of continually challenging ideals insofar as they are worthy of pursuit. In an intriguing — and epistemologically controversial — move, Stone takes the pursuit of truth as a paradigm of this ideal aspect of the transcendent (1992:16). The concept of "truth" then continues to function for him as a goal in relation to which our theories are but approximations. As such truth is an ideal never fully attained, but (much as in

Nicholas Rescher's thought) functions as a kind of *focus imaginarius,* as a continual demand that we push toward. For Stone, the divine (or God) is then the collection of situationally transcendent resources and continually challenging ideals of the universe, i.e., the sum of what are worthy and constructively challenging aspects of our experienced world. Stone's model thus carefully articulates a concept of this-worldly transcendence. The question remains, of course, whether this transcendent could in any sense be the same as what we normally see as God. In answering this Stone wants to move beyond a mere "yes" or "no": on the one hand he acknowledges that it is a long way from traditional and even revisioned beliefs about God; on the other hand this transcendent can function in a person's life much like the traditional God. Whether or not one then chooses to call the transcendent by the traditional name "God" is a matter of personal judgment, choice, and context (1992:18). For Stone, however, a minimal requirement would be to stop short of affirming any form of transcendent or ontological unity.

It has now become abundantly clear, I think, that Stone's approach is characterized by pushing toward a pragmatic or functional justification for using minimalist religious language. His naturalism relies on a phenomenology of the transcendent, and the resulting focus is on a pluralistic understanding of the divine. When we now move to a more critical assessment of Stone's proposal, the focus will be on one fairly simple question: How religious is the religious experience that follows this clear and well-argued-for minimalist vision of transcendence? I hope to make it clear that I have no problems with Stone's carefully constructed theory of experience as such. What does, however, seem to be problematical is the way some epistemic decisions and value judgments, because they are essentially shaped by his prior choice for naturalism, are made in advance: decisions that in the end very specifically determine the boundaries between maximalist and minimalist forms of theism. His choice for minimalism thus not so much results from an argument, but in fact exemplifies the earlier and more comprehensive commitment to religious naturalism. The strength of Stone's proposal, however, is precisely that he opens up this choice to public and cross-contextual conversation.

Stone's proposal has, of course, never been that the transcendent *is* God, but that the "transcendent" and "God," minimally understood, are both referents of transcendent resources and challenges. The transcendent may in reality be more than what our experience reveals and this experience may eventually even point to some form of unity, ultimacy, and intelligent purposiveness. There is, however, not enough support for these affirmations for us to make them as publicly responsible assertions, nor to take them as the basis for personal faith. The crucial question now becomes the following: What exactly, for Stone, is the key to the publicness and accessibility of this discussion? I think the key to this cross-contextual conversation, instead of identifying a notion of rationality that is performative in various contexts and across different reasoning strategies, is clearly found in the minimalist notion of transcendence, which provides the religious epistemologist with an accessible, and fairly innocuous, inoffensive, generic notion of the divine.

It is difficult to comprehend, however, how such a minimalist vision of transcendence, as an abstract and general concept of the divine, if not at some point immersed in the language and practice of a living religious tradition, can avoid becoming not only a-contextual (even a-historical), but also too remote and empty — in a word, too universalist. It is precisely at this point that I again raise the question: How *religious* is religious experience within the context of this radical empiricism? For a model of transcendence to be, religiously speaking, experientially adequate, it has to somehow relate to an ultimate commitment of faith, i.e., if it wants to avoid the label of being intellectually esoteric. Of course Stone wants to avoid this, and the key question for him is not whether a person uses language about God, but whether a person is open to transcendent resources and demands. But if Stone wants to avoid ultimacy, what would be the distinctive trait of this religious self-actualization that would go beyond and distinguish it from, say, psychological self-actualization? When the term "God" is adequately understood, so Stone argues (cf. 1992:20f.), it will be found to refer to inner-worldly transcendent resources. It can, however, be convincingly argued that the belief itself in the inadequacy of natural explanations to account for all our experiences may even be more invariant across cultures than the belief in any specific God (cf. also Proudfoot 1985:77). Stone's minimalist vision thus seems to be firmly rooted in a prior commitment to and faith in a worldview of naturalist metaphysics, and not in good reasons or arguments why a minimalist vision of transcendence would be experientially more adequate to the way in which religious people of various stripes live and practice their daily lives of faith.

Closely linked to this issue is the fact that Stone does not really show why maximalist theistic views fail, but only why highly restricted — and already problematical — arguments for maximalist positions on theism fail (cf. 1992:28ff.). He renounces the full ontological affirmation of the transcendent which normally is contained in such religious notions as Brahman or God. He does, however, acknowledge that the major traditions provide a clue to the notion of the transcendent which is useful. The reason for this minimalism is his faith in naturalism, but the position taken on the broader spectrum between minimalism and maximalism remains vague, a line to a certain extent even arbitrarily drawn. Stone's faith in naturalism gives each of the themes of his empiricist philosophy a carefully constructed agnostic boundary, which is, however, never completely crossed precisely because of his accompanying — and intriguing — commitment to realism. Because of his generic minimalist vision of transcendence, however, Stone can also stop short of asking what is the "more," the religious aspect of reality to which his notions are referring.

Stone concedes that no rigorous proof for the adequacy of his or any other model can be given (1992:27). An existential choice for an all-encompassing view of life can certainly never be "proved," but it can indeed be argued for. Helpful arguments for Stone turn out to be arguments on clarity, empirical fit, and especially pragmatic adequacy. I have no problems with clarity and pragmatic adequacy, but how a naturalistic minimalist vision can manage to empirically fit (or be experientially adequate to) the way religious people live their everyday lives — normally in commitment to some extra-human grounds for their faith — remains unclear to me, except, of course, if it is meant all along only for a selected intellectual few. Stone's view of God is a stance of ontological modesty, but he also wants to argue that this view is indeed the most adequate. Stone realizes that his position of ontological restraint is in itself a metaphysical position (cf. 1992:27). It remains highly questionable, however, whether this position can be argued for only on the basis of his radical empiricism. The reasons and the place for pinning down the boundaries of Stone's minimalism thus remain unclear, although Stone is to be applauded for moving beyond epistemological foundationalism in his careful, albeit restricted, focus on the shaping role of interpreted experience.

Jerome Stone's radical empiricism is in fact his attempted

postfoundationalist move beyond the certainty and despair of foundationalism, relativism, and cultural provincialism (cf. 1992:135). It is deeply rooted in the crucial importance he attaches to sensitive discernment, the historical rootedness of all empirical inquiry, and the transactional or interpreted nature of experience. Stone develops a theory of experience (and of religious experience) in which experience is seen as a transaction, a transaction between the individual person or "self" (as a combination of social choices and genetic legacies) and "world" (as both construct and reality). As such, experience is a complex interaction between language and lived feelings, between organism and environment. From this, it can be gleaned that Stone's focus on interpreted experience clearly epistemically shapes the rationality of (also) religious reflection. Here too there are no foundationalist points of "pure" experience that could be used as epistemological anchors or sure foundations to solve our quest for religious certainty. With this Stone moves remarkably close to the current discussions on critical realism in religious and theological reflection: we are indeed never out of touch with our world, i.e., it is not language all the way down (cf. Stone 1992:128). In our religion too we are therefore not adrift on a linguistic sea, but experience is a relational transaction, and interpreted experience reveals that language is a crucial and determining part of this transaction.

However, when Stone finally discusses the historical rootedness of all inquiry (cf. 1992:142ff.), the problems we raised earlier are back to haunt us: Can a minimalist naturalistic view, which eschews theistic explanations for religious experience, indeed provide adequate explanations for what is experienced as the essentially religious in religious experience? Stone is right to argue that a theory of experience has to affirm — both in theory and in practice — that all experience and all inquiry is historically rooted. A generous empiricism like that proposed by Stone will therefore recognize that present experience is, to a large degree, a reconstruction of past experience. Thus experience is a chain or series of interpretations, informed but also restricted in its range by the past. This means — and Stone would agree — that our experiences of the divine are also always rooted in the past (cf. Stone 1992:143). In his move beyond the foundationalist confines of cultural provincialism, Stone moves from theism to minimalism and radical empiricism. But again, what really warrants this move? The only apparent answer seems to be a prior metaphysical commitment to naturalism as a comprehensive view of life. This of course is fine, but if so, what we have here is not just a pragmatic argument for greater experiential adequacy, but an argument dependent on a prior commitment to, or faith in, naturalism. We have also seen, however, that for us to rationally hold on to our beliefs never means that we are also rationally compelled to agree with one another. Precisely the way that interpreted experience, as embedded in our rich and diverse traditions, necessarily leads to religious (and theological) pluralism and a healthy "dissensus management," will be the focus of the next and last chapter.

We saw earlier that postmodern thought challenges those of us who are Christian theologians to account for the fact of Christianity. Jerome Stone's important book challenges us to rediscover the explanatory role of religious experience in postfoundationalist theology, but it also shows how a postfoundationalist notion of experiential rationality makes a conversation between widely divergent contexts possible. I agree with Stone that religious language can never only be seen as just a useful system of symbols that can be action-guiding and meaningful for the believer without having to be referential or reality depicting in any stronger sense of the word. Within Stone's minimalist model, however, the divine functions as a placemaker (cf. 1992:40), and not as the — for him — illegitimate move beyond the available evidence to an ontological ultimate. This transactional realism, as well as the accompanying notion of reference, may be the most intriguing notion of Stone's minimalist vision, but it is also the point where this model is most vulnerable. When in moments of extremity, moments of existential defeat or despair, joy or victory, we reach a profound awareness of our own limits, what will the language and experience of our limitation refer to? For Stone the reference is to generic resources of minimalist transcendence, which is at the same time a (bold?) step outside any particular religion. Stone's initial embracing of pluralism might indeed have allowed for the ultimate and even passionate commitment to truth that many of the historic religions presuppose. But his move to a generic minimalist vision of the divine almost borders on a modernist commitment to a universalist notion of rationality.

As we saw in Chapters One and Two, one of the most distinguishing marks of postmodernity is its preoccupation with (nonfoundationalist) narrative. Narrative in this broader epistemic sense certainly not only implies the composition of stories, but much more involves our actions and discourses, as well as ourselves as engaged participants. We have also discussed the fact that in the postmodern challenge to rationality, the rejection of the role of metanarratives always implies skepticism about any rational resources that may want to unify our diverse discourses and practices. Calvin Schrag has convincingly argued that narratives do not have to have this totalizing role, and can still bind, integrate, assimilate, synthesize, and grasp together the multiplicity of our modes of discourse, the plurality of perspectives, and the diversity of our actions and various disciplines. Narrative thinking thus articulates patterns and lines of continuity in human experience, and transforms stories into cohesive and powerful social instruments (cf. Schrag 1992:92f.). It does not, however, appeal to the kind of timeless essences and atemporal transcendence that modernist metanarratives would appeal to.

From this emerged a clear task for rationality to discern and articulate how our discursive and nondiscursive practices hang together, however loosely, within the texture of everyday life. In this sense rationality can now be seen as the skill that enables us to gather and bind together the patterns of our interpreted experience through the resources of discernment, articulation, and disclosure. This is also what Calvin Schrag, as we saw earlier, has called *praxial critique as a performance of discernment* (Schrag 1992:97). In contrast to metanarratives that claim to bind together the totality of discourse and action into overarching unity, local narratives are more responsive to the diversity of micro-practices in everyday life and the plurality of language games that pervade our discourse. Narrative knowledge certainly also yields the interpretative character of all our knowledge and experience — a point that not only blurs some of the stereotypical distinctions between scientific knowledge and other forms of knowledge, but also between epistemology and hermeneutics. Thus was revealed the interpretative moment in all forms of knowledge. Calvin Schrag thus very convincingly argued that hermeneutics is neither an extension of, nor a supplement to, nor a substitute for the project of the reconstruction of our knowledge in epistemology (cf. 1992:100). It is thus that we find in a postfoundationalist rationality the refigured fusion of hermeneutics and epistemology: interpretation is as much at work in the process of scientific discovery as in other forms of (narrative) knowledge. Interpretation goes all the way down and all the way back, whether one is playing the language game of science, morality, art, or religion (cf. Schrag 1992:101). In all of these domains the choice of a research program or tradition is at once a project and strategy of interpretation.

In science too interpretation is therefore at work in selecting and choosing research programs, a specific vocabulary for a specific science. The scientist, in concert with other investigators, and therefore with theologians too, thus constitutes the parameters of inquiry and his or her data in what Schrag has called a *hermeneutical performance* (1992:101). In this sense one could say that in setting the stage for inquiry, demarcating a domain or field of inquiry, there really is no interesting distinction between the physical and the social and other sciences. All of these reasoning strategies respond to the hermeneutical demand of setting up their disciplinary practices and boundaries. And these practices are always informed by a community of investigators and are contextualized within a history of ideas, emerging within the specific research traditions of that scientific practice. The constitution of a disciplinary matrix — whether in the social sciences, the natural sciences, or theology — is a corporate performance by a community of investigators and interpreters.

The performance of rationality in the diverse domains of our disciplinary reflections was also characterized by Schrag as a moment of *incursive disclosure*. By using this concept, Schrag wanted to articulate a response to the otherness of phenomena in our rational reflection. This moment is tied very closely to that of articulation and can be explained as a postulate of reference, a claim for reality that brings us out of the "closure" of the isolated subject. In Schrag's own words: it is disclosure that keeps articulation from circling back upon itself to a space where there is nothing outside of language, nothing beyond the text (1994:72). Disclosure in this sense is the achievement of reference that ultimately leads us beyond language and textuality. This revisioning of epistemological reference does not fall back onto a modernist truth theory of correspondence, and it does not objectify. Disclosure in this sense brings us face to face with the fact that we relate to our world(s) only through interpreted experience, and that the world as a phenomenon shows itself precisely in the manifold forms of human experience. The performance of reference thus supplies that which our articulatory gestures of discourse and action *are about* (Schrag 1994:73). But what do we mean when we talk about disclosure as *incursive?* The feature of incursivity points to the resistance, the en-

211

counter with otherness, that is implied by referential disclosure, and as such it is an effect of the transversal lines of force that issue from that which is other (cf. Schrag 1994:74).

By using this concept to indicate an important moment in the performance of rationality, Schrag wanted to focus on a very specific sense of uncovering, making manifest, letting something be seen, but in a way that effectively places this disclosure outside the matrix of epistemology, either of a realist or idealist sort, and which at the same time frees it from the aporia of a representational truth (cf. Schrag 1992:111). Most importantly there is no foundationalist given that answers to the question about what it is that our discourse or action refers to, because the reference that is displayed through disclosure is often multiple and pluralist. This notion of disclosure finds important depth in what I have called here the emerging patterns of our narrativical experiences: our narratives reveal the meaning structures of our diverse practices (also our theologies and our sciences), which thus become vehicles of reference. The stories of our lives, of our traditions, our religious faiths, our sciences, and our theologies are therefore *about* something, and it is this moment that Jerome Stone has so adequately captured in his notion of transactional realism. But this moment of disclosure does not lead us down the modernist path back to imposed, generic notions of realism that would prescriptively totalize all our domains of inquiry by expecting all disciplines to be similarly "realist" in some or other generic, epistemological way. It does, however, open up the way, modestly and minimally, to retain the speech of reference, of "otherness" for those domains of reflection that feel it would appropriately express what knowledge in those domains is about.

When earlier we pursued the crucial epistemic role of responsible judgment in the ongoing interpretation of our experience, it became clear that relating to our world only through the medium of interpreted experience also means that theology and the sciences in a sense offer different interpretations of very different aspects of the manifold dimensions of our experience. Regardless of the epistemic extent to which the reality we focus on in theology and science may be "mind-independent" or not, our knowledge of this reality represents information yielded only in an interpretation of our experience. What is epistemically relevant for us therefore depends on how we go about experiencing our world, and how we interact with what we presuppose as real in our experience. On a postfoundationalist view of rationality, furthermore, fallibilism becomes our only viable option when we realize that our only access to whatever our reasoning strategies are *about* is via the construction of theories, models, or world-pictures in which our intellectual resources play a crucially conditioning and shaping role.

On a postfoundationalist view no generic, universal claims for realism (or even critical realism) can be made for the domains of our intellectual inquiry in general. For specifically theology I would still claim a mild form of critical realism as we try to understand the specific nature and standards of rationality of this specific mode of knowing. The form of modest critical realism I am arguing for sees exactly our experience as a transaction or relation between the rational agent and the world. And on this postfoundationalist view, although there are indeed no points of "pure" experience that could be used as epistemological anchors or sure foundations to solve our quests for certainty, we are indeed never out of touch with our world, i.e., it is indeed not language all the way down (cf. Stone 1992:128). Also in theology we are not adrift in a linguistic sea; experience is a relational transaction, and interpreted experience reveals that language is always part of this transaction. What does this tell us, however, about the epistemic reasons why we presuppose some form of reality in religious epistemology? I do believe that in religious epistemology a plausible form of modest realism can be maintained only on experiential and pragmatic grounds, and even then only within the broader, shaping context of the narrative patterns of our traditions. A postfoundationalist notion of rationality that wants to plausibly and adequately leave room for realist presuppositions in religious faith and theological reflection will therefore always see this modest realism as first of all an empirical thesis: its credibility and acceptance as a presupposed worldview can be determined only on experiential and pragmatic grounds, and thus for the good reasons that humans still make responsible judgments in favor of the reality they believe in. This is the reason why believers can pragmatically point to the fact that throughout human history, and in various cultures — including our own — human beings have found it fruitful and liberating to make room for a transcendent interpretation of the ultimate questions about our world and ourselves. The postfoundationalist choice for the relational quality of religious experience thus opens up, as we saw earlier, the possibility of interpreting religiously the way we believe God comes to us through the manifold of our experiences of nature, persons, ideas, emotions, places, things, and events.

This issue of the role and ramifications of realist assumptions in religious knowledge is greatly clarified by carefully looking at the related philosophical question: Why is natural science possible at all? What happens so that the lawful order of nature becomes intelligible to us in the conceptual terms that we have devised? Philosophers like Nicholas Rescher and scientists like Paul Davies have persuasively argued that the problem of the intelligibility of nature is eminently expressed in the question of the cognitive accessibility of nature to mathematizing intelligence (cf. Rescher 1992:99). In fact, the belief that the underlying order of the world can be expressed in mathematical form lies at the very heart of science, and is rarely questioned (Davies 1992:140).

Nicholas Rescher's answer to this crucial question not only reveals a postfoundationalist move to an interactionist model of rationality, which enables him to transcend the rigid realism/nonrealism debate, but also gets him to a position that is very close to Jerome Stone's notion of transactional realism. The answer to the question of the cognitive accessibility of nature to mathematizing intelligence can only be found in a somewhat complex, two-sided story in which both sides, intelligence and nature, must be expected to have a part (Rescher 1992:99). This of course is consonant with the most basic thrust of a qualified or weak form of critical realism: it is precisely the interaction between our thoughts and the world that conditions our sense of order, beauty, regularity, symmetry, and elegance. Evolutionary pressure thus coordinates the mind with its environment. For Nicholas Rescher, as we also saw earlier, this leads to a crucial epistemological insight: the mathematical mechanisms we employ for understanding our world reflect the structure of our (interpreted) experience. In this sense it is no more a miracle that the human mind can understand the world through its intellectual resources than that the human eye can see it through its physiological resources (Rescher 1992:100).

A model of rationality which, in this interactionist way, allows us to acknowledge that we devise our mathematics and science to fit nature through the mediation of experience, reveals unexpected epistemological consonances between scientific and theological modes of reflection. As I have argued before, all religious (and certainly all theological) language reflects the structure of our interpreted experience (cf. also van Huyssteen 1993:253-65). In science our concepts and theories can therefore also be seen as products of an interaction in which both nature and we play a formative role. Talking abstractly about the intelligibility of nature, about the regularities of nature and the laws that express them, indeed remains incomplete until we answer the more basic question: intelligible for whom? This implies that reality can never be described or presupposed in any absolute, generic way, but provides investigator-relative results that will differ with various modes of interactions between our world and us (cf. Rescher 1992:111).

What is at stake in this postfoundationalist model of rationality is therefore not so much the existence or not of the "real world" (mind-independent or not, as in the realism/antirealism debate), but the status of our knowledge about it (cf. van Huyssteen 1998b:38f.). Rescher also convincingly argues, that however "mind-independent" reality may be, our knowledge of this reality represents information gleaned only from an interpretation of experience (1992:119). What is relevant and important for us thus depends on how we go about experiencing our world, and how we interact with what we see as reality. For the theology and science discussion a plausible epistemological consonance emerges only on this level. As we have seen, the resources of rationality are indeed broader than just cognitivity. However, it is only when we realize that our only cognitive access to reality is via interpreted experience, i.e., via the construction of a "world picture," or models in which our own intellectual resources play a crucially conditioning and shaping role, that epistemological fallibilism and rational accountability become viable options.

Obviously the issue of objectivity (in the sense of mind-independence) is pivotal for any form of realism. Rescher argues that realism in this broad sense has two inseparable and indispensable constituents, the one existential and ontological, the other cognitive and epistemic (cf. 1992:256). The former maintains that there is indeed a real world, a realm of mind-independent, physical reality. The latter maintains that we can to some extent secure information about this mind-independent realm. What is crucial about Rescher's position on realism — *vis-à-vis* strong forms of scientific realism (which argue for realism on the basis of the success of science), and also some modernist forms of critical realism (cf. Shults 1995), which attempt to ground reference to reality in a correspondence view of truth — is that the ontological component of this philosophical realism is not a matter of discovery or the result of argument, but rather a functional or pragmatic presupposition for our inquiries (cf. 1992:257). Without this presupposed conception of reality it would be hard to maintain a fallibilist epistemology. The justification of this fundamental presupposition of objectivity is not evidential, and therefore not foundationalist; it is, rather, functional. The validation for this postulate is therefore a *pragmatic* one and lies in its utility, since we need it to operate our conceptual schemes.

This account of the pragmatic basis for a pragmatic form of critical realism thus results in a truly postfoundationalist move: on this view, realism is a position to which we are constrained not by the push of evidence, but by the pull of purpose (cf. Rescher 1992:270). Critical realism in this mode does not represent a discovered fact or justified position, but an acknowledged methodological presupposition for our praxis of inquiry. Within the context of the epistemic aims and purposes of rational inquiry, realism here is a practical postulate justified by its utility, and as such ultimately rests on a pragmatic basis. This finally also enables the following challenging statement: our commitment to a mind-independent reality thus arises not *from* experience, but *for* experience (cf. Rescher 1992:271).

Finally, this pragmatic form of critical realism clearly does not argue from the success of science (or theology) to a mind-independent reality. The very fact of fallibilism and limitedness — our absolute confidence that our provisional knowledge does not do justice to what reality is actually like — is surely one of the best arguments for a realism that pivots on the basic idea that there is more to reality than we can know about (cf. Rescher 1992:274). Traditional scientific realists see the basis for realism in the progress and success of science (cf. Leplin 1984:1-8). The epistemic humility that is implied in a weak, pragmatic form of critical realism, however, finds the basis of this realism in the inevitable provisional character of all our knowledge, whether scientific or theological. Rescher's fairly strong statement is thus justified: there is no realistic alternative for a cognitive fallibilism (1992:275).

This kind of pragmatic form of critical realism in theology will of course bring with it its own challenges (cf. van Huyssteen 1997a:40ff.). The juxtaposition of critical realism and God is especially challenging for anyone concerned with the epistemic values that shape our religious and theological reflections. Critical realism, of course, is neither a theological nor a scientific thesis; it is a philosophical, or even more accurately, an epistemological thesis about the goals of scientific knowledge and the implications of theoretical models in science (cf. McMullin 1985:41). Hence it should not be seen as a theory about truth, but rather as a theory about the values that shape scientific rationality. In theology, a pragmatic form of critical realism should be seen as a response to the question: What sort of philosophical account is possible of the aims and structure of religious/theological reflection and of the epistemic attitudes presupposed by this kind of reflection?

This very specific epistemological focus distinguishes critical realism from the many realisms that dot the history of philosophical thought. What I am proposing here is that, first, the traditional realist assumptions of the Christian faith, as all-important values that shape the rationality of theological reflection, cannot just be sheltered in protective fideist strategies; and second, in theology a pragmatic form of critical realism will in fact have a quite limited claim: it purports to explain why it makes sense not to abandon some of the Christian faith's most basic realist assumptions. As such, a pragmatic form of critical realism will turn out to be at least in part an empirical thesis and never just a metaphysical claim about how the world must be. From this, however, it follows that a choice for critical realism in theological reflection does not necessarily imply a choice for some form of realism in either the social or the natural sciences. Philosophers of science have convincingly argued that there can be no undisputed and monolithic notions of "reality" or of "explanation" in science. As we saw earlier, the objects of our interest not only dictate different strategies, but also different views on what could be regarded as adequate forms of explanation in the different sciences.

I have dealt extensively with the complex nature of critical realism in post-Kuhnian philosophy of science elsewhere (cf. van Huyssteen 1987; 1988; 1989; 1997a). I have also argued against the uncritical, superficial transference of realism in science to the domain of religious belief and to theology as reflection on the claims of this belief. In a pragmatic or weak form of critical realism in theology, the focus is only on the very limited epistemological conviction that what we are provisionally conceptualizing somehow really exists. Talking about "critical realism" and "God" in this sense thus becomes an attempt to find a promising and suggestive hypothesis that can help us deal with some of the traditionally realist and meaning-giving assumptions of the Christian faith within a pluralist, postmodern context. A pragmatic or weak form of critical realism, therefore, does not at all offer a strong defense of theism, but rather attempts to deal pragmatically with the realist assumptions and cognitive claims of religious language and theological reflection.

Against this background it should already be clear why critical realism has developed into one of the most important positions in the current philosophy of science debate. It not only highlights the role of metaphorical reference in scientific theory formation, while at the same time honoring the provisionality and sociohistorical nature of all knowledge, but it also enables us to retain the ideals of truth, objectivity, rationality, and intellectual progress in a radically reconstructed way. Certainly the strength of the critical realist position lies in its insistence that both the objects of science and the objects of religious belief often lie beyond the range of literal description (cf. McMullin 1985:47). In their respective quests for intelligibility, the scientific and theological enterprises share alike the groping and tentative tools of humankind: words, ideas, and images that have been handed down and which we refashion and reinterpret for our context in light of contemporary experience (cf. Peacocke 1984:51). "Realism" in a pragmatic form of critical realism thus enables us to speak of disclosure, and refers to the attempt at reliable cognitive claims about domains of reality that may lie beyond our experience, but to which interpreted experience is our only epistemic access.

Thus is confirmed what we already learned from being in dialogue with Jerome Stone's notion of transactional realism: critical realism, in this particular sense, is an empirical thesis since its credibility and acceptance as a belief system is determined on experiential, pragmatic grounds. Also in theology, therefore, our rational inquiry and our quest for intelligibility will always include a response to what we experience, and experiential adequacy thus becomes one of the most important epistemic values that shape the rationality of theological reflection. The high degree of personal involvement in theological theorizing not only reveals the relational character of our being in the world, but epistemologically again implies the mediated and interpretative character of all religious experience. It also points to the epistemic role of personal religious commitment, which certainly is

218

no irrational retreat to commitment, but, on the contrary, reveals the committed nature of all rational thought, and thus the fiduciary rootedness of all rationality.

We saw earlier that religious experience, and the way we define it, serves as a matrix out of which meaning and knowledge arise as a basis for theological theorizing, and that the theory-ladenness of all data in the sciences therefore parallels the interpreted nature of all religious experience. This also revealed, however, that the under-determination of theories by data is epistemologically as important in theology as in the other sciences. Furthermore, the use of metaphors and models in religious cognition — a use which parallels that in sci-entific cognition — also supports the claim that the structure of reli-gious cognition is that of interpreted experience. Models also provide a way of speaking of the unknown in terms of the known and, as com-prehensive interpretative networks, they open up new dimensions through their suggestiveness and fertility.

In my attempt to focus on experiential adequacy as perhaps the most important epistemic value that shapes theological rationality, theology has come to be defined, in the broadest sense, as a reflection on religious experience. This is consistent with the important post-foundationalist task of retrieving interpreted religious experience as a valid methodological starting point for theological reflection. In terms of a qualified and pragmatic form of critical realism, it now becomes possible to construct an imaginative approach to theological reflec-tion that begins with ordinary human experience and reflection, ex-plores possible "signals of transcendence" to be found in it, and then moves from there to religious affirmations about the nature of reality. On this view critical realism in theology implies a fallibilist, experi-ential epistemology that not only opens up new common ground between religion and science, but also confronts the current challenge to incorporate theology and science in the broader interdisciplinary dialogue.

A postfoundationalist model of rationality should therefore in-clude an interpretation of religious experience which not only facili-tates the evaluation of the problem-solving effectiveness of religious and theological traditions, but which also transcends pitfalls like the kind of dualism that sets up a false dichotomy between "natural" and "supernatural," and then demands a reductionist choice between the two. Surely our choices here cannot be restricted to either the dualist notion of seeing the divine as interrupting or intruding on the natural, or the reductionist option of a naturalist interpretation of experience (cf. Gill 1981:117ff.). Precisely because of the transactional and relational nature of all interpreted experience, religious experience can indeed be thought of as arising out of, and yet transcending, the social, ethical, moral, and aesthetic dimensions of reality. Because of this, from my point of view, Stone's transactional realism may prematurely be giving up on what may be discovered — contextually and through traditioned experience — about the scope and the richness of the presence of transcendence in the natural world. The strongest point of this radical empiricism, however, remains its claim to the public nature of religious rationality.

This postfoundationalist choice for a cognitive dimension in religious experience thus opens up the possibility of interpreting religiously the ways we believe God comes to us in and through the manifold of our experiences of nature, persons, ideas, emotions, places, things, and events. And because of this religious quest for ultimate meaning, each dimension and context of our experience may contain within itself not just a potential element of minimalist transcendence, but an element of mystery, which when responded to, may be plausibly said to carry with it the potential for divine disclosure. With this we have also arrived at possibly the most crucial and telling difference between theology and the sciences. This kind of mystery is unique to the experiential resources and epistemic focus of theology, and very definitely sets it apart from the very focused empirical scope of the natural sciences.

It is also the element of mystery in all religious reflection that has often led to modernist claims that theology and the sciences, if not in conflict, should at least be seen as incommensurably different paradigms from one another. This element of mystery, when followed by a religious commitment, does indeed again seem to force theology out of the shared domain of interdisciplinary discussion, and now confronts us with the serious question: Are deep and personal religious convictions radically opposed to and different from other forms of knowledge, and does this again imply a radical difference between scientific and theological rationality? The postfoundationalist notion of rationality for which I have been arguing above claims, of course, the exact opposite: because of the nature of human rationality, we should be able to enter the pluralist, interdisciplinary conversation with our full personal convictions intact, and at the same time be theoretically empowered to step beyond the limitations and boundaries of our own contexts or forms of life. How do we, however, in this discussion justify the pragmatic move of choosing for or against a commitment, a theory, a model, a tradition? More importantly: Have we really gained by moving from the modernist dilemma, opposing "objective" scientific knowledge with subjective religious "opinion," to the seemingly radical pluralism of our postmodern culture today? To enable us to begin to construct an answer to these difficult questions in the final chapter, we need to take one more careful look at precisely what the role is of interpreted experience in a postfoundationalist model of rationality.

Evidence and Inquiry

If in both theology and the sciences our rational inquiry always is profoundly shaped by a response to interpreted experience, and if our own experiences are indeed rationally compelling because rationality by nature is person-relative, then it becomes clear that precisely our experiences — in the broadest sense of the word — in some important sense must be the source of what we normally regard as good reasons, or convincing evidence, for shaping and determining our choices and responsible judgments. It is precisely against this background that the distinct profile for a postfoundationalist notion of rationality has already emerged: a postfoundationalist model of rationality is revealed when we find a careful balance between, on the one hand, the way our beliefs are anchored in interpreted experience, and, on the other hand, the broader networks of belief in which our rationally compelling experiences are already embedded. But this experience is a complex interaction between language, self-awareness, and lived feelings, between the rational agent and his or her immediate historical and social context. And in exactly this sense it has become clear that our interpreted experience clearly epistemically shapes the rationality of all our reflection. Furthermore, whether in the sciences or in religion (and, therefore, also in theological reflection), we now know that we never have access to foundationalist points of "pure" experience that could be used as secure epistemological evidence or indubitable foundations in our quests for knowledge in either theology or the sciences.

221

In her important book *Evidence and Inquiry: Towards Reconstruction in Epistemology* (1995), Susan Haack has argued along similar lines that, as far as theories of justification for our beliefs go, none of us should be forced to have to choose between foundationalism and coherentism (what I have called nonfoundationalism). In this book she also explodes the idea that the distinction between foundationalism (which typically holds that some of our beliefs are certain, or basic, and could justify other beliefs that are nonbasic) and nonfoundationalist coherentism (which typically denies that there are such basic beliefs, and holds that all our beliefs require support from other beliefs) can in any sense be exclusive or exhaustive, and then goes on to develop her own third option, which she has called *foundherentism* (cf. 1995:73ff.). In defending this attempt at a reconstructed epistemology, Haack argues that all our knowledge is anchored in experience (like some forms of experiential foundationalism) but is then justified by means of claims to coherence (like nonfoundationalist coherentism). What Haack is effectively attempting, therefore, is a "splitting of the difference" between the best intentions of foundationalist and nonfoundationalist/coherentist worldviews.

Haack is famously critical of postmodern, nonfoundationalist philosophers (especially Richard Rorty) who claim that projects of epistemology are misconstrued and should be deconstructed. In a marked contrast to these attempts, Haack now sets out to reconstruct epistemology beyond the foundationalism/nonfoundationalism dichotomy. In her model too the universal intent of human rationality is strongly presupposed. Eventually Haack justifies this universal intent of rationality by linking it to the truth-indicativeness of our rational criteria of evidence, and both of these issues by a further appeal to evolutionary considerations: if human rationality has been a very specific survival strategy for our species, then it is our greater cognitive capacity to interact with the world, and hence to predict and manipulate it, that offers us some modest reassurance that we have an innate ability to classify certain things, and at least the minimal explanatory competence to deal with them (cf. Haack 1995:220). This basically is the reason why evolutionary epistemology is such a successful tool to explain how our minimal, fallibilist explanatory competence, exactly by revising and correcting our beliefs in the face of further experience, has enabled us to develop and build a praxis like science.

In developing her foundherentist position, Haack now wants the best of both worlds: as in foundationalism, foundherentism recognizes the crucial importance of experience for all forms of empirical justification. Unlike foundationalism, however, foundherentism does not require that any of our beliefs should be justified exclusively by experience, or (most importantly) that in justifying our beliefs the evidential support for these beliefs must always flow one-directionally from experience to beliefs. As in coherentism, Haack wants her foundherentism to allow for exactly the kind of mutual support our beliefs receive from the wider networks of belief in which they are always already nonfoundationally embedded. But unlike nonfoundationalist coherentism, Haack's foundherentism also requires some degree of experiential support for the justification of our beliefs. Haack's foundherentism thus moves into the logical space between foundationalism and coherentism (cf. 1995:19) and while allowing for the crucial relevance of experience to all forms of justification, requires no class of privileged beliefs justified exclusively by experience with no support from other beliefs. Foundherentism thus combines two important claims (cf. 1995:19ff.):

- A subject's experience is relevant to the justification of his or her empirical beliefs, but there need be no privileged class of empirical beliefs justified exclusively by the support of experience, independently of the support of other beliefs.
- Justification of our beliefs is never exclusively one-directional, but involves relations of mutual support between them.

In combining these two claims, Haack's foundherentism clearly dovetails with the postfoundationalist affirmation that we relate to our worlds, and to one another, only through complex networks of belief that reflect our interpreted experiences. And since a subject's experience plays such an important role, the way we account for our experiences will never be impersonal, but always personal. My reading of Haack at this point precisely yields a model of rationality that is person-relative, and thus one where one's own experience will always be rationally compelling. Foundherentism also yields a healthy fallibilism and therefore on this point closely overlaps with postfoundationalism: precisely because the good reasons we have for our beliefs are always partially justified by experience and partially justified by other beliefs, the justification for holding our beliefs will never be complete, but will rather be *gradational*. In the in-between space between our compelling experiences and our networks of belief, the justification of our beliefs is therefore never categorical, but comes in degrees (cf. Haack 1995:20, 222). And precisely for this reason I have argued earlier that responsible judgment, so crucial a notion for a postfoundationalist rationality, will always imply a choice between good, better, and best reasons for hanging on to certain beliefs. This kind of responsible choice, then, will also determine whether we are more or less justified in holding certain beliefs. Foundherentism thus clearly points beyond the kind of infallible certitude promised by foundationalism, but also beyond the new conventionalism and tribalism (1995:222) of nonfoundationalist coherentism, and illuminates why an experiential epistemology will always necessarily imply fallibilism.

On this point foundherentism also supports my earlier argument that radical nonfoundationalist views may actually imply a covert crypto-foundationalism: if our contextual *standards* for rationality are confused with the *nature* of rationality as such, then a nonfoundationalist position can easily posit "basic" or hard core beliefs by which all our justified beliefs must be supported. But these will be construed, in the typical protective strategy we discussed earlier, as beliefs which, in the epistemic community in question, do not stand in need of any justification whatsoever. And because this kind of nonfoundationalist contextualism in fact undermines the legitimacy of our rational obligation to critically account for our beliefs, opinions, and our strong convictions, it is actually covertly anti-epistemological (cf. Haack 1995:20). More typically, however, nonfoundationalist views of knowledge make justification depend solely on the relations among beliefs that are coherent or consistent with one another. Haack calls this argument for the claim that empirical claims can be justified by nothing but relations of mutual support, the *drunken sailors argument:* the claim that our beliefs can be justified by nothing but mutual support from other beliefs, is as absurd as suggesting that two drunken sailors could support each other by leaning back to back — when neither was standing on anything (cf. 1995:27). The fundamental problem with this kind of nonfoundationalist coherentism is that it allows no role for experience, and for the fact that we relate to our world only through the mediation of interpreted experience. Foundherentism wants to creatively fuse the ideas that, on the one hand, all our beliefs and networks of belief are experientially anchored, and, on the other hand, our beliefs always also need mutual support from other beliefs.

To help capture the notion of epistemic justification she has in mind, Susan Haack now introduces the image of the *crossword puzzle* (cf. 1995:81ff.). In a normal crossword puzzle entries must, first of all, answer to the clues, and, secondly, also fit well with one another. On this view, the clues in the crossword puzzle become the analogies for experiential evidence, while other already completed and intersecting entries are comparable to our background beliefs. The clues thus represent experiential evidence, while the entries represent the results of how we have reasoned and justified our beliefs about our experiences. The reasonableness of any entry into the "crossword puzzle," representing our experientially anchored networks of belief, ultimately depends on how well it fits with the clues and other already completed entries, the degree of confidence we have in the correctness of the other entries, and how much of the crossword puzzle has actually been completed. Our justified beliefs must therefore answer to experience, but these justified beliefs must also cohere with all others, as proper entries do. Therefore, just as the clues provide evidence for the correctness of response with respect to the individual rows and columns of a crossword puzzle, so empirical experience provides evidence for our epistemic claims. And just as the probability of the correctness of one's answers increases as the answers gradually fit together in the grid, so the degree of certainty or conviction with regard to one's own knowledge claims increases as bits of empirical evidence fit together. A significant upshot of all of this is that ultimately the degree of justification we have for believing what we believe is a product both of *the quality of the available and recognized experiential evidence,* and *the way we enquire about and account for our beliefs* (cf. Crawley 1997:8). This essentially captures how what I earlier called the experiential and theoretical adequacy of our networks of beliefs will function in a postfoundationalist model of rationality.

The great advantage of Susan Haack's foundherentism is that it so clearly shows that a coherentist account of our beliefs cannot allow the crucial relevance of experience to justification, while a foundationalist account can do that, but only in a forced and unnatural fash-

225

ion.[5] Haack's vision that a foundherentist conception of justification is always gradational in character (1995:42) also offers a strong argument for the epistemic fallibilism that is so much a part of a post-foundationalist notion of rationality. Haack also presents us with a rich notion of experience that includes a wide spectrum of sensory, introspective, and memory experiences (1995:36ff.), and argues that all these experiences are necessary for justified empirical beliefs. Much in the way that Mikael Stenmark has argued, Haack also argues for a wider notion of rationality that is intended to be person-relative. And when Stenmark argues that the standards of our rationality are always context-dependent or domain-specific, Haack too argues that, like rationality, a foundherentist notion of justification is always person-relative and therefore domain-dependent. What we see as good reason for believing such and such not only differs across time, but also differs from place to place. The performative presence of rationality in all domains of our lives certainly affirms the universal nature of human rationality. However, just as there is a history of rationality, there also is a geography of rationality (cf. Crawley 1997:9). In the next chapter we will carefully review the epistemological significance of the local and situated nature of our standards of rationality, as well as the special challenge that the pluralism which so naturally flows from this will entail.

Although Haack implicitly (and explicitly) argues for broader notions of rationality and justification, as well as for a richer notion of experience, it does become clear that she covertly harbors a carefully constructed preference for a highly theoretical natural scientific rationality. In spite of her person-centered notion of rationality, the kind of experience that turns out to be rationally compelling for Haack is still *empirical* evidence, narrowly and scientifically construed (cf. 1995: 214f.). This ultimately narrows down her notion of experiential evidence to empirical evidence, and again leaves us with an idealized rational agent devoid of the rich experiential resources of human rationality. Nowhere will this be more clear than in Haack's reluctance to deal with the problem of religious experience.

In her development of a foundherentist position, Haack has successfully combined the positive aspects of foundationalism (its appeal

5. I have benefited very much from discussions with Clifford Blake Anderson and Evica Novacovic on these and related issues.

to experience in the justification of theories) with the positive aspects of a nonfoundationalist coherentism (its insistence on mutual support for beliefs within wider networks of belief). In doing so she has also made the important move of linking the nature of rationality and of justification to the individual person. In placing her whole project within the broader scope of the justification of natural scientific knowledge, however, Haack has significantly narrowed the scope of what experiential justification may mean in rational reflection. If we recall for a moment Nicholas Rescher's argument for a rich notion of human rationality that reaches beyond the strictly cognitive and theoretical, to a rational agent embedded in the resources of the experiential, evaluative, and pragmatic dimensions of human lives, Haack's rational agent emerges as narrowly individualist and highly idealized. Criticizing her for prioritizing exactly such an idealized individual over the community in epistemology, Clifford Blake Anderson has characterized Haack as a traditional modernist epistemologist (1997: 20). This, I think, is true for at least two reasons: first, Haack narrows down rationality to natural scientific rationality by reducing experiential accountability to empirical accountability, and second, as a result of this she finally chooses to exclude the problem of religious experience from her experiential epistemology.

As we have seen, in her retrieval of a rich notion of experience Haack acknowledges that the individual person is embedded in a mesh of interconnected beliefs, perceptual experiences, desires, and fears (cf. 1995:76ff.). She then goes on, however, and distinguishes between *evidential* and *nonevidential* components within our web of beliefs. Our belief states, our perceptual states, our introspective awareness and memories — all of these will count as evidential components (the experiential "clues" of her crossword puzzle) and are embedded in our webs of belief. Other states such as our desires, preferences, and fears, however, have a nonevidential status, even if they belong to the causal nexus that explains how it is that we believe something. Haack thus excludes all existential feelings and attitudes (such a crucially and determining part of our experience) from the category of rational evidence, and seems to effectively disqualify many of the causes that prompt and sustain our beliefs from counting as rational evidence (cf. also Anderson 1997:21). But if we now recall that we relate to our worlds and one another only through interpreted experience, then it becomes unintelligible how the interpretation of empirical experiences, and especially introspective or memory experiences, could in principle be distinguished from the interpretation of fear- or desire-experiences — unless these kinds of personal experiences are somehow still regarded as foundationalist points of "pure" experience, something Haack strongly would deny. Haack's narrowing of her notion of experience to what is relevant in natural scientific rationality, and the resultant (arbitrary?) demarcation between experiences that have or do not have evidential value, therefore seems to be inconsistent with the rest of her foundherentist program. Although Haack makes an important shift to a person-relative notion of rationality, this idealized rational agent now turns out to be stripped of any epistemic characteristics that may make that individual particular (cf. Anderson 1997:23). It also, however, seems to persistently continue the modernist distinction between objective, empirical scientific knowledge, and subjective, experientially based opinion. It does seem, therefore, that a web of beliefs is already so firmly in place here that it shapes and determines which kinds of experiences should qualify as clues to the credibility of our beliefs. On this view, of course, the "experiential anchoring" of our webs of belief becomes a highly selective and empiricist affair. That this is true for Haack's foundherentism quickly becomes clear when one looks at her views on *religious* experiences.

Within the wider context of foundherentism, religious experience certainly is the first casualty of Haack's modernist notion of an idealized rational subject. In Haack's text there are in fact only two brief references to the issue of religious experience. The first is a throwaway line in which Haack almost casually states that religious propositions are in principle incapable of settlement by evidence (cf. 1995:202). In the second she briefly considers whether the problem of religious experience should have been included in her foundherentist program. Her interesting answer to this is unambiguous:

> The question reveals an interesting unclarity in what is meant by "empirical" in "empirical beliefs"; if one takes it as "to do with the natural world," the question of religious experience can perhaps be put aside as not relevant, whereas if one takes it as "not purely logical, to do with how things contingently are," the question cannot be avoided. Since the present task is already formidable, I shall take the easier path, and construe "empirical" narrowly enough to keep the issues of religious experience at bay. (1995:214)

Haack thus clearly and unambiguously narrows down the crucially important epistemic role of interpreted experience to empirical evidence, and although *empirical* evidence for her includes both *sensory* evidence (our senses are sources of information about the world) and *introspective* evidence (introspection as a source of information about one's own mental goings-on, but — as we saw earlier — arbitrarily demarcated from existential feelings and attitudes), empirical evidence still remains the *only* ultimate evidence we have with respect to our empirical beliefs, which as such are specifically relevant for *scientific* investigations only (cf. 1995:214). It seems strange that Haack, who so obviously wants to move beyond foundationalist and scientistic notions of scientific investigation, would at the outset categorically state that religious experience is in principle incapable of being settled by experiential evidence. If, as we saw earlier, we relate to our world and to ourselves only through the mediation of interpreted experience, and if in reasoning strategies as diverse as theology and the sciences the same interpretative procedures are at work in spite of their very different experiential resources and epistemic scopes, then surely there could in principle be no valid epistemological reasons for excluding religious experiences as important "clues" or evidential resources for finding religious meaning in life.

The very different *standards* of rationality in the practice of science should therefore not be normative and decisive for determining the value of religious experiences (and whether they are in or out of an evidentialist program). On the contrary, the postmodern challenge to modernist, totalizing views of human rationality has precisely broken down these unnatural epistemic distinctions, and has freed us to rediscover the performative presence of rationality in *all* our reasoning strategies. Religion (and by implication also theological reflection) can be excluded from this process only if a decision to favor a strictly empiricist, narrow notion of scientific rationality has already been made in advance and is now serving as a grid for determining which experiential clues, and which networks of belief, are ultimately going to qualify as empirical evidence for our knowledge claims. It therefore seems that Haack may still be giving preference to the "foundationalism" part of foundherentism, and could still be working covertly with foundationalist points of "pure" experience as "clues" that have to be interpreted and supported by our networks of belief. What is clearly not accepted in this experiential epistemology is the ubiquitous nature of all experience as already interpreted experience, and that we have no access to any non-belief input that is not already interpreted. Furthermore, what seems even more inconsistent is the fact that Haack does in fact grant an "indirect" dependence on broad notions of experience to philosophy (cf. 1995:213), a privilege that is obviously denied to our reflection on religious experience.

Another interesting perspective on Haack's inconsistent and seemingly arbitrary demarcation of religious experience from all other kinds of experience is found in her acceptance of the role of testimonial evidence (1995:79). Here Haack acknowledges that our beliefs are often maintained, in whole or part, by our hearing, seeing, and our remembering hearing and seeing, of what someone else says or writes. But surely such testimonial evidence is always and everywhere highly interpreted. William Crawley, consistent with Haack's jargon, has ironically called this a rather subversive *in through the back door argument* (1997:12), and rightly so: not only does Haack's acknowledgment of the role of testimonial evidence imply an argument for a much richer notion of experience than she actually claims to be working with, but with this acknowledgment she certainly is leaving an opening ("through the back door!") for precisely the broader class of interpreted experiences that she claims to have excluded earlier by declaring them in principle incapable of being settled by (her narrow definition of) empirical evidence. It is certainly true that at least some of our religious beliefs are testimonial in character, since we all find ourselves embedded in rich traditions. But traditions are, among other things, long-established testimonial chains, and if Haack accepts the implications of the *in through the back door argument* for nonreligious testimonial evidence, there could be no reason left for not accepting it for the category of religious testimonial evidence too (cf. Crawley 1997:12).

In Conclusion

In this chapter I have attempted to construct a modest theory of experience that might help to understand better the crucial experiential dimension of a postfoundationalist notion of rationality. We first of all turned our attention to what it might mean that our self-awareness as rational agents lies at the heart of human rationality. The answer to this question was found in the fact that human rationality is always person-relative. As we probed deeper the differences between the nature and standards of rationality, the true richness of rationality's experiential and contextual dimensions was revealed: if our own personal experiences are always rationally compelling, then the pattern of our ongoing, contextualized experiences will be altogether decisive for the way we cope rationally with our worlds. Furthermore, if rationality requires that we attune our beliefs, personal convictions, and critical evaluations to our own self-awareness, then a postfoundationalist notion of rationality will also require that we attune our beliefs, personal convictions, and critical evaluations to the overall pattern of our experience.

In the meantime we have already established that significant epistemological overlaps between theological and scientific rationality (as we have identified them in the quest for optimal understanding, responsible judgment skills, and progressive problem-solving) in fact reveal a breakdown of the traditional modernist demarcation between scientific and nonscientific rationality. As a reasoning strategy science differs from theological reflection only in degree, and through an emphasis on diverse epistemic scopes, experiential resources, and different heuristic structures. At the end of the day, however, diverse theologies and various sciences all grapple with what we perceive as real aspects of our experience. Because of this crucial experiential dimension in the nature of rationality, we have also established that, whether in theology or in the sciences, we relate to our worlds epistemically only through the mediation of interpreted experience. And in this sense it could be said that theology and the sciences offer alternative interpretations of our manifold experiences. In a postfoundationalist context, both reasoning strategies have to make do without any "pure" points of foundationalist, uninterpreted, given experiences. Not only in theology, but also in the sciences we therefore relate to our worlds only through interpreted experience: even empirical scientific observation is theoretically selected and interpreted, and functions only within the network of those presupposed theories that constitute a specific reasoning strategy. For both theology and the sciences this then is the definitive move beyond foundationalism (and for attaining the "post"-status in postfoundationalism): if our beliefs are the results of our interpreted experiences, then the content of this belief can never be given immediately or directly in the experience itself.

231

To claim, then, that in neither theology nor the sciences is there such a thing as an uninterpreted experience is to claim that all our experience and observations are theory-laden. This claim, as we saw, also reached deeply into the pragmatic, cognitive, and evaluative dimensions of a postfoundationalist epistemology, and would make it impossible to arbitrarily distinguish "objective" experiential data from "subjective" experiential data. To say that all interpretations are always interpreted is to say that all our experiences are shaped by the fiduciary rootedness of human rationality, and that we interact with our worlds, ourselves, and others in terms of the comprehensive life-views we are already committed to. On this view the distinguishing mark of a *religious* experience cannot anymore be found in its subjective nature, and in the fact that therefore it supposedly is incapable of being experientially justified (contra Susan Haack), but rather in the individual rational agent's judgment that the experience, and the beliefs that shape the experience, can only be accounted for in religious terms. A postfoundationalist model of rationality is therefore attained when we find a careful balance between, on the one hand, the way our beliefs are anchored in interpreted experience, and, on the other hand, the broader networks of beliefs in which our rationally compelling experiences are already embedded.

As we now move to the final chapter, we seem to be closer to our goal of locating theology within the broader context of interdisciplinary reflection. In spite of important differences in focus, experiential resources, and interpretative scope, theological and scientific reflection do share the same rich experiential and interpretative resources of human rationality. Each of these reasoning strategies therefore exemplifies how rationality is performatively present in different domains of our lives. But this can never again yield a modernist and universalist notion of rationality, because human rationality is never housed within any one specific genre of discourse or reasoning strategy. A postfoundationalist notion of rationality has revealed the richness of our species' most distinguishing survival strategy as operative between different modes of knowledge, as lying across diverse reasoning strategies, and as performatively present in all the various domains of our lives.

As we now turn to the reality of pluralism in theology and the sciences in the wake of postmodernism, then to the role of tradition in the shaping of theological and scientific rationality, and finally, to the problem of interdisciplinary conversation between theology and the sciences, we will ask what it means to affirm that rationality, so closely linked to social praxis and historical context, also is our only instrumentality that may make interdisciplinary and cross-contextual conversation possible. As we will see, it will at least mean that our seemingly remote epistemologies are integral parts of a whole web of theories about the world and ourselves, and that the standards of rationality, although always contextually shaped, are not hopelessly culture-bound (cf. Haack 1995:222).

Chapter Five

Rationality and Pluralism

"Our hopes, however, go in a different direction: the emergence of an intellectual culture that would be rationalist but not dogmatic, scientifically minded but not scientistic, open-minded but not frivolous, and politically progressive but not sectarian. But this, of course, is only a hope, and perhaps only a dream."

Alan Sokal and Jean Bricmont, *Intellectual Impostures*
(London: Profile Books, 1998:198)

I n our search for a notion of rationality that would somehow bind together diverse cultural domains and different disciplines, it became clear that the nostalgia for one, unified form of knowledge after postmodernity still very much defines who we are intellectually. This became eminently clear with the recent publication of E. O. Wilson's controversial new book *Consilience: The Unity of Knowledge* (1998). In this work Wilson explains how, at a young age, he experienced the "Ionian Enchantment": a conversion to a strong belief in the unity of the sciences — a conviction far deeper than a mere working proposition, that the world is orderly and can be explained by a small number of natural laws (cf. Wilson 1998:4). For Wilson this comprehensive vision soon, however, becomes completely dominated by the superiority of science and scientific thought, and the spell of this enchantment ultimately extends beyond the natural sciences to absorb also the social sciences, the humanities, and ultimately religion and theological reflection too.

235

E. O. Wilson is quite clear about the fact that as a species we yearn to have ultimate meaning and a purpose larger than ourselves: we are obliged by the deepest drives of the human spirit to make ourselves more than animated dust, and we must have a story to tell about where we came from and why we are here (cf. Wilson 1998:6). For Wilson, however, it is science that will ultimately be a continuation of, and a better tested ground than even conventional religion, and his ideal of consilience, a unified form of knowledge, will only be reached on strictly natural scientific grounds. Wilson's scientism is truly breathtaking, for if the natural sciences can attain this unity of knowledge, then the classical Christian Scriptures can be demoted as "the first literate attempt to explain the universe and make ourselves significant in it" (cf. 1998:6). If this were to be true, then science would in fact be a better way to attain the original goals of religion, and in that sense science would be religion liberated and writ large. For Wilson, then, the scientistic search for a unified form of knowledge leads directly to this preference for what he calls "objective reality" over "revelation," and should be seen as another — and better — way of satisfying religious hunger (cf. 1998:6).

This search for the unification of all knowledge, according to Wilson, found its apex in the Enlightenment, where we saw best illustrated the greatest enterprise of the mind, i.e., the attempted linkage of the sciences and the humanities. In stark contrast to this view, the current postmodern fragmentation of knowledge and the resulting "chaos in philosophy" are not at all reflections of the real world, but are "artifacts of scholarship" only (cf. 1998:8). The way out of this fragmentation, the key to the unification of all forms of knowledge, Wilson finds in what he has termed *consilience*. As we saw earlier, Wilson believes that the concept "consilience," through its rarity of use, has retained a precision which a concept like "coherence" does not have anymore. Consilience points to an integration, literally a "jumping together" of knowledge by the linking of facts and fact-based theory across disciplines to create a common groundwork of explanation (cf. 1998:8). Wilson's reductionist scientism, however, becomes even more overt when he proceeds to argue that the only way to either establish or refute consilience is by methods developed in the natural sciences (1998:9). Not just this rather blatant scientism, however, but also an astounding lack of epistemological awareness shines through when Wilson proceeds to argue that, as we approach the new age of synthesis and epistemic integration, philosophy too is (allegedly) revealed to have a shrinking dominion, and he goes on to say: "We have the common goal of turning as much philosophy as possible into science" (cf. 1998:12). The emergence here of a totally imperialist, modernist notion of scientific rationality is complete when philosophy and epistemology now follow religion and theology in a glorious transformation into "real science."

Wilson knows, of course, that the pluralism we find in the wake of postmodernism poses a very real threat to his attempt at unifying all forms of human knowledge. Without the necessary philosophical tools to deal with this complex issue, the only way out is now to caricaturize postmodernism itself. *Postmodernism,* as the ultimate polar antithesis of the Enlightenment, is interpreted by Wilson as follows: Enlightenment thinkers believed we can know everything, and radical postmodernists believe we can know nothing. Blissfully unaware of the important work of postmodern philosophers of science like Joseph Rouse, Wilson goes on and typifies philosophical postmodernists as a rebel crew milling beneath the black flag of anarchy, challenging the very foundations of science and traditional philosophy (1998:40). Echoing the "early" Alan Sokal, he sees all postmodernists as proposing that reality is a construction of the mind, and in its most extreme form actually denying reality, as well as all objective truths.

Wilson is, of course, right in warning against the extreme forms of postmodern cultural and epistemic relativism, but careless in indiscriminately grouping together all forms of postmodern thinking under this generic vision. Only if one first take seriously what postmodern philosophers of science say about the local and social nature of all scientific work and praxis, can one — as we saw before — via a process of standardization come to the valid point that Wilson later wants to make: the laws of physics are indeed so accurate as to transcend cultural differences; they boil down to mathematical formulae that cannot too flippantly be given Chinese or Ethiopian or Mayan nuances, or be carelessly reinterpreted in masculinist or feminist variations (cf. 1998:49).

Wilson's solution for what he sees as the trials and tribulations of postmodern thinking is to simply walk away from Foucault and existentialist despair (1998:43). The vocabulary of postmodernism has indeed become standard fare in the postmodern literature and is used to flag the plurality of our language games, the plurality of our narratives, and the plurality of our social practices. Plurality therefore indeed seems to infiltrate our grammar, our concept formations, our social attitudes, our principles of justice, and our institutions (cf. Schrag 1992:30). This pluralism is indeed to be taken extremely seriously, but dissensus, incommensurability, irretrievable conflicts of interpretation, and hermeneutical nihilism are not at all necessary consequences of plurality and multiplicity. This of course explains why Calvin Schrag has proposed that it might be more fruitful to think of postmodernism as a radicalization and retrenchment of modernity, than as a period of history that comes "after" the modern (cf. 1992:45). I have also argued in this book that the only way to deal with this issue epistemologically is to revision a notion of postfoundationalist rationality that would respect diverse forms of human knowledge and find unifying links between these domains without totalizing them, while at the same time taking very seriously the pluralism we find in the wake of postmodernity. Therefore, the only way to deal with this issue epistemologically is to forge ahead through this pluralism, take it absolutely seriously, and instead of a nostalgia for scientistic, modernist metanarratives, to rediscover rationality as alive and well in the many and varied domains of our discourses, practices, communities, arts, sciences, religion, and also in our theological reflection. Postmodernism has indeed embraced the opportunity to expose the failures of all foundationalist, totalizing metanarratives, but we have seen that we are not left to just accept and make do with this inescapable pluralization and relativization of all our beliefs and practices.

In our ongoing conversation with philosophers like Harold Brown, Nicholas Rescher, and Calvin Schrag, we have seen that, instead of having to choose between modernist objectivism and postmodern pluralism, consensus or dissensus, commensurability or incommensurability, imperialist science and privatized religion, it is indeed possible to respond to the postmodern challenge by *refiguring* our notion of rationality, and the resources of this rationality, into a postfoundationalist vision of this remarkable skill and ability which most defines who we are as a species. This notion of rationality has not only helped us to steer a course between the Scylla of modernity and the Charybdis of postmodernity, but it has also helped us to appropriate a constructive notion of postmodernism precisely by navigating around the directionless pluralism of so much of skeptical postmodernity (cf. Schrag 1989:86). This refigured and broadened notion of rationality not only now includes an awareness of the shared cognitive, pragmatic, and evaluative dimensions of rationality, but also reveals rationality as a social practice in which the narrative patterns of our interpreted experience contain resources for responsible judgment and critical evaluation as communicative projects. As we saw earlier, in modernity rule-governed judgment and critical discernment were construed as a quest for certainty, and finally fused into the impossible epistemological requirement of finding indubitable foundations for our claims to knowledge. On a postfoundationalist view of rationality, however, critical, responsible judgment pursues neither the modernist desire for foundations, nor its hope for certainty and final truths.

We now seem to be closer to our goal of finding a space where both theology and the sciences can be located within the broader context of interdisciplinary reflection. In spite of important differences in focus, experiential resources, methodologies, and interpretative scope, theological and scientific reflection do share the same rich resources of human rationality. Each of these reasoning strategies, in their many diverse forms, therefore exemplifies how rationality is indeed performatively present in different domains of our lives. But this can never again yield a modernist and universalist notion of one, unified form of knowledge, one overarching rationality, because the dynamics of human rationality is never housed within any one specific genre of discourse or reasoning strategy only. It is to this issue that we will ultimately turn: how a postfoundationalist notion of rationality reveals the richness of our species' most distinguishing survival strategy as operative between different modes of knowledge, as lying across diverse reasoning strategies, and as performatively present in all the various domains of our lives. It is in such a safe space that the dialogue between theology and the sciences will ultimately find a home.

The Postmodern Challenge to Rationality, Revisited

The contemporary North American theological landscape is currently dominated by an almost overwhelming sense of pluralism within the domain of theological reflection. In a sense this pluralism is, as we saw

239

before, what many would see as a typically postmodern phenomenon. Whatever else this may mean, it certainly also means that theology today has no single, ultimate question or focus, and no one overriding concern that defines and shapes its current image. In this sense it has become not just wrong, but plain pointless to talk of "theology" in the singular in today's ongoing dialogue between theology and the sciences. There is, however, a sense in which theological pluralism itself can be seen as the emergence of a valid contemporary problem, a fact that surfaces in our times in questions like the following: Is pluralism a phenomenon that should be seen as an integral part of the theological enterprise, or is it in fact a passing cultural fad that is best avoided when doing theology? Is pluralism, in a more positive sense, more about theology's relationship with the culture(s) in which it is embedded, or should it in fact rather point to Christianity's problematic relationship to the other religions of the world (cf. Wegter-McNelly 1996:1f.)? Ultimately the focal point of this question is, of course, whether this pluralism in theological reflection enhances or problematizes theology's ongoing conversation with other disciplines and with our culture in general.

In contemporary Christian theology the current form of the problem of pluralism is directly related to the rather dramatic emergence of contextual theologies since the 1970s. When contextual theologies first began to appear, their main purpose was to rebel against typically Western, academic forms of theological reflection with its equally typical universal, a-contextual, intellectualist scope, and a preoccupation with issues like atheism and secularization — issues often never even raised in local, highly contextualized situations. In spite of their universalizing tendencies, however, these comprehensive, or so-called "universal" Western theologies did not reach far enough and ignored what were often the most pressing issues in local contexts: the burden of poverty, oppression, multiple forms of discrimination, and in the so-called "third world," the struggle to create a new identity after a colonial past. The reaction to such experiences understandably led to a search for what made our different experiences of the one Christian faith so different, and the answer seemed to lie in the radically different contexts, traditions, and experiences in which Christian communities found themselves. Theologians who were aware of this problem came to realize that if Christianity was to engage the hearts and minds of believers, then it would have to take the specific experiences, contexts, and traditions that shape their lives much more intentionally and seriously (cf. Schreiter 1997:1ff.). The universalizing theologies of modernity have therefore now been forced to take seriously not only context and tradition, but to be open also to the possibility of seeing the Christian tradition itself as a series of local theologies. The inescapable pluralism that resulted from this certainly leaves theology today with the complex task of taking both its contextual and universalizing dimensions seriously (cf. Schreiter 1997:3).

Christian theology at the end of the twentieth century is, therefore, certainly marked by an inescapable pluralism which not only seems to threaten the intellectual integrity of traditional academic theology, but which makes cross-contextual and interdisciplinary dialogue almost impossible. Instead of "one true theology," the discarding of modernity's metanarratives has now led both to the recognition of the importance of discrete experiences and specific traditions in theological reflection, and so to the inevitable emergence of so-called "local theologies" (cf. Byrne 1994:6). These theologies are local not only in the sense of being ethnic or cultural theologies, but "local" also in the specific sense of growing from very particular experiences. The radical demise of objectivist understandings of rationality has thus left us with an almost breathtaking pluralism of theologies, such as liberation theologies, womanist and feminist theologies, Black theologies and Asian theologies, eco-theologies, empirical theologies, process theologies, postliberal and revisionist theologies, gay and queer theologies, as well as various forms of confessional and evangelical theologies which now also often claim to be forms of postmodern theology. The way in which these diverse and pluralist forms of theological reflection involve a serious and conscious choice for very specific traditions, or even neglected aspects of the Christian tradition, not only shows that tradition and local context always go together closely, but also why contemporary theological pluralism has almost rendered it meaningless to talk about "theology" today as if the existence of one true theology could still be posited in such a generic, uncomplicated way.

Even the briefest overview of this pluralist, contemporary theological landscape, therefore, reveals the startling fragmentation caused by what is often called "the postmodern challenge" of our times. And as we saw earlier in our discussion of nonfoundationalist theologies, the radical pluralization following skeptical forms of postmodern cri-

241

tique has not only affected different theologies in different ways, but has seriously undermined any attempt to construct a safe epistemological space where, as theologians, we might be taken seriously in interdisciplinary dialogue. For the Christian theologian this has profound implications, and questions like the following haunt some of us all the time: In a radically pluralist world where epistemological foundationalism has been so successfully deconstructed, will it still be possible for theology to join other modes of knowledge and other reasoning strategies in some form of interdisciplinary, public discourse? Or is the only coherent and consistent way to defend theological truth claims to give up this public voice and fall back massively on our respective preferred traditions, and to hope that some form of local consensus will emerge there and pave the way to whatever a specific group may be claiming as the "truth"?

Talking about the problem of pluralism and tradition in this way inevitably leads us to reflect on how the problem of cognitive pluralism relates to tradition, and how this relationship as such is deeply embedded in the more general problem of *rationality*. Have highly contextualized, nonfoundationalist local theologies now taught us that theological rationality only makes sense within the sharply demarcated context of tradition, and that therefore tradition itself should be seen as rationality's only destiny? As theologians who are being forced to take pluralism seriously, we have hopefully now learned to avoid the arrogance of prescribing overarching, foundationalist rules for interdisciplinary dialogue. But surely, as we saw, we should as seriously avoid the insular comfort of fideism, and of a nonfoundationalist isolationism, where what we see as our preferred tradition can easily transform that tradition from being rationality's *destiny* (cf. Schrag 1992:49) to being more like rationality's *prison*. Nonfoundationalist attempts to rely solely on the uniqueness of confessional traditions can in fact, as we saw in an earlier chapter, turn out to be just the other side of the great modernist debate (cf. Bell 1996:179), where, *vis-à-vis* the objectivist claims of a unified science, theological traditions too are easily transformed into privatized matters of individual or communal belief only. I argued earlier for the critical rejection of all unified forms of knowledge, but this critical rejection of modernist, universalist notions of rationality will still imply that it is the destiny of all our reasoning strategies — therefore of theology and the sciences too — to somehow stay with their own tradition(s). The fact that rationality is so closely tied to tradition, however, should never simply mean a choice for only contextual consensus and internalist rules, or for social standards and ideals that define only particular communities. Over against an objectivist foundationalism, on the one hand, and the extreme pluralism/relativism of most forms of nonfoundationalism, on the other hand, I have been arguing here for a postfoundationalist notion of rationality (cf. also van Huyssteen 1997a; 1998a:214f.) which implies the following important moves for theological reflection:

1. It acknowledges contextuality and the embeddedness of all our theological reflection in human culture, and therefore, in specific traditions.
2. It takes seriously the epistemically crucial role of interpreted experience or experiential understanding, and the way that tradition shapes the epistemic and nonepistemic values that inform our reflection about God and what some of us believe to be God's presence in the world.
3. However, a postfoundationalist notion of rationality in theological reflection also claims to point beyond the boundaries of the local community, group, tradition, or culture, toward a plausible form of interdisciplinary conversation.

Postfoundationalism in theological reflection has therefore shown itself as a viable third epistemological option beyond the extremes of absolutism and the relativism of extreme forms of pluralism. The overriding concern here is therefore as follows: while we always come to our cross-disciplinary conversations with strong beliefs, commitments, and even prejudices, epistemological postfoundationalism enables us to identify the shared resources of human rationality in different modes of knowledge, and then to reach beyond the boundaries of our own traditional communities in cross-contextual, cross-disciplinary conversation. As such an interdisciplinary, public space is cleared for thinking between more than one knowledge system or reasoning strategy, in what Sandra Harding has aptly called a "borderlands epistemology" (Harding 1996:15ff.).

In this final chapter I will, therefore, argue that to talk about pluralism and interdisciplinary reflection is indeed to talk specifically about the problem of rationality, and about the values that shape the

243

rationality of theological reflection. This quest for a refigured notion of theological rationality — which also implies how good theology ought to be done — is presented here in terms of three claims that reach back directly to our earlier discussions of the notions of rationality and experience:

1. I have argued that we always relate to our world through interpreted experience only. As such we will have no standing ground, no place for evaluating, judging, and enquiring, apart from that which is provided by some specific tradition or traditions. In this sense interpretation is as much at work in the process of scientific discovery as it is in different forms of narrative knowledge: it goes all the way down and all the way back, whether we are moving in the domain of science, morality, art, or religion.

2. Because we cannot think and act except through experiential understanding and an engagement with tradition, our task is to stand in a *critical* relation to our tradition, and thereby — as we saw before — split the difference between modernity and postmodernity. This will imply a step beyond the confines of particular traditions, a step that is warranted by a revisioned and postfoundationalist notion of rationality where the task and identity of theology is revealed as definitively shaped by its location in the living context, of not only tradition, but also of interdisciplinary reflection.

3. This contemporary interdisciplinary context is — epistemologically, at least — significantly shaped by the dominant influence and the ubiquitous presence of scientific rationality in our culture. Theologians, often focusing on the unique hermeneutics of theological reflection, have notoriously neglected this profound epistemological challenge by ignoring, or not recognizing, the pervasive influence of the sciences on the epistemic and other values that shape theological rationality.

As we saw earlier, Calvin Schrag, in his important work on the postmodern challenge to rationality, has pointed out how common it has become to ascribe antireason and "end of philosophy"–talk to what is broadly referred to as *postmodernism:* although there is no unified voice of postmodernism, it has always been clear that the problematization of rationality has been one of its recurring themes. Indeed, the postmodern celebration of pluralism, multiplicity, heterogeneity, and incommensurability makes the task of finding a valid place for the "claims of reason" (1994:61) a particularly demanding one. Schrag's recent work, however, has been presented here as a response to exactly this kind of postmodern challenge to the resources of rationality.

Schrag's attempt to move beyond both the totalizing meta-narratives of modernity and the unmitigated pluralism and self-isolating relativism of extreme forms of postmodernism is found — as we saw earlier — in his proposal for a notion of *transversal rationality* (cf. Schrag 1994). It is to this important notion that we have to return one more time in order to harvest the full richness of a postfoundationalist rationality for the problem of interdisciplinary reflection. We saw that much of Schrag's recent work has been an exploration of the powerful resources of reason as revealed in the dynamics of rationality's crucially important dimensions of critique, articulation, and disclosure. We also saw earlier that the notion of transversal rationality charts a new course between the classical and modern over-determination of cognitive rationality, on the one hand, and the dissolution of the rational subject in much of postmodern philosophy, on the other hand. Schrag's notion of transversal rationality has indeed significantly enhanced what I have been naming *postfoundationalist rationality*. This refigured notion of rationality can now be seen as a constructive response against any modernist attempts that would first want to carve out the different cultural domains of science, morality, art, and religion, and then afterwards search for some unifying perspective between them (cf. Schrag 1992:5).

In stark contrast to the totalizing nature of modernist notions of rationality and the pluralism of extreme forms of postmodernism, a postfoundationalist, transversal notion of rationality revealed reason as present and operative in and through the interrelated domains of our discourses and actions, our words and deeds, speaking and writing, hearing and reading (cf. Schrag 1992:9). These are indeed the multiple forms of life that make up our communicative practices. But it is especially the postmodern jettisoning of "critique" that Schrag wanted to confront: in his own refigured notion of rationality the difference between modernity and postmodernity is split, and a refigured notion of critique as praxial critique is retained. Here the dynamics of responsible judgment and evaluative critique has been refigured as a dynamic communal and cross-disciplinary discernment and assessment of all our various discourses, beliefs, and actions. Our earlier discussion of praxial critique, then, was all about a refiguration of critical rationality, a resituation of critical thinking within the spaces of our communicative practices and the dynamics of our lifeworld involvements.

The fitting response of responsible judgment, which earlier we found at the heart of rationality, was thus contextualized and revealed as a true communicative project. For Schrag, rationality as praxial critique fills the void that results from the displacement of the theoretico-epistemological paradigm of modernity. Critique in this sense is never about modernity's zeal for foundations, nor about the hopes for indubitable certainty. A postfoundationalist critique of our uncritically held assumptions wants to attain exactly the opposite and reveal the viability of cognitive pluralism. In this sense praxial critique aligns itself with the prejudgments operative in the many different dimensions of our communal existence, since there clearly is no discernment possible without prejudgments (cf. Schrag 1992:64f.). For the theology and science dialogue this had far-reaching consequences: in this kind of pragmatic understanding there is no discernment possible that could still be decontextualized from the background of our prejudgments, habits, and skills that inform our participation in the communal world. However, there is also no discernment possible apart from at the same time placing these prejudgments, habits of thought and action, into question in a relentless ongoing criticism of the (often) crypto-foundationalist assumptions with which we enter our cross-disciplinary conversations with one another.

In proposing the use of the metaphor of transversality in a creative new way, Calvin Schrag takes his cue from mathematicians (who take up the vocabulary of transversality when speaking of the transversality of a line as it intersects a system of other lines or surfaces), but also from physicists and physiologists: in the interdisciplinary and varied use of this concept a shared meaning emerged, having to do principally with the related senses of extending over, lying across, and intersecting (cf. Schrag 1994:64). All of these notions in fact enrich and enlighten what happens in concrete, contextual situations where we start down the risky and precarious road of interdisciplinary conversation. When we discussed the notion of rationality earlier, it also became clear that Schrag goes even further and follows Sartre in using the notion of transversality to indicate how human consciousness and self-awareness are unified by a play of intentionalities which includes concrete retentions of past consciousness. In this sense rationality is taken up directly into our consciousness and self-awareness, and this consciousness is then unified by an experience of self-presence, emerging over time from a remembering self-awareness/consciousness in which diverse past experiences are integrated. In using the notion of transversal rationality in this truly rich and creative way, Schrag wanted to justify and urge an acknowledgment of multiple patterns of interpretation as one moves across the borders and boundaries of the different disciplinary matrices (cf. 1994:65).

In making this important move Schrag acknowledged that he shares the postmodern suspicion about various subject-grounded and consciousness-centered approaches to rationality within modernity. But, importantly and correctly, for him this does not automatically lead to the jettisoning of the vocabulary of subjectivity *per se* (cf. 1994:66). And on exactly this point I took my cue when earlier I argued that the vocabulary of *epistemology* should also not just be jettisoned too easily in a revisioning of rationality as transversal or postfoundationalist rationality. Talk about the human subject, then, has now been revisioned and moved from seeing the self as a pure epistemological point, to resituating the human subject in the space of communicative praxis. Thus the notion of transversal rationality opened up the possibility to focus on patterns of discourse and action as they happen in our communicative practices, rather than focusing only on the structure of the self, ego, or subject. It also became clear, however, that transversal rationality is not just a "passage of consciousness" across a wide spectrum of experiences and held together by our memory. It is, rather, a lying across, extending over, and intersecting of various forms of discourse, modes of thought, and action. Transversal rationality thus emerged as a place in time and space where our multiple beliefs and practices, our habits of thought and attitudes, our prejudices and assessments, converge.

In interdisciplinary conversation the degree of transversality achieved depends on the effectiveness of our dialogue across different domains and different meanings. What is at stake in this notion of a transversal rationality is to discover, or reveal, the shared resources of human rationality precisely in our very pluralist, diverse assemblages of beliefs or practices, and then to locate the claims of reason in the transversal passage or overlaps of rationality between groups, discourses, or reasoning strategies. This is exactly what Calvin Schrag meant when he argued that reason is operative in the transversal play of thought and action in the guise of three interrelated moments/phases of communicative praxis, i.e., evaluative critique, engaged articulation, and incursive disclosure (cf. 1994:69ff.). For Schrag, as we saw, the adjective "praxial" qualifies all three of these moments, and distinguishes the operation of rationality as critique, articulation, and disclosure from the theory-grounded, subject-centered paradigm of modernity. This clearly involves a radical shift from a focus on thought and experience as a-contextual systems of belief, to an acknowledgment of the relocation of thought, experience, and belief systems in our assemblages of social practices (cf. 1994:69). In this move the concepts of theory and practice are themselves refigured: theory is here no longer viewed as a system of a priori rules and principles, and practice is liberated from its subordination as a mere application of theory. What now emerged was a third option, the third dimension of *praxis,* which indicates a fusion of thought and action that displays its own discernment, insight, and disclosure, no longer needing a transcendental ego or a system of rules to swoop down from on high.

The implications of the notion of transversal rationality, however, went even further than this. Schrag also distinguished between *discursive* (the performance of articulation in language and conversation) and *nondiscursive* practices. The latter specifically refers to the performance of rationality beyond the realm of language and the spoken word. Thus, "as there is a time and space for discourse, so there is a time and space of action, mood, desire, bodily and institutional inscriptions — a vast arena of *nondiscursive* dispositions and practices that also exhibit an articulatory function" (Schrag 1992:83). Our actions, desires, and emotions are all ways of also understanding and articulating ourselves and our world(s). And in this sense, what Schrag calls the event or articulation lies transversally across both our discursive and nondiscursive actions in time and space. Thus our experiences as "events of interpretation" are always situated temporally and spatially (cf. 1992:83). And it is at this point that Schrag appropriates Russian philosopher and historian Mikhail Bakhtin's notion of the *chronotope* as the marker of the intrinsic connectedness of time and space: but not, then, portrayed as an *a priori* and abstract form of perception, but rather as concrete dwellings for our varied discourses. In this concrete sense, time and space become vitalized and vibrant as existential dwellings rather than as dead frames of reference. Most importantly, when we take the radical situatedness of our existence seriously in this sense, a multiplicity of language games and cultural domains come into play as we attempt to articulate our situatedness in historical time and historical space. In this sense one could say that the texts of our discourses always remain embedded in the *con*-texts — scientific, moral, legal, economic, aesthetic, and religious — from which they emerge (cf. Schrag 1992:84).

In this way, then, a postfoundationalist notion of rationality enables us to retain the language of epistemology by fusing it with hermeneutics. Our different genres of discourse can now certainly be identified by our making of scientific claims, moral statements, aesthetic evaluations, religious judgments, and theological assessments, or by our participating in the praxis of prayer. This determination of whether a certain discourse should be recognized as scientific, ethical, political, aesthetical, or religious, unfolds against the background of a wide spectrum of social practices and linguistic usages. But such an understanding is never complete, because it always again is threatened by ambiguity. In this sense it is the task of explanation to focus on the more detailed parts of discourse and to provide an analytical explication of their functions, but always while aware of the role of these specific functions within the gestalt of discourse as an emergent whole. It is thus that understanding and explanation move to and fro between whole and part, enabling understanding and explanation to work together side by side as twin halves of the same interpretative event, enabling us to understand as we explain and explain as we understand (cf. Schrag 1992:86).

This discussion gives new depth to the important notion of *transversal rationality*. The modern epistemological paradigm, as we saw, was typified by claims for universality. The postmodern challenge typically calls into question any search for universals: instead of a "God's-eye view," a perspective from the other side of history, we are offered only a fragmented vision from this side of history that typically leaves us with a complete relativization of all forms of thought and all contents of culture. Schrag's response to this has been the pursuit of a third option, i.e., the "splitting of the difference" between modernity and postmodernity. In this move the postmodern problematization of the classical and modern claims for universality is embraced, but then postmodernism is used against itself by showing how the figure of transversality can more productively address the issues at hand. On this view, therefore, transversality replaces universality (cf. Schrag 1994:75). On this view, too, the knowing subject is not just jettisoned, but is refigured in a praxial performance of critique, articulation, and disclosure. As we discover the resources of reason in transversal/postfoundationalist rationality, modernist epistemology finally has to make room for a fusion of a refigured epistemology and hermeneutics in postfoundationalist rationality.

Transversal/postfoundationalist rationality thus enables us to shuttle in the space between modernity and postmodernity: the space of interpreted experience and communicative praxis which enables praxial critique, articulation, and disclosure. Here, finally, transcontextual, even transhistorical judgments and assessments can be made without gravitating into an empty universalization on the one hand, or a pluralism of culture-spheres, particularized language games, and relativized moral claims on the other hand (cf. Schrag 1994:75). A postfoundationalist notion of rationality thus creates a safe space where our different discourses and actions are seen at times to link up with one another, and at times to contrast or conflict with one another. It is precisely in the hard struggle for interpersonal and interdisciplinary communication that the many faces of human rationality are revealed in critique, articulation, and disclosure. A postfoundationalist notion of rationality thus yields the kind of shared rational space that David Tracy has rightly called *an authentic public realm:* a shared rational space where all participants, whatever their other particular differences, can meet to discuss any claim that is rationally redeemable (cf. Tracy 1992:19).

On this view transhistorical judgments and interdisciplinary assessments, therefore, are still possible, and indeed required, thanks to the transversal play of our social practices, our webs of belief, and our societal engagements, which demand from us an ongoing response to that which is said and done. It is this "performance of the fitting response" (cf. Schrag 1994:76), the practice of responsible judgment, that is at the heart of a postfoundationalist notion of rationality, and that enables us — through the strategies of critical discernment, articulation, and disclosure — to reach fragile and provisional forms of coherence in our interpersonal and interdisciplinary conversations.

Hopefully it has now become clear that in my mind theological reflection too will find its identity only as a reasoning strategy in an ongoing, if not tenacious, public dialogue with contemporary culture. And, as we saw earlier, an all-important focus for this dialogue with our contemporary culture is indeed found in two seemingly unrelated issues: on the one hand, the tremendous problems that would arise if theology should choose to abandon its cross-contextual and interdisciplinary obligations and retreat to the insular comfort of its own preferred tradition in an exclusivist theological isolationism; and on the other hand, contemporary theology's uneasy relationship with what is often perceived to be a superior scientific rationality. Both of these challenges, however, now look different when we realize that not only theology but also contemporary science — as we saw earlier — has been profoundly influenced by postmodern culture. This gave an unexpected and complicating twist not only to the problem of interdisciplinarity, but also to the question how different modes of reflection may relate to the traditions they are embedded in: not only theology, but also postmodern science and postmodern philosophy of science have moved away quite dramatically from positivist and technocentric conceptions of scientific rationality, with its closely aligned beliefs in linear progress, objectivity, guaranteed success, deterministic predictability, absolute truths, and some uniform, standardized form of knowledge. As we saw earlier, some contemporary philosophers of science now explicitly argue for a postmodern philosophy of science that, along with feminist interpretations of science, rejects all global interpretations of science as well as the power-play implied by scientific progress. The focus, instead, is on trust in local, contextual scientific practice (cf. Rouse 1991a).

However, this kind of postmodernism turned out to not only sharply deconstruct and reject the autonomy and cultural dominance of especially the natural sciences as the accepted paradigm for rationality in our time, but also to seriously challenge and deconstruct any attempt to develop a meaningful and intelligible relationship between the sciences and Christian theology today. In this extreme form, postmodernism, as a complex phenomenon with a clear-cut option for pluralism and diversity (cf. D. Harvey 1989:9ff.), often indeed seems to leave both theology and the sciences fragmented. It is in the

251

rich resources of a postfoundationalist notion of rationality, however, that we have discerned an answer to one of the most perplexing challenges we had to deal with: how to meaningfully relate the fragmented, specialized world of contemporary science to the equally fragmented intellectual world of contemporary theology. It is to the ramifications of this proposal that we now turn.

Rationality and Tradition

With the advent of postmodern thought we all witnessed the spectacular collapse of the classical model of rationality as well as the demise of various forms of foundationalism, metanarratives, and positivist philosophies. The movement from confidence to skepticism about the foundations of our knowledge claims, our methods, and our rational criteria of evaluation has indeed not been limited to philosophy alone (cf. Bernstein 1983:3f.). Furthermore, this kind of postmodern challenge not only makes it impossible to speak in general, a-contextual terms about "theology," "God," "tradition," "rationality," or "science": it finally is rationality itself that has been fundamentally challenged and problematized by postmodernism.

Whatever notion of postmodernity we eventually opt for, all postmodern thinkers see the modernist quest for epistemic certainty, and the accompanying program of laying foundations for our knowledge, as a dream for the impossible, a contemporary version of the quest for the Holy Grail (cf. Schrag 1989:84; cf. van Huyssteen 1998a:216). Postmodern thinkers from Foucault to Rorty have also coupled this deconstruction of the epistemological paradigm of modern philosophy with a marked recognition of the contextual and social resources of rationality. On this view human reason no longer issues from an isolate, epistemic consciousness, but unfolds in a variety of sociopolitical functions in a focused attention for the marginalized, that which is left out and those who are constructed as the other (cf. Rossouw 1993:902). Michel Foucault in particular, in his celebrated attack on a totalizing and hierarchical rationality, has made much of "regimes of knowledge" as forms of social practices that reflect — consciously or unconsciously — certain power relations within the existing social order. For Foucault it is precisely *tradition,* and the progressivist perspective of uninterrupted continuity we project onto

252

it, which preserves the power relations that underlie all conventions and oppressions (cf. Foucault 1980:89). For Foucault, power is the fundamental characteristic of human culture and tradition, and as such produces knowledge. But power and knowledge are so integrated with one another that there would be no point in dreaming of a time when knowledge will cease to depend on power: it is not possible for power to be exercised without knowledge, and it is impossible for knowledge not to engender power (cf. Foucault 1980:52). What is clear, however, is his sharp criticism of all thinking that situates itself in the context of an ongoing, continuous tradition (cf. Byrne 1992:335). In his own words: "I adopt the methodical precaution and the radical but unaggressive skepticism which makes it a principle not to regard the point in time where we are now standing as the outcome of a teleological progression which it would be one's business to reconstruct historically" (Foucault 1980:49).

Clearly, one of the most distinguishing characteristics of the "postmodern" is precisely the crisis of continuity which now disrupts the accepted relationship between an event and a tradition that gains its stability from that relationship. The writings of Michel Foucault offer a vivid picture of precisely the kind of postmodern thinking that seeks to purge history of any such overtones of metaphysical continuity (cf. Byrne 1992:335). This view of tradition certainly presents a radical challenge to a Christianity that generally tries to live in continuity with the event and person of Jesus Christ, and for whom the relationship to this kind of tradition is based on the witness of Scripture and the preaching and tradition of the church. By seeking to disturb any easy relationship with our past by arguing that our assertion of continuity is itself an invention of our need to control the destiny of our culture and society, a skeptical form of postmodern critique of continuity thus calls into question the very possibility of tradition (cf. Byrne 1992:337).

James Byrne has argued, though, that even Foucault's antimetaphysical critique — while stressing abrupt changes in history — never in fact glorified discontinuity to the extent of denying the continuity of traditions completely (1992:341). In fact, it should be possible to recognize both the continuity and discontinuity of traditions; what is to be rejected is any claim to impose a necessary, modernist, or metaphysical continuity onto history. In this sense tradition is not something we can presume as an ontological datum, but is rather something we create out of the phenomena of history. The same post-foundationalist awareness of the vulnerability and ambiguity of all traditions is found in Delwin Brown's carefully constructed theory of religious traditions. Brown also sees continuity and change as primary categories in the dynamics of tradition, and by acknowledging that the behavior of traditions is fundamentally pragmatic and has to do with survival, power, and legitimation, he argues that tradition creates, sustains, and recreates communal and individual entities (cf. D. Brown 1994:24-28).

This opens up a door, beyond the postmodern crisis of continuity, to theologize with a tradition whose continuity does not have to be guaranteed anymore by a foundationalist metaphysics of history. In this way we are empowered to criticize our traditions while standing in them, but also to allow a particular history to speak for itself without being subsumed under the umbrella of an all-encompassing theory, based on a series of texts and interpretations we have endowed with a particular authority, and which then function as the accepted ideology of a specific community. It is on this view that our traditions, and also our research traditions — those interpretative sets of theories we construct to make sense of the continuities and discontinuities of our traditions — do not at all have to reflect a *consensus of authority*, but can rather, and in a broader sense, be seen as representing a comprehensive *field of concerns* (cf. Rouse 1991b:614) within which both consensus and dissent, continuity and discontinuity acquire coherence and intelligibility (cf. van Huyssteen 1998a:218).

In this very specific sense one can then say that the primary task of the critical theologian is to examine the tradition, not just to repeat it, and through critically examining the tradition to allow the present to be reshaped more closely along the lines of what the tradition truly stands for (cf. Byrne 1992:347). But this critical engagement with traditions (or with research traditions) never happens in epistemic isolation. The postfoundationalist notion of theological rationality for which I am arguing here claims exactly the opposite: we should be able to enter into cross-contextual and interdisciplinary conversations with our strong personal convictions intact, but at the same time be theoretically empowered to reach beyond the boundaries and limitations of our own traditions and forms of life.

If we relate to the past and to our traditions through interpreted experience, and if we accept the fact that the continuity of tradition can no more be a foundationalist premise from which we can deduce other truths, then we have arrived in the pluralist world where many interpretations of the same tradition are alive and well. How, then, do we justify the pragmatic move of choosing for or against a specific commitment, specific theories, and a specific tradition? To try to answer this question adequately, I now want to take the ramifications of this fact — that we relate to our world epistemically only through the medium of interpreted experience — one step further by exploring what it might mean for theology that our interpreted experience is always contextual and as such determined — epistemically and nonepistemically — by living and evolving traditions. In a postfoundationalist context our communicative evaluations, our responsible judgments, and our problem-solving theory choices ultimately constitute the true nature of rational reflection. This implies that not just those beliefs we regard as our rational beliefs, but also those compelling reasons we may want to identify as plausible notions of problem-solving progress, are therefore located within the context of living, changing, and developing traditions. Any time we choose, in our critical relationship to our traditions(s), to modify or replace a theory with another theory, that change is meaningful and progressive if and only if we regard the later version as more compelling, i.e., as a better or more adequate problem-solver than its predecessor (cf. van Huyssteen 1989:172ff.).

On a fallibilist view then, as we saw earlier, the real meaning of intellectual growth or qualified progress is found in our ability to find compelling and good enough reasons for choosing one theory or one framework of ideas above another. Larry Laudan has argued that it is these more general, global theories (research traditions or paradigms), rather than more specific ones, which turn out to be our primary tools for understanding and appraising good/progressive theory choices (cf. Laudan 1977:71f.). These comprehensive or global frameworks of theories, because of the interpreted nature of all human knowledge, form an essential part of the structure of all forms of human cognition, and are as such firmly embedded in specific traditions. Thomas Kuhn called them paradigms, Lakatos called them research programs, and Laudan calls them research traditions. These research traditions are complex and comprehensive theoretical frameworks, and when carefully analyzed always reveal a network of conceptual, theoretical, and metaphysical commitments that give the research tradition its particular identity.

In a sense theology has maybe always known what philosophy of science is again teaching us today: in a pluralist world there is no way that we can claim that these broader traditions, unlike specific theories in, say, the natural sciences, are in any way directly testable or justifiable. This does not mean, however, that they are outside the problem-solving process of our ongoing evaluation of our traditions. Because a progressive or successful research tradition leads one, through its component theories, to what a community may regard as an adequate solution of a broad range of conceptual problems, the tradition itself could claim a very specific form of theoretical and experiential adequacy. The degree of this adequacy, of course, tells us nothing about the truth or falsity of the tradition itself (cf. Laudan 1977:82), but rather points to pragmatic criteria for choosing — through responsible judgment — between frameworks of thought, frameworks that may in reality be very different from one another. In this sense the role of critical judgment in all cognition not only implies a distinctly pragmatic move, but also enables us to retain the idea of intersubjective rational appraisal, and the idea of theoretical adequacy or progress, in a clearly postfoundationalist way.

In theology our research traditions or paradigms, like all other traditions, are historical creatures (cf. D. Brown 1994:24ff.). As such they are created and articulated within a particular intellectual milieu, and like all other historical institutions, they wax and wane (cf. Laudan 1977:95). We saw earlier that in all theological reflection, as in other modes of knowledge, we relate to our worlds epistemically through the medium of interpreted experience. This interpretation of experience, however, always takes place within the comprehensive context of living and evolving traditions, and it is these traditions which are epistemically constituted by broader paradigms or research traditions. Because of their historical nature, research traditions in all modes of human knowledge can change and evolve through either the internal modification of some of their specific theories, or through a change of some of their most basic core elements. Larry Laudan correctly points out that Kuhn's famous notion of a "conversion" or paradigmatic revolution from one paradigm to another (cf. Kuhn 1970:92ff.) can most probably be better described as a natural evolution within and between research traditions. Traditions, however, not only imply ongoing change and evolution, they also exhibit continuity. In this sense, as we saw, it is right to claim that in any adequate theory of traditions, continuity and change would be primary categories (D. Brown 1994:24f.).

To understand what continuity and change might mean in the dynamic of evolving traditions, Larry Laudan — like Lakatos — suggests that certain elements of a research tradition are sacrosanct and can therefore not be rejected without repudiation of the tradition itself. Unlike Lakatos, however, Laudan insists that what is normally seen as sacrosanct in traditions can indeed change with time (cf. Laudan 1977:99). Lakatos and Kuhn were right in thinking that a research tradition or paradigm always has certain nonrejectable elements associated with it. They were, however, mistaken in failing to see that the elements constituting this core can actually shift through time. From this Laudan concludes: "By relativizing the 'essence' of a research tradition with respect to time, we can, I believe, come much closer to capturing the way in which scientists and historians of science actually utilize the concept of tradition" (1977:100).

This not only reveals again the radical historical nature of all research traditions, but reveals also that intellectual and scientific revolutions take place, not necessarily through complete shifts, but through the ongoing integration and the grafting of research traditions. From this we can now glean the following characteristics of research traditions (also cf. D. Brown 1994:44f.; van Huyssteen 1998a: 220f.):

1. Because we belong to history, tradition is constitutive of the present and finally explains why we relate to our world epistemically only through the mediation of interpreted experience.
2. Research traditions — like all traditions — are not reducible to the activities of individuals and groups within them, but neither do they have reality except as they are instantiated by the epistemic communities (the "experts") of specific traditions.
3. Research traditions are dynamic, evolving phenomena that live precisely in the dialectic of continuity and change.
4. Research traditions are never isolated from one another, because the borders separating traditions from their milieus and from other traditions are usually, if not always, exceedingly porous (cf. D. Brown 1994:26).
5. All traditions have sacrosanct elements which, even if they shift or change over time, form the canons of, and define the identity

of traditions. These canons serve as the source of creativity as well as the principle of identity of traditions (cf. D. Brown 1994:45).

These characteristics of research traditions now take us back again to a problem which, while exceedingly difficult for theology to deal with, has become impossible to ignore if we want to make the epistemological move beyond both the extremes of foundationalism and nonfoundationalism: If the context of tradition is the ultimate destiny for human rationality, are we then ultimately, and fideistically, the prisoners of our research traditions and commitments? Any uncritical retreat to, or fideist commitment (cf. Bartley 1964) to, a specific tradition would seriously jeopardize the epistemic status of theological reflection as a credible partner in a pluralist, interdisciplinary conversation. Within a fideist context all commitment and religious faith seems to be irrevocably arbitrary. But the most serious limitation to any fideist epistemology, however, would be its complete inability to explain why we choose certain viewpoints, certain networks of belief, certain traditions over others. Surely, there must be more to the using of religious language than just understanding and adopting the internal workings of some specialized linguistic system that is not answerable to anything or anybody outside itself (cf. Frankenberry 1987:13). There also should be more to the making of commitments than just being embedded in traditions that can never be questioned. Theology's critical relation to tradition thus shows us that all religious and theological language are indeed human conventions, the result of creative intellectual construction, which — along with the commitments they serve to express — should be examined and critiqued too.

A theology that takes seriously its embeddedness in postfoundationalist rationality moves out of the protective shelter of all forms of fideism and on to a location in the interdisciplinary discussion, where it *ipso facto* will be challenged to cross-contextual explanations. This kind of interdisciplinary dialogue will be possible precisely because our different discourses share the rich resources of human rationality. But in the specific contexts where our varied discourses unfold, the standards for rational reflection will indeed be domain specific and definitively shaped by the nature of these discourses. For this reason interdisciplinary reflection will demand of us the strenuous task of keeping in mind the different forms of interpreted experience, and thus the different forms of explanation that operate in different discourses and disciplines. I have argued elsewhere that in theological reflection the theological explanation of religious beliefs obviously plays a central role (cf. van Huyssteen 1997a:231ff.). Religious beliefs of course have many important functions for the believer. As beliefs they describe the rites and practices of believing communities, express psychological and sociological needs in the language of faith, and also answer philosophical questions in religious terms. In short, religious beliefs help to explain the world and the place of believers in it. In doing this, religious beliefs reflect a general sense of meaningfulness on the part of the believer, a meaningfulness that extends from an existential level to the level of particular theories and dogmas (cf. Clayton 1989:1f.). But on a postfoundationalist view, where hermeneutics and epistemology are fused so closely, of central importance among the various functions of religious beliefs is the fact that they obviously *explain* something.

In the light of the postmodern challenge, the question as to whether or not there is some unitary theory of explanation that would allow us to speak of "explanation" in the singular when referring to the broader spectrum of academic disciplines, has obviously become a moot one. But if theology and the sciences share the rich resources of human rationality, then it is to be expected that there will be important parallels between the role of explanation in the sciences and in theology. However significant these parallels might be, religious and theological explanations do have unique aspects as well: they are normally all-encompassing and deeply personal, they often arise from vague and elusive questions concerning the meaning of life, and as religious answers they provide ultimate meaning in life. Religious, and eventually theological, explanations thus provide a context of security for the believer and also involve a faith commitment to God. This implies that both the scope and content of theological explanations may set them apart from explanations in other areas. In assessing the explanatory role of religious experience and beliefs we therefore should assess the continuities as well as the discontinuities between theological and other types of explanations. Scientific explanations, of course, are never completely impersonal, but they are usually capable of achieving a high degree of interpersonal agreement. Art and ethics are much more personal than science and as such may not represent areas in which a high degree of agreement is attainable. Even more personal is the realm of religious experience, where also the refracting influence of culture is always powerfully present (cf. Polkinghorne 1991:54).

The central goal of natural scientific theories is to explain the empirical world. To call an explanation "scientific" is to say that the explanation draws on science for its information, and that the criteria of evaluation for an explanation are applied, using a scientific theory (cf. van Fraassen 1989:156). Theories of explanation, however, have been directly influenced by important shifts in the discussion of natural scientific rationality, especially since the advent of Thomas S. Kuhn's revolutionary paradigm theory (cf. van Huyssteen 1989:47-70). This contextualist shift in the philosophy of the natural sciences clearly indicates a very specific hermeneutical awareness, as well as the realization that even criteria for scientific explanation function only within a particular paradigm. Seen in the light of this contextualist shift, later so much more intensified by postmodern philosophy of science, the unique role of explanation in science is indeed relativized and should be seen as an important element within the broader hermeneutical task of science (cf. Clayton 1989:39).

In the social and human sciences a long and learned tradition has opposed explanation to empathic understanding. Explanation in the social sciences, however, does not need to be downplayed in the light of the broader hermeneutical purpose of the social and human sciences. It also would be incorrect to claim that the social and human sciences, because of their subject matter, are more subjective than the natural sciences: the role of subjective factors in the formulation of natural as well as social scientific explanations is today widely accepted. We already saw that not only in theology, but also in the social, human, and natural sciences, the subjectivity of interpreting belongs right in the heart of the explanatory task. On another level, the explanatory task in the social sciences is closer to explanations in theology than to explanations in the natural sciences. Both in the social and human sciences and in theology the object of research is itself already symbolically structured, mainly as a result of a long and ongoing history of interpretation. Therefore, if all science is hermeneutical, then in the human and social sciences, and especially in the history of theological ideas, we encounter what some scholars have called a "double hermeneutic" of having to interpret again the already preinterpreted world of our experience (cf. Clayton 1989:88). To therefore summarize some of our earlier conclusions: from this we may conclude that explanation — whether in the natural, social or human sciences, or in theology — is always a form of rational reconstruction, that rational thought is never purely objective, that context greatly influences the interpretative theoretical process, and that any research program and its explanations can only be partially evaluated at any given time.

Our quest for some form of interdisciplinary consonance between theology and the sciences thus brings us to the need for philosophical explanations. Philosophical explanations, like other explanations, aim to address and coherently answer some specific question. They are philosophical in that they are not limited in scope to any particular discipline, or aspect of experience (cf. Clayton 1989:104). In trying to understand the explanatory role of religious experiences and the interpreted beliefs that shape them, it is important to note that religious explanations share some very significant features with philosophical explanations. The most important of these are their greater generality or depth and an emphasis on systematic coherence and meaningfulness.

For philosophical and religious (and eventually also theological) explanations, both context and the coherence of our networks of belief are of prime importance. Therefore, when we reflect on a portion of our experience, it is possible to locate this reflection on a specific problem within an ever-broadening horizon of contexts until we reach a context that reaches out to the whole of human experience. At this level, one is involved in making sense of total experience, and this broadest context could be labeled metaphysical or religious. Within this broader context of religious experience, Philip Clayton (1989:5, 113ff.) has identified at least three types or forms of explanation:

1. Private explanations: these explanations are warranted solely by the fact that they make sense of experience for the individual believer. Private explanations can be quite comprehensive in scope and can account for broad areas of human experience, but the justification of these explanations is rooted in personal evaluation only.
2. Communal explanations: here the standards of adequate explanations are set by the particular believing and practicing community.
3. Intersubjective or transcommunal explanations: this category of

explanation supposes that even religious beliefs can be accounted for in a way that transcends the boundaries of the individual or the religious community in interdisciplinary and cross-contextual dialogue.

The importance of these distinctions for theology is apparent: any comparison between theology and the sciences would be meaningful only if some form of transcommunal or interdisciplinary explanation is at least one viable form of epistemic accountability in theological reflection. As far as theological explanations go then, theologians should first and foremost beware of the fideist misconstrual where religious faith is seen as evidence for the truth of religious or theological propositions. Faith — as the "heart" of religion — implies a total commitment to the object of one's belief. In the context of rational argumentation, however, faith does not make the object of faith more probable and thus should not be seen as an epistemic virtue, nor, of course, as an epistemic vice (cf. Clayton 1989:143). It now becomes clear that the believer's effort to understand and come to terms with her or his faith displays a structure quite similar to what we earlier identified as a strictly scientific rationality. Seen against this background, theological explanations attempt to establish a link between the inherited beliefs and practices of a specific religious tradition and the contemporary experience of its adherents (cf. van Huyssteen 1997a:231ff.). These explanations arise out of traditioned experience and can be phrased in terms of traditional doctrines, the practices (liturgies and rites) of a religious community, and its norms or codes of behavior; or they can be constructed in terms of the broader intellectual, social, and ethical intersubjective life-experience of believers.

As such, theological explanations function to continually ensure a tradition's relevance to the challenges posed by contemporary contextual questions. Philip Clayton is therefore right when he states that theology is not primarily a descriptive (first order) but an explanatory (second order) endeavor. There are indeed good reasons for theology to pursue explanatory adequacy and academic excellence (1989:149). All theological explanations should therefore be open to intersubjective examination and criticism, which means that theological statements should at all times be construed as hypotheses (cf. van Huyssteen 1989:143ff.). And since all attempts to clarify Christian beliefs necessarily involve dependence on categories not drawn from the Christian tradition, as well as the use of general notions such as truth, meaning, coherence, and reference, Christian theology will always find itself in necessary discourse with other theologies, and with the science and philosophy of its time.

The theology and science discussion in a very specific way reveals how the explanatory role of interpreted experience in theology can only be adequately accounted for in terms of a postfoundationalist notion of rationality. This not only means that religious experience is better explained theologically, but that in explaining the role of experience, the philosophical theologian will have to move from the question of rationality to intelligibility, from intelligibility to the question of personal understanding, and from personal understanding to personal experience. This is something the scientist need never do. Dealing with personal commitment in this way may show that the rationality of theology is often shaped by values different from those of science. However, the dependence of theology on experiential adequacy for determining and maintaining its explanatory adequacy need never again mean that theology is less rational than the sciences. The nature of the ongoing discussion between theology and the sciences should help us to realize that the complex relationship between scientific and religious epistemology, in spite of the promising emergence of new interdisciplinary studies, is more challenging than ever. But a postfoundationalist notion of rationality that respects the uniqueness of standards of rationality in theology and the sciences, respectively, now reveals that sciences are eminently competent when it comes to theory construction and to experimental and justificatory enterprises, but they are incompetent when it comes to finding answers to our deepest religious questions.

In a cross-disciplinary conversation the fundamental differences between theology and the sciences should therefore be respected. This includes the different forms of explanation not only in the different sciences, but also between theology and the other sciences. However, in spite of important differences and sometimes radically different levels of explanation, theology and science do share — as we have now seen extensively — the rich resources of rationality. A theology and a science that come to discover this kind of mutual quest for intelligibility in spite of important differences will also be freed to discover that nothing that is part of, or the result of, natural scientific explanation, need ever be logically incompatible with theological reflection. In recognizing the importance of the natural sciences, we should then have an openness for that which reaches beyond the world of the natural sciences, i.e., to those aspects of our world on which the social sciences, history, philosophy, and theology all focus. In this wider context we could discover that theology and science, as two of our most important modes of inquiry, share not only a mutually enriching quest for intelligibility, but — each in their own way — also the importance of tradition and of the explanatory role of interpreted experience. An honest analysis of the differences between the sciences and between theological and scientific explanations might then yield more intelligibility in our attempts to understand our postmodern world as truly God's own world.

Against this background, we are again confronted with an unavoidable question: Why then do we choose to commit ourselves — often passionately — only to certain explanations, certain theories, certain traditions, and certain viewpoints? In trying to answer these complex and challenging questions, I will argue that, *first,* we should be able to enter the pluralist, interdisciplinary conversation between disciplines and research traditions with our full personal convictions intact, while at the same time reaching beyond the strict boundaries of our own intellectual contexts; *second,* we should indeed be able to justify our choices for or against a specific research tradition in interdisciplinary conversation. As we saw earlier, the fact that our broader research traditions can as such never be directly tested or justified does not mean that they are outside the problem-solving process.

Rationality and Interdisciplinarity

In his recent *Boundaries of Our Habitations: Tradition and Theological Construction,* Delwin Brown takes up some of these same issues and proposes a constructive historicism where theology retrieves its transcontextual obligation precisely by being *the caregiver of tradition* (1994:111-55). Seeing tradition as the matrix of creative theological reflection may help us to develop a form of theological thinking that would be both culturally and religiously more effective, by achieving an integration of inheritance and imagination, continuity and discontinuity, in a theological reflection that is as adequate as possible. The central theme of Brown's book thus explores the idea that tradition is one type of cultural strategy, one way of negotiating chaos and order, or — as I would put it — one way of facilitating responsible critical judgment in our theory choices.

I believe Delwin Brown's important views on transcontextual conversation and evaluation will be significantly enhanced when supported by the kind of postfoundationalist epistemology I have outlined above. It also relates closely to what Andy F. Sanders has recently called "traditionalist fallibilism" (1995). On this view tradition is acknowledged, not just as part of our background knowledge, but as the main source of our knowledge. In cross-contextual conversation the background of beliefs, commitments, and expectations — as embedded in our tradition(s) — is taken to be something more than a common platform to start our inquiries from. This "more" consists in the trust in and the reliance on the traditions in terms of which we define our lives (cf. van Huyssteen 1998a:224). This does not only mean that we practice our shared trades of theologies, the sciences, humanities, and philosophy in the light of their respective disciplinary traditions, but also that we rely on a complex variety of political, moral, and religious traditions to define and shape our lives.

For theology, then, being part of the interdisciplinary conversation would mean at least the following: we begin our conversations by bringing our fallible views and judgments to those who traditionally make up our epistemic communities. In a postfoundationalist evaluation of the beliefs, opinions, and viewpoints in which our commitments are embedded, the epistemic movement thus goes from individual judgment to communal evaluation to intersubjective conversation. Because each judgment and each rhetorical argument always takes place in some community, and each community has a particular tradition and history, the broader research tradition(s) in which communities are embedded will now epistemically shape (but not completely determine) the questions one asks, the assumptions one can make, and the arguments one will find persuasive. For theology, this interdisciplinary location not only opens the way to genuine conversation, but also reveals a judgment about how theology should be done and the criteria to which theological claims should be obligated. Delwin Brown puts a similar conclusion succinctly: theology, even specifically Christian theology, is answerable to canons of critical inquiry defensible within the various arenas of our common discourse, and not merely within those that are Christian (cf. D. Brown 1994:4f.).

The fact that there are no more foundationalist, universal, cross-cultural, or interreligious rules for theology also does not necessarily mean that all the criteria we employ in the task of doing theology are now always going to be strictly local or exclusively contextual. If none of our criteria were to be acceptable beyond the boundaries of a specifically chosen research tradition, the giving of rational reasons beyond the boundaries of any tradition would be impossible (cf. D. Brown 1994:6). The crucial problem for a theology located in interdisciplinary conversation therefore remains the following: Is it at all possible to make sensible and rational choices between different viewpoints and alternative research traditions? At this point Larry Laudan's admonition to scientists and theologians comes to mind: unless we can somehow articulate criteria for choice between research traditions, we neither have a theory of rationality, nor a theory of what progressive growth in knowledge should be (cf. Laudan 1977:106). In theology, as in other forms of inquiry, providing warrants for our views thus becomes a cross-contextual obligation (cf. D. Brown 1994:6f.).

Remarkable parallels have surfaced here between theology and other modes of knowledge. A good example is again found in modes of knowledge as different as theology and the sciences. In both of these reasoning strategies we are required to trust our traditions as we reach out beyond them in interdisciplinary conversation. Earlier, in our discussion of Joseph Rouse's response to the postmodern challenge in the sciences, we saw that the intelligibility, significance, and justification of scientific knowledge stem from the fact that it already belongs to quite specific research traditions which yield continually reconstructed narrative contexts supplied by the ongoing social practices of scientific research (cf. Rouse 1990:181). Scientific knowledge on this view clearly and fundamentally is *local* knowledge, situated in the praxis of specific traditions. Through experimentation scientists artificially create "microworlds" in their laboratories which enable them to isolate, manipulate, and monitor phenomena, and to construct theories with which to reciprocally interpret these microworlds. Rouse also argued that the belief that scientific knowledge is always nonlocal, universal knowledge, arises from its wide technological applicability and the universal dissemination of scientific research in scientific literature. Scientific knowledge, however, is always first of all local knowledge, and whatever universal applicability it may then attain arises not from some form of theoretical or universal decontextualization that may be seen to be typical of scientific knowledge, but rather from a process of "standardization" (cf. Rouse 1987:113). In science, as in theology, we therefore find a general trusting attitude toward local contexts of practice, and what this trust is about is a deeper trust in the narratives and traditions of a specific discipline, where these are understood, not as an imposed consensus of authority, but rather as a creative field of concerns.

In both theology and the sciences, so deeply embedded in praxis, we should therefore be able to identify some criteria to warrant our theory choices, and neither scientific nor theological knowledge can ever claim demonstrably certain foundations for making these choices. Epistemic similarities between theology and the sciences do not mean, of course, that scientific knowledge is "just like" theology, but it does mean that methods in science do not provide a uniquely rational and objective way of discovering truth. In both theology and science good arguments should therefore be offered for or against theory choice, for or against commitment to a tradition, and for or against the problem-solving ability of a research program. Obviously, our good arguments and value judgments rest on broader assumptions and commitments that can always again be challenged. This does not mean, however, that any opinion is as good as any other, or that we can never compare radically different points of view (cf. Placher 1989:51).

The postfoundationalist challenge always to critique our own foundationalist assumptions certainly means that there are no universal standards of rationality against which we can measure other beliefs or competing research traditions. The fact that we lack a clear and "objective" criterion for judging the experiential adequacy or problem-solving ability of one tradition over another, however, should not leave us with a radical relativism, or even with an easy pluralism. Our ability to make rational judgments and share them with various and different epistemic communities also means that we are able to communicate with one another meaningfully through conversation, deliberation, and evaluation in an ongoing process of collective assessment. Sharing our views and judgments with those inside and outside our epistemic communities can therefore lead to a truly postfoundationalist conversation, which we should enter not just to persuade, but also to learn from. Such a style of inquiry can provide a way of thinking about rationality that respects authentic pluralism — it does not force us all to agree or to ever share the same assumptions, but it finds ways we can talk with one another and criticize our traditions while standing in them.

The way toward a responsible epistemic pluralism is enhanced if we briefly recall the experiential basis of rationality, and the fact that we always relate to our world(s) through interpreted experience. As we saw earlier in Chapter Three, in a postfoundationalist notion of rationality the predicate "rational" first of all characterizes an individual's responsible decisions and beliefs, not propositions as such, nor communities. Even if — as in science — a community of experts is necessary for an individual to arrive at a rational belief, it still first of all is the individual's belief that is rational, and not the community as such (H. Brown 1990:193). In a postfoundationalist notion of rationality, those agents who exercise responsible judgments are therefore central to rational procedures, and it is the fallibility of these agents' judgments that leads to the requirement of ongoing critical evaluation by others. And, as we saw earlier, it is precisely this resituation of critique and communal judgment within the spaces of our communicative practices, that Calvin Schrag has called *praxial critique* (Schrag 1992:57f.). In a postfoundationalist theology it is precisely the much neglected role of personal, responsible judgment and discernment in rational decision-making that will be retrieved as crucially important, but always within the larger context of the community. And because of the way we exercise our value judgments, as well as choose and construct our theories, the mediating role of our interpreted experience was revealed as crucial for the process that leads to rational judgment, even if we cannot always capture the complexity of interpreted human experience in exact propositions.

An important dimension of a postfoundationalist notion of rationality was therefore revealed when it became clear that rationality not only involves evaluation against the standards of a community of inquiry, but also and precisely assures that the personal voice of the individual rational agent is not silenced in this ongoing process of collective assessment (cf. van Huyssteen 1998b:29). The rationality of a given claim is indeed to be found in an ongoing process of collective assessment, but at the same time there is no reason to hold that *any* presently existing community fully represents a rational agent's sense of what a community is or should be (cf. Clayton and Knapp 1993:152). What was forcefully revealed in our earlier discussion of this issue is precisely the very specific limits of communal rationality, when — for instance — a visionary, a genius, or a prophet relies almost exclusively on the standards of an as-yet-nonexistent communal rationality. This also again reveals the richness of the resources of human rationality, as the cognitive, pragmatic, and evaluative dimensions of rationality merge in the rational agent's own reasons for believing, acting, and judging. This means that our good reasons for making certain judgments, which will lead to certain strong convictions which will and should be critically evaluated in our epistemic community's ongoing process of collective assessment, are first of all evaluated against the standards implicit in each rational agent's *self-conception* (cf. Clayton and Knapp 1993:152). By recognizing how a rational agent's personal judgments, beliefs, and actions are shaped by his or her self-conception, we were truly moved beyond any modernist attempts to argue for a universal, rule-governed, general account of human rationality. As human beings we are characterized by self-awareness, and our individual, personal motivations or reasons for believing, acting, and choosing are not only closely tied in with some sense of who this "I" is, but are indeed epistemically shaping the value judgments we make in terms of this self-conception.

The key to understanding a postfoundationalist notion of rationality is therefore found in exactly the fact that the human (rational) self can partake in and live through a plurality of language games and disciplinary or cultural domains, precisely while holding on to a sense of self-identity — a sense of this same self being present to its self in its remembered past, its engaged present, and its projected future. The rational agent is, therefore, as Calvin Schrag would put it, present to itself as it shifts from one genre of discourse and one language game to another (cf. 1997:33). We also saw earlier that the individual's self-conception and self-awareness not only is intrinsically connected to rationality, but it is indeed an indispensable starting point for any account of the values that shape human rationality. In the absence of the availability of modernist rules, metanarratives, or transcendental standards for rationality, each of us is left with only one viable option: in assessing what rationality is, I must assess it as I see it, from where I stand. As a human being with a distinct self-awareness, and a very specific quest for intelligibility, I can step into the reality of communicative praxis/praxial critique only from where I stand, and begin any intersubjective conversation only by appealing to *my* rationality (cf. Rescher 1993:110). Thus not only rationality and context, but also rationality and strong personal commitments inextricably go together. And as long as I participate in a rationally conscientious way in the back and forth of the feedback process that makes up our communal discourse, I am rationally justified in holding on to my commitments and strong convictions.

As a rational agent I can therefore enter any conversation — also our interdisciplinary conversations — only from my own perspective on what the rational explanation of the diverse dimensions of our experience is. It does *not* follow from this, as we have seen, that for my standards to be rational, they should ultimately always be in agreement with those of others who are differently situated (cf. Rescher 1993:110). As we saw earlier, the belief that consensus or interpersonal agreement plays a leading role in matters of rational inquiry, and in the way we come to our decisions and judgments, is among the oldest and most pervasive ideas in philosophy. However, on precisely this point Nicholas Rescher has convincingly argued that diversity and dissensus can often play a highly constructive role in our communal discourses, and that rationality thus does not necessarily have to lead to consensus. It is therefore rational to optimize our choices rhetorically by providing the best available reasons for our beliefs, actions, and choices. *Vis-à-vis* all our attempts to attain a uniformity of consensus as interpersonal agreement, Rescher has argued instead for a legitimate pluralism of diversity: the fact that different people have different experiential situations makes it normal, natural, and rational that they should proceed differently in cognitive, evaluative, and practical matters. In this sense consensus is revealed as (at most) an ideal and not a realizable "fact of life" (cf. Rescher 1993:9). As rational agents we are embedded in and live out of concrete contexts and traditions, and the diversity of our traditions will yield a diversity of experiences, epistemic situations, cognitive values, and methodologies. Consensus is therefore not a prerequisite for, nor a necessary consequence of, rationality. It also never is the "highway to truth" (cf. Rescher 1993:52).

Also in interpersonal and interdisciplinary conversation, rationality therefore does not presuppose consensus. The epistemic tolerance that should emerge from this pluralism flows from the experiential and contextual nature of human rationality, and should never lead to relativistic indifference. Precisely at this point it can be argued that when it comes to making good rational choices for the right reasons, all perspectives that are taken to be normative are *not* going to be equally acceptable. If the experiential bases and the values that shape our judgments are at issue, then the patterns of our own ongoing, contextualized experience are going to be altogether decisive — for us at any rate — in communal discourse. And because rationality requires that we attune our beliefs and judgments to our own self-conception and self-awareness, rationality also requires that we attune our beliefs, convictions, and evaluations to the overall pattern of our experience. On this view it should be clear that a postfoundationalist notion of rationality could never be some kind of superimposed metanarrative, but rather develops as an emerging pattern that unifies our interpreted experience without totalizing it (cf. Schrag 1992:154ff.). In this sense, the claim that rationality is always embedded in the rational agent's self-awareness also implies that one's own experience is always going to be rationally compelling (Rescher 1993:119).

This notion of a postfoundationalist rationality clearly takes a stand against any easy relativism, or relativistic individualism, and defends the fact that it is rationally appropriate to take up a definite and committed position in interpersonal and interdisciplinary conversation. In this way not only the dogmatic absolutism of all forms of foundationalism is avoided, but also the indifferent relativism of extreme forms of postmodernist relativism that would imprison every position we take in the isolated context of personal interests, matters of taste, and group custom. *Vis-à-vis* the uniformity promised by consensus, Nicholas Rescher too has argued for a legitimate diversity of opinions in conversation, a diversity where cooperation and coordination would still be possible — and rational! — even in the face of disagreement over facts and values (cf. Rescher 1993:2ff.). The fact that different people have different experiential situations indeed makes it normal, natural, and rational that they should proceed differently in cognitive, evaluative, and practical matters. Constructive interaction should therefore be possible as we learn to acquiesce in difference, i.e., come to terms with the fact that others will not only differ from us in their opinions, customs, evaluations, and modes of action, but that it is perfectly rational for them to do so. For theologians this "consensus downgrading" should be liberating and energizing: also in theological reflection — in spite of a shared commitment to the Christian faith — consensus in general is in fact unattainable. What we should learn to do in our interpersonal and cross-disciplinary conversations, therefore, is to constructively manage dissensus, to accept the rationality of a healthy pluralism and the fact that diversity can play a highly constructive role in human affairs (cf. Rescher 1993:5f.).

The fact that different human minds, in and across different domains and disciplines, share in the same resources of human rationality does not therefore mean that rational persons must ultimately reach agreement on all meaningful issues. Rescher convincingly argues that rationality ultimately consists in effecting an appropriate alignment between our beliefs and the way we experience "bodies of evidence" differently: different individuals will generally confront different bodies of evidence and will accordingly — through responsible judgment — evaluate it differently. This kind of "perspectival pluralism" thus reveals consensus or agreement as at most an ideal, but as not morally or epistemically necessary for our commitment to rationality. The diversity of our traditions, our experiences, our epistemic situations, and cognitive values, of our disciplinary domains and methodologies, all make for a difference in the beliefs, judgments, and evaluations of otherwise perfectly rational people (cf. Rescher 1993: 9ff.). Our moral obligation is therefore not first of all to coordinate our beliefs with those of others, but rather with what we, through ongoing critical conversation, have come to accept as correct, right, or true. This kind of intellectual honesty may of course lead to agreement with others; agreement, as such, however, is not something to which we are morally — or rationally — obligated.

In religion — and certainly in theological reflection — the rejection of a "consensus epistemology" and the acceptance of a healthy pluralism is liberating for those of us who are trying to find our ways to one another in cross-contextual conversation. It does, however, also reveal an important difference to the domain of natural scientific reflection. In theology, because of the highly complex and diverse role of religious experience, it is important to move away from consensus as an all-important epistemic instrument. It is clear, however, that in science consensus may indeed play an important role. In especially the natural sciences the quest for consensus has always been a defining characteristic: the justification or verification of claims through the reproducibility of experiments to yield one and the same outcome ultimately warrants the acceptability of scientific results. This kind of communal acceptance certainly represents a touchstone of scientific rationality (cf. Rescher 1993:38f.).

This idea also formed the heart of Joseph Rouse's notion of *standardization:* precisely because of the differences in the way we relate to our worlds through interpreted experience, under- or overdetermination in the natural sciences is dealt with by demanding the robustness of experiments, the verifiability of measurements, and the reproducibility of experiments. Nicholas Rescher has correctly pointed out, however, that these strivings for consensus in the natural sciences, where the scientific community indeed seems to achieve substantial consensus on certain concrete issues, are not to be seen as mechanisms for obtaining truth, but rather as safeguards for eliminating errors. This kind of fallibilism indeed leaves ample room for disagreement and diversity, even in the natural sciences.

Scientific traditions or paradigms can indeed be seen as the product of community consensus, but even so science itself is not first of all about agreement or consensus. In Rescher's words:

> In natural science the answer to existing questions always opens up further questions and leads us into new areas of uncertainty and disagreement. As science "progresses," we do, no doubt, achieve the equilibrium of a consensus on some issues, but this equilibrium is an unstable one because generally as we push our inquiries more deeply we encounter further unresolved and inherently controversial problems. At and near science's creative edge there are always disagreements. (Rescher 1993:39)

The "progress" of science can therefore indeed be seen as an ever-widening area of agreement, but the area of disagreement also increases as the areas near a research frontier always contain controversial issues that may divide the research community into conflicting schools of thought. What we learn from this is that, in spite of the epistemic importance of agreement and consensus in scientific reflection, dissensus or disagreement is always prevalent in science too. Rescher takes the next step and calls the pluralist views generated by this kind of disagreement the lifeblood of science, that as such provides one of the main stimuli to scientific progress (1993:40). On this view not only rational behavior in everyday life, but also the rationality of theological and scientific reflection benefits from the kind of epistemic pluralism that leaves room for disagreement. Clearly the acceptance of this pluralism also implies the embracing of precisely the value of cognitive interaction with others through conversation, controversy, and information-sharing, as well as the probing of the roots of our disagreements with others (cf. Rescher 1993:59).

In the previous chapter I argued at length for the fact that we always relate to our world(s) only though interpreted experience. What now has become clearer is why the experiential basis of rationality unavoidably leads to cognitive diversity and a pluralism of beliefs. We saw earlier that rational inquiry is always a matter of aligning our views with the substance of what we experience: it calls for making responsible judgments that might achieve the most harmonious overall coordination between the information afforded us by our ever-widening range of experiences. What is true for theology is on this level true for science too: in our rational reflection we attune our beliefs, expectations, and evaluations to the course of our ongoing experiences. And experience is something that differs from age to age, culture to culture, person to person. This is what Nicholas Rescher means when he states that a pluralism of cognitive commitments is an unavoidable part of the natural scheme of things (1993:67), and that given the diversity of human experience, empiricism naturally entails pluralism (1993:77). Both for the issue of theological pluralism and for the interdisciplinary conversation between theology and the natural sciences, this has important ramifications: different temporal, historical, and social contexts equip different inquirers with different experiential resources, and the pluralism that results from this is rationally justified. The fact that others may sometimes fundamentally disagree with us should not keep us from having a warranted confidence in the appropriateness and correctness of our own convictions.

The acceptance of cognitive pluralism, therefore, does not imply the suspension of strong convictions and opinions. Our cognitive commitments in theology (and in the sciences) are therefore never mere opinions, but they are, in fact, "fitting responses," the kinds of judgments, as we saw previously, that are inextricably linked to human rationality: a fitting response, as a proper rational judgment, is not to be confused with simple accommodation, but rather involves discernment, evaluation, and critical judgment. This notion of responsible, rational judgment clearly places a premium on context and on the contingency of local and historically specific social practices, without leading to moral or epistemic relativism. We escape this relativism because our criteria, as resources for critical evaluation and grounds for critique, are *conditioned* by historically specific contexts, but they are not completely *determined* by such contexts (cf. Schrag 1997:107). In the making of moral and epistemological judgments in the shared domain of a rational public realm, the distinction between "context-conditioned" and "context-determined" is therefore crucial. Although richly conditioned by its context, human rational thought is nonetheless able to transcend the particularities of its social and historical contexts.

This is the reason I argued earlier that we can critique our traditions while standing in them; and this refusal to be completely determined by a particular tradition, a particular isolated conceptual system, or a particular form of behavior, enables a standpoint of critique that delivers us from the kind of relativism in which all interpretations and perspectives are granted equal status (cf. Trigg 1993: 58ff.). Whereas the relativist embraces this kind of contextuality and contingency, the absolutist simply reflects the obverse side of the same mistake: by assuming that contextuality entails determinism, the absolutist appeals to a priori and context-free conditions and yearns for a foundationalist universality to ground a transcending critique that is wholly contextless. It is exactly these *bogus dichotomies* (cf. Schrag 1997:108) of the absolute versus the relative, the universal versus the particular, the necessary versus the contingent, the natural versus the supernatural, that needed to be exposed for what they are — namely, conceptual constructs of a theoretical position-taking that has been revealed as no longer compelling at all. Truth claims and effective critique, as we saw earlier, thus retain a central place in postfoundationalism, but the space for this is now communicative praxis, transversally textured, where personal judgment and communal feedback guide a fitting response that is neither a-historically absolutist nor historically relativist. The rational self is therefore always a self in community, a self situated in the space of communicative praxis, historically embedded, existing with and for others; but these others will always include our predecessors, our contemporaries, and our successors.

Our opinions, then, result from these kinds of responsible judgments as matters that we have good reasons for. We therefore not only have epistemic justification to stand by our own convictions, we also have a moral duty to do so (cf. Rescher 1993:122ff.). But does this entitlement to one's own position not take us back to the relativism of extreme individualism or the parochialism of communal nonfoundationalism, where we are reduced to only addressing others who think like us? At this point we should remind ourselves that, even if we think differently, or inhabit different intellectual domains, we all still share the resources of human rationality, and that — on a postfoundationalist view of rationality — the aim of the cognitive enterprise is still to reach beyond one's own context in interdisciplinary, transcontextual conversation. The fact that on this postfoundationalist view of rationality, human reason is never exclusively housed within or represented by one form of knowledge only, has had far-reaching implications for understanding the shaping of rationality in discourses as diverse as theology and the sciences. On this view, and certainly as far as the presence and quality of rationality in different disciplines go, there will be no hierarchy of disciplines with the natural sciences emerging on top as "the most rational" of all our reasoning strategies. In this sense one could indeed say that science does not constitute rationality, but constitutes one human response to the question how we can gain knowledge, intelligibility, and understanding (cf. Trigg 1993:62). Even if, as we saw earlier, we were to regard mathematics and the natural sciences as representing the most manicured forms of cognitive rationality, then human rationality still has richer resources than just the cognitive — resources that stretch out and include the pragmatic and evaluative dimensions of all our actions. But rationality is not only performatively present in our different cultural domains and diverse disciplines, it also enables us to reach beyond the boundaries of our disciplines and cultural domains by being operative *between* cultural spheres, *between* our different forms of knowledge, linking different disciplines and lying across diverse disciplinary boundaries.

This postfoundationalist notion of rationality has been enhanced and enriched by what Calvin Schrag has called *transversal rationality*. The notion of transversality indeed provides us with a window to the wider world of thought and action. As such it now enables us to resist any attempts at totalizing different forms of knowledge into one, unified (or "consilient") worldview where the natural sciences can imperialistically emerge as somehow paradigmatic and normative for all other discourses. A postfoundationalist notion of rationality thus helps us resist the rationalistic impulse to combine different modes of knowledge into a higher concept that totalizes the different disciplines and reasoning strategies into a seamless unity viewed from above (cf. Schrag 1992:149). And it also, however, helps us to resist all forms of scientism and the positivistic impulse to determine a usage where one form of rationality would somehow become normative for all the rest.

Furthermore, and most importantly for the conversation between theology and the sciences, a postfoundationalist notion of rationality opens up the possibility for dialogue across disciplinary boundaries. And since rationality is always first of all person- and domain-specific, it heightens our understanding of the uniqueness of each of these discourses while at the same time enabling us to reach beyond the boundaries of our disciplines in cross-disciplinary dialogue. On this view rationality can never be something that is superimposed on diverse disciplines and discourses as a unifying factor, but develops, rather, or is discovered as, an emerging pattern that does indeed give us a degree of unification and dynamic integration in a conversation that can now reach across disciplinary boundaries. For Schrag it was the binding rationality of critique, articulation, and disclosure, as overlapping moments of rationality, that enabled the achievement of shared understanding and solidarity: a shared understanding that is very different from the kind of consensus grounded in universal claims (cf. 1992:169). This shared understanding is indeed the achievement of a hard struggle for communication across the spectrum of various life forms and diverse disciplines. So, although all our critical judgments are indeed context-dependent, this does not preclude an assessment and evaluation of different localized contexts as one discerns the interaction between and among them: every context-dependency is always situated within a wider context-interdependency (cf. Schrag 1992:173).

A postfoundationalist model of rationality thus enables us to communicate across boundaries, from context to context, from one form of life to another, from one discipline to another. The tentative and shared understanding that we achieve through this was provocatively and effectively named a *wide reflective equilibrium* by various scholars (cf. Nielsen 1987; Fiorenza 1984:301f.; Schrag 1992:176;

Davaney 1999:327). This "wide reflective equilibrium" is never just some kind of interior mental event, but is from the bottom up social, and thus emerges from the heart of our communicative practices. A wide reflective equilibrium thus points to the fragile accomplishments of our interpersonal and interdisciplinary communication, and establishes the necessity of a multiplicity of voices and perspectives in our ongoing processes of mutual assessment. So, in this "wide reflective equilibrium" we finally find the safe but fragile public space we have been searching for: a space for shuttling back and forth between deep personal convictions and the principles resulting from responsible interpersonal judgments. The dynamics of a postfoundationalist rationality is thus finally revealed in this fragile process where we strive to attain the most coherent and most consistent sets of beliefs in interdisciplinary conversation. When we have attained that, we have — for a while, at least — attained a wide reflective equilibrium (cf. Nielsen 1987:148f.; Schrag 1992:177). The wide scope of a postfoundationalist notion of rationality thus encompasses the separated cultural domains of modernity (science, morality, art, religion), but it is the dynamics of this process of intercontextual and cross-disciplinary reflection that enables one to move across discourses, effecting a binding and integration of sorts that finally could yield the "wide reflective equilibrium" of interdisciplinary understanding also in reasoning strategies as diverse as theology and the sciences.

This reflective equilibrium now emerges as the deeper and richer sense of what early on in this book was indicated as the most important epistemic goal of human rationality, namely intelligibility or optimal understanding. This accomplishment of postfoundationalist equilibrium in interdisciplinary conversation is *reflective* precisely because it is never static, but rather consists in a constantly revising movement as we move back and forth between personal commitments, doctrinal convictions, and the public accomplishments of natural scientific research. Francis Schüssler Fiorenza eloquently captured this postfoundationalist strategy by stating that, through a back and forth movement the method of reflective equilibrium seeks to bring into equilibrium the principles reconstructed from practice with the practice itself (cf. 1984:301). On this view our already agreed-upon principles and background theories provide a critical, independent constraint that prevents these principles from being mere generalizations of our contextual judgments and practices, while at the same time these principles can be critically questioned too. The epistemic goal of a wide reflective equilibrium is therefore truly postfoundationalist because it could never accept any one tradition of responsible judgments or practices or principles as foundational (cf. Fiorenza 1984:302). Also, in any theology's conversation with any of the sciences, a postfoundationalist strategy therefore acknowledges that one always starts an interdisciplinary conversation with initial commitments that could be anything from moral judgments to religious convictions, to strong commitments to science or scientific worldviews. These disciplinary or philosophical commitments are often brought into the conversation as principles or rules for discussion. As principles they are in part independent of those strong commitments and should actually be able to modify them if interdisciplinary argument and rhetoric justify it, even as they themselves remain open to revision.

The epistemic goal of attaining this wide reflective equilibrium in interdisciplinary conversation will have far-reaching implications for theology, and also for the theology and science dialogue. On this view genuine theological pluralism emerges as normal and natural, and ought to allow for conversations between people from different traditions or cultural domains who may enter the conversation for very different reasons, and who may in fact disagree about many issues. This pluralism also allows for a legitimate diversity: the fact that different people have different experiential situations because they come from different traditions, and in addition commit themselves to different research traditions, makes it normal, natural, and rational that they should proceed differently in cognitive, evaluative, and practical matters. We therefore have to accept that also, and maybe especially in theology, cognitive agreement or consensus is unattainable, and that exactly what Nicholas Rescher called *dissensus tolerance* could prove to be a positive and constructive part of theological pluralism (cf. Rescher 1993:3f.). It is at this point that we reach beyond our specific traditions in cross-contextual conversation, to a shared "wide reflective equilibrium" where the diversity of our traditions will yield the diversity of our experiences, the diversity of our epistemic situations, the diversity of our values and methodologies. Also in the theology and science dialogue the most sensible posture is therefore to accept the reality of cognitive pluralism within a shared public realm of discourse, to accept the unavailability of consensus, and to work at creating a communal framework or wide reflective equilibrium of thought and action. This is what true coherence is about: a coherence where dissensus and a variety of opinion provide for the creative enhancement rather than impoverishment of our intellectual culture. To be able to live with diversity and cognitive pluralism, and with the idea that others think differently from us, is to finally transcend the kind of conformism that insists that "I think like them," or the kind of chauvinism that insists that "they think like me" (Rescher 1993:193).

This also means that, even if we lack universal rules for rationality, and even if we can never judge the reasonableness of statements and beliefs in isolation from their cultural or disciplinary contexts, we can still meaningfully engage in cross-contextual evaluation and conversation and give the best available cognitive, evaluative, or pragmatic reasons for the responsible choices we hope to make. True interdisciplinarity in theology will therefore be achieved when our conversations proceed, not in terms of imposed "universal" rules, nor in terms of purely *ad hoc* rules, but when we identify this (postfoundationalist) space where both strong Christian convictions as well as the public voice of theology are fused in public conversation. A postfoundationalist acknowledgment of the pluralist character of such an ongoing process of collective assessment should open our eyes to how the richness of our various traditions — our various discourses, our communities, our sciences, our practices — makes up our social and intellectual domains and shapes our behavior and our different modes of understanding. Each of our domains of understanding may indeed have its own logic of behavior, as well as an understanding unique to the particular domain, but in each the rich resources of human rationality remain (cf. Bottum 1994:379). When we discover the shared richness of the resources of rationality without attempting to subsume all discourses and all communities under one universal reason, we have discovered the richness of a postfoundationalist notion of rationality.

Finally, as we aim for a wide reflective equilibrium by judging the degree of adequacy or the problem-solving ability of one tradition over another, what modes of appraisal should we now be looking for? Larry Laudan has identified the following as the two most important modes of appraisal: first, the *momentary adequacy* of a research tradition, i.e., how effective the latest theories within a research tradition are at adequately solving problems; and second, the *progressiveness* of a research tradition, i.e., whether a research tradition has, in the course of time, increased or decreased the problem-solving effectiveness of its components, and thus its own adequacy (cf. Laudan 1977:106f.). What emerges from this as a criterion for theory choice is the following: we ultimately choose the theory or research tradition which we find the most compelling, and which we judge to have the highest problem-solving adequacy for a specific problem within a specific context. The choice for the problem-solving ability of a research tradition, as for a specific theory, is therefore always a strategy of interpretation. If — for a given epistemic community — a research tradition has solved more problems than its rivals, then accepting that tradition would be the rational thing to do. Interdisciplinary cross-contextual conversation as a highly interpretative and pragmatic way of appraising research traditions thus simultaneously offers an account of rational acceptance and of qualified progress. This model of rational theory choice thus implies that in any appraisal of the rationality of a particular belief, theory, or research tradition, this specific belief, theory, or tradition is always relative to its contemporaneous competitors, to prevailing doctrines of theory assessment, and to the previous theories within a research tradition. By thus linking rationality to not just community, but also to cross-disciplinary adequacy and progressiveness, we can now have a theory of rationality without first presupposing anything about the truth or verisimilitude of those traditions we judge to be rational or irrational (cf. Laudan 1977:125ff.). In this open, postfoundationalist way, tradition is indeed rationality's destiny.

Laudan's major contribution to our discussion has therefore been his arguments for showing that different modes of human cognition, and therefore also theology and the various sciences, are all systems of inquiry for the solutions of very specific problems. To talk about the shaping of rationality is therefore not only to talk about accountability, optimal understanding, and responsible judgment, but should also reveal the intellectual activity of judgment and decision-making as a progressive, problem-solving process that takes us closer to exactly the kind of fragile epistemic equilibrium that constitutes interdisciplinary conversation. On this view, where responsible, rational judgment was revealed as an effective form of problem-solving, the scope of human rationality again goes far beyond the narrow confines of a strictly natural scientific rationality. Linking the role of rational judgment to theory choice and progressive problem-solving has therefore made it clear that the adoption of theories or doctrines in nonnatural scientific fields of inquiry does not have to be more arbitrary or more subjective than the use of rational judgment in scientific decision-making. And although, as we saw earlier, scientific rationality shows itself as a very disciplined and manicured (cf. Puddefoot 1994:10) form of rationality, this kind of problem-solving reaches beyond the sciences and already forms part of the preanalytic or common sense reasonableness we live by every day. Furthermore, a broadened notion of postfoundationalist rationality has shown that the "intrusion" of seemingly "non-scientific" factors into the process of theological and even scientific decision-making is, or can be, an entirely rational affair. Far from viewing the introduction of philosophical, religious, and moral issues into science as the triumph of prejudice, superstition, and irrationality, postfoundationalist rationality claims that, through the role of responsible judgment in interdisciplinary conversation, the presence of such elements may be entirely rational. In fact, the suppression of such elements may itself be irrational and prejudicial.

In Conclusion

Over against the very helpful but more limited and traditional ways of relating theological reflection to the sciences through models of either conflict, dialogue, independence, or integration (cf. Barbour 1990:3-30), and the rigorous demarcation these models imply between the domains of science and religion, I have argued for a constructive, postfoundationalist affirmation of various research traditions in diverse disciplines as the proper domain and destiny of human rationality. On this view our multiple forms of theological reflection, as well as the many disciplines in the sciences, are now revealed to be more like an unmappable geography of dynamic intellectual practices (cf. Bottum 1994:379) which transcend the rigorously defined cultural domains of modernity, and which each in its own way informs and contributes to our passionate goal for understanding ourselves and the world we live in. On this view, rationality and context are not only mutually compatible, but are in fact inseparable. What this means is that in each of these domains of inquiry the standards of rationality, the methodologies, the scope of critical inquiry, and the objects of study will be unique and different. But in each, the resources of rationality are alive and well and interdisciplinary dialogue becomes a live and real option. So, if in the wake of postmodernism we abandon the attempt to integrate all our discourses and research strategies under one, unified form of knowledge, we discover rationality as performatively present in domains even as widely different as Christian theology and the natural sciences.

On a postfoundationalist view we will discover the resources of rationality in overlapping but often also in conflicting domains of inquiry. This refigured notion of rationality has thus opened up the possibility of affirming the creative continuity of our preferred traditions within our various disciplinary domains: precisely by discovering the epistemic resources and the problem-solving abilities of these traditions, we are freed from being the fideistic prisoners of our preferred traditions, and liberated to the difficult task of interdisciplinary conversation. In our quest for the values that shape the rationality of theology and the sciences, a broader and richer notion of human rationality with distinct cognitive, evaluative, and pragmatic resources has thus emerged. Whether in faith, in religion, or theology, or in the various sciences, we normally have good reasons for hanging on to certain beliefs, good reasons for making certain judgments and moral choices, and good reasons for acting in certain ways. Possibly the most plausible of these good reasons has turned out to be the epistemic goal of intelligibility, the passion for finding some form of fragile equilibrium in our interdisciplinary attempts to understand ourselves and the world we live in. Also in theology, as an ongoing critical reflection about the content of faith and religious experience, rationality implies the ability to give an account, to provide a rationale, for the way one thinks, chooses, acts, and believes. In all of our disciplines, theory-acceptance has a distinct cognitive dimension. When we asked, however, what besides belief is involved in theory-acceptance, the pragmatic and evaluative dimensions of theory-acceptance were revealed. I have therefore claimed that the quest for intelligibility and meaning in theology, as in the various domains of the sciences, is inexorably linked to the living research traditions of those domains, and that precisely because of that, it also is dependent on broader resources than just the purely cognitive. I have also claimed that rationality makes its presence known in theological reflection — as in other reasoning strategies like the sciences — when we discern and argue for those theories, models, or research traditions that are judged to be the most progressive, and thus the most effective problem-solvers in our ongoing search for epistemic equilibrium and deeper understanding.

Theology's indispensable link to tradition thus revealed the evolving nature of the epistemic and nonepistemic values that have shaped theological rationality through its long history. But what does this concretely imply for theology? At the very least it implies that the assumptions and faith commitments of the praxis of experienced Christian faith are relevant epistemic issues that deserve to be taken seriously in interdisciplinary discussion. By doing this, theology could in fact move away from the absolutism of foundationalism, but also from the relativism of nonfoundationalism. This was achieved by showing that, because theological reflection is always embedded within the broader context of an epistemic community, there can be no way to prescribe a rationality for that community without also considering its actual practice, along with the way this reflective and traditioned praxis grows out of the way Christian believers live their daily lives of faith. In reflecting on the presence of rationality in theological reflection we were therefore able to refocus on the crucial role of individual judgment as an all-important epistemic skill. Linking the crucial role of individual judgment to an ongoing process of collective communal assessment also helped us to move beyond abstract, generic, and universalist notions of rationality, precisely by rediscovering the experiential and interpretative nature of the contexts in which we live as rational agents.

In a postfoundationalist Christian theology the focus will always, however, first of all be on a relentless criticism of our uncritically held crypto-foundationalist assumptions. This should allow us to freely and critically explore the experiential and interpretative roots of all our beliefs, and to be open to the fact that, also in matters of faith, religious commitment, and theological reflection, we relate to our world primarily through interpreted experience. The theologian is thus freed to speak and reflect from within a personal faith commitment, and in cross-disciplinary conversation with the sciences, to discover patterns that might sometimes be consonant with the Christian paradigm. The persuasiveness of these patterns should be taken up in critical theological reflection, where its problem-solving ability should be evaluated and judged in an open, postfoundationalist conversation which will allow for the creative exchange of critical, cross-disciplinary reflection. In this conversation the shaping role of experi-

284

ence and of tradition should be carefully evaluated, as we ask whether or not these shaping criteria themselves may or may not manage to still plausibly and critically determine why and how we hold on to our beliefs about God.

Finally, in this book I have argued for a revisioning of theology's public voice by taking on the challenge to locate theological reflection within the broader context of interdisciplinary reflection. In our search for an integrative, nontotalizing model of human knowledge, human rationality was adequately revealed as our species' most distinguishing survival strategy, performatively present in all the various domains of our lives. Also, the seemingly remote, isolated epistemologies of reasoning strategies as different as theology and the sciences can now be recognized as integral parts of webs of theories about the world and ourselves. On this view, religious and theological reflection can now be recognized as equal partners in a democratic, interdisciplinary conversation where the voice of authentic religious commitment might actually be heard in a postmodern, pluralist situation. This kind of theological reflection will share in interdisciplinary standards of rationality which, although always socially and contextually shaped, will not be hopelessly culture and context bound: even with widely divergent personal, religious, or disciplinary viewpoints, we still share in the rich resources of human rationality.

I have therefore argued for the clearing of an interdisciplinary space where not only very diverse and pluralist forms of theological reflection, but also theology and other disciplines/reasoning strategies might explore shared concerns and discover possible shared epistemological overlaps in an ongoing interdisciplinary conversation. On this view, our various research traditions have been reconfirmed as the origin and destiny of constructive dialogue between diverse reasoning strategies. In rediscovering that, in spite of our diverse theologies and our pluralist approaches to various reasoning strategies, we still share in the resources of human rationality, we have opened up the possibility of affirming the creative continuity of our various, diverse traditions: by discovering the shared epistemic resources as well as the interdisciplinary ability for critically evaluating our problem-solving traditions, we are freed from being the fideistic prisoners of our preferred traditions and respective disciplines. Precisely by allowing ourselves to freely and critically explore the experiential and interpretative roots of all our beliefs in our various domains of knowledge, we as

285

theologians too are freed to speak and reflect publicly, but from within a personal faith commitment, and in this cross-disciplinary conversation with those of other traditions and other disciplines, to discover patterns that may be consonant with or complementary to the Christian worldview. In genuine interdisciplinary conversation this accomplishment, however fragile, should be the definitive move beyond the kind of fideism where our own unique experiences and appropriate explanations are never challenged, and the need for transcommunal conversation is never taken seriously.

Bibliography

Anderson, Clifford B. 1997. *Scientific Laws and Divine Agency.* Princeton Theological Seminary (unpublished paper).

Barbour, Ian G. 1974. *Myths, Models and Paradigms.* San Francisco: Harper and Row.

Barbour, Ian G. 1989. "Creation and Cosmology," in *Cosmos and Creation,* Peters, Ted (ed.). Nashville: Abingdon Press.

Barbour, Ian G. 1990. *Religion in an Age of Science.* San Francisco: Harper and Row.

Barbour, Ian G. 1997. *Religion in the Age of Science.* San Francisco: Harper and Row.

Barker, Eileen. 1981. "Science as Theology: The Theological Functioning of Western Science," in *The Sciences and Theology in the Twentieth Century,* Peacocke, Arthur R. (ed.). Notre Dame: University of Notre Dame Press.

Bartley, W. W. 1964. *The Retreat to Commitment.* LaSalle: Open Court.

Bell, Catherine. 1996. "Modernism and Postmodernism in the Study of Religion," in *Religious Studies Review.* 22/3.

Bernstein, Richard J. 1983. *Beyond Objectivism and Relativism.* Oxford: Basil Blackwell.

Bottum, Joseph. 1994. "A Review of the Resources of Rationality: A Response to the Postmodern Challenge, by Calvin O. Schrag," in *International Philosophical Quarterly.* 34/3.

Bowker, John W. 1998. "Science and Religion: Contest or Confirmation," in *Science Meets Faith,* Watts, Fraser (ed.). London: SPCK.

BIBLIOGRAPHY

Brown, Delwin. 1994. *Boundaries of Our Habitations: Tradition and Theological Construction*. New York: SUNY Press.

Brown, Harold I. 1988. "Normative Epistemology and Naturalized Epistemology," in *Inquiry*. 31.

Brown, Harold I. 1990. *Rationality*. London and New York: Routledge.

Byrne, James. 1992. "Foucault on Continuity: The Postmodern Challenge to Tradition," in *Faith and Philosophy*. 9/3.

Byrne, James. 1994. "Theology and Christian Faith," in *Concilium*. 6.

Cahoone, Lawrence. 1995. *The End of Philosophy*. Albany: SUNY Press.

Clayton, P. 1989. *Explanations from Physics to Theology*. New Haven: Yale University Press.

Clayton, Philip; Knapp, Steven. 1993. "Ethics and Rationality," in *American Philosophical Quarterly*. 30/2.

Comstock, Gary L. 1987. "Two Types of Narrative Theology," in *Journal of the American Academy of Religion*. 55/4.

Comstock, Gary L. 1989. "Is Postmodern Religious Dialogue Possible?," in *Faith and Philosophy*. 6/2.

Crawley, William H. G. 1997. *Haack's Foundherentist Proposal: An Epistemological Third Way?* Princeton Theological Seminary (unpublished paper).

Davaney, Sheila G. 1991. *Theology at the End of Modernity: Essays in the Honor of Gordon D. Kaufman*. Philadelphia: Trinity Press International.

Davaney, Sheila G. 1999. *Pragmatic Historicism: Reconstructing the Theological Task.* In press.

Davies, P. 1992. *The Mind of God: The Scientific Basis for a Rational World*. New York: Simon and Schuster.

Dean, William. 1988. *History Making History, The New Historicism in American Religious Thought*. New York: SUNY Press.

D'Espagnat, B. 1989. *Reality and the Physicist*. Cambridge: Cambridge University Press.

Echeverria, Edward J. 1986. "Rationality and the Theory of Rationality," in *Christian Scholar's Review*. 15/4.

Fine, Arthur. 1984. "The Natural Ontological Attitude," in *Scientific Realism*, Leplin, Jarrett (ed.). Berkeley: University of California Press.

Fiorenza, F. S. 1984. *Foundational Theology: Jesus and the Church*. New York: Crossroad.

Foucault, Michel. 1980. *Power/Knowledge: Selected Interviews and Other Writings*. New York: Pantheon Books.

Frankenberry, Nancy. 1987. *Religion and Radical Empiricism*. Albany: SUNY Press.

Geertz, Clifford. 1973. *The Interpretation of Cultures; Selected Essays*. New York: Basic Books.

Gilkey, Langdon. 1992. Foreword to Stone, Jerome A. *A Minimalist Vision of Transcendence*. Albany: SUNY Press.

Gill, Jerry. 1981. *On Knowing God*. Philadelphia: The Westminster Press.

Glanville, Helena. 1989. *What Is a Bongaloo, Daddy? On Narrative Knowledge, Religious Truth, and Pluralism*. University of Port Elizabeth (unpublished paper).

Green, Garrett. 1989. *Imagining God: Theology and the Religious Imagination*. San Francisco: Harper and Row.

Gregersen, Niels; van Huyssteen, J. Wentzel (eds.). 1998. *Rethinking Theology and Science: Six Models for the Current Discussion*. Grand Rapids: Eerdmans.

Griffin, David Ray; Beardslee, William A.; Holland, Joe. 1989. *Varieties of Postmodern Theology*. Albany: SUNY Press.

Haack, Susan. 1995. *Evidence and Inquiry: Towards Reconstruction in Epistemology*. Oxford: Blackwell.

Habermas, Jürgen. 1984. *The Theory of Communicative Action*. Vol. 1, *Reason and the Rationalization of Society*. Boston: Beacon Press.

Habermas, Jürgen. 1987. *The Philosophical Discourse of Modernity: Twelve Lectures*. Cambridge: MIT Press.

Harding, Sandra. 1996. "Science Is Good to Think With," in *Social Text*. 46-47.

Harvey, David. 1989. *The Condition of Postmodernity: An Enquiry into the Origins of Cultural Change*. Oxford: Blackwell.

Harvey, Michael G. 1994. *Personal Conviction and Rational Justification*. Princeton Theological Seminary (unpublished paper).

Hauerwas, Stanley. 1994. "The Church's One Foundation Is Jesus Christ Her Lord Or, In a World without Foundations All We Have Is the Church," in *Theology without Foundations: Religious Practice and the Future of Theological Truth*, Hauerwas, Stanley; Murphy, Nancey; Nation, Mark. Nashville: Abingdon Press.

Hauerwas, Stanley; Jones, L. Gregory. 1989. *Why Narrative? Readings in Narrative Theology*. Grand Rapids: Eerdmans.

Hauerwas, Stanley; Murphy, Nancey; Nation, Mark. 1994. *Theology without Foundations: Religious Practice and the Future of Theological Truth*. Nashville: Abingdon Press.

Hesse, Mary. 1998. "Is Science the New Religion?," in *Science Meets Faith*, Watts, Fraser (ed.). London: SPCK.

Hodgson, Peter. 1989. *God in History: Shapes of Freedom*. Nashville: Abingdon Press.

Hoering, Walter. 1980. "On Judging Rationality," in *Studies in the History of the Philosophy of Science*. 11/2.

Horgan, John. 1996a. "Science Set Free from Truth," in *The New York Times*, July 16, 1996.

Horgan, John. 1996b. *The End of Science. Facing the Limits of Knowledge in the Twilight of the Scientific Age*. Reading, MA: Addison-Wesley Publishing Company.

Jeanrond, Werner. 1988. "Response to Janet Martin Soskice," in *Proceedings: 7th European Conference on Philosophy of Religion*. Utrecht: Utrecht University.

Jones, Stanton. 1994. "A Constructive Relationship for Religion with the Science and Profession of Psychology: Perhaps the Boldest Model Yet," in *American Psychologist*. 49/3.

Kerr, Fergus. 1992. "Simplicity Itself: Milbank's Thesis," in *New Blackfriars*. 73/861.

Kline, Stephen Jay. 1995. *Conceptual Foundations for Multidisciplinary Thinking*. Stanford: Stanford University Press.

Kuhn, Thomas. 1970. *The Structure of Scientific Revolutions*. Chicago: University of Chicago Press.

Lakatos, Imre. 1970. *Criticism and the Growth of Knowledge*. Cambridge: Cambridge University Press.

Laudan, Larry. 1977. *Progress and Its Problems: Toward a Theory of Scientific Growth*. Berkeley: University of California Press.

Leplin, Jarrett (ed.). 1984. *Scientific Realism*. Berkeley: University of California Press.

Lindbeck, George A. 1984. *The Nature of Doctrine*. Philadelphia: The Westminster Press.

Lötter, H. P. P. 1994. "A Postmodern Philosophy of Science?," in *Journal of South African Philosophy*. 13/3.

Lötter, H. P. P. 1997. *The Complexity of Science*. Johannesburg: Randse Afrikaanse Universiteit.

Lyotard, Jean-François. 1984. *The Postmodern Condition: A Report on Knowledge*. Manchester: Manchester University Press.

McMullin, Ernan. 1985. "Realism in Theology and Science: A Response to Peacocke," in *Religion and Intellectual Life*. 2.

McMullin, Ernan. 1986. "Explanatory Success and the Truth of Theory," in *Scientific Inquiry in Philosophical Perspective*, Rescher, Nicholas (ed.). Lanham, MD: University Press of America.

McMullin, Ernan. 1988. *Construction and Constraint: The Shaping of Scientific Rationality*. Notre Dame: University of Notre Dame Press.

Merleau-Ponty, Maurice. 1962. *Phenomenology of Perception*. London: Routledge & Kegan Paul.

Milbank, John. 1990. *Theology and Social Theory: Beyond Secular Reason*. Oxford: Blackwell.

Moore, Gareth. 1994. "A Scene with Cranes: Engagement and Truth in Religion," in *Philosophical Investigations*. 17.

Murphy, Nancey. 1990. *Theology in the Age of Scientific Reasoning*. Ithaca: Cornell University Press.

Murphy, Nancey. 1994. *Reasoning and Rhetoric in Religion*. Valley Forge, PA: Trinity Press International.

Murphy, Nancey. 1996a. *Anglo-American Postmodernity: Philosophical Perspectives on Science, Religion and Ethics*. Boulder: Westview Press.

Murphy, Nancey. 1996b. *Beyond Liberalism and Fundamentalism*. Valley Forge, PA: Trinity Press International.

Murphy, Nancey; Ellis, George F. R. 1996. *On the Moral Nature of the Universe*. Philadelphia: Fortress Press.

Murphy, Nancey; McClendon, James W. 1989. "Distinguishing Modern and Postmodern Theologies," in *Modern Theology*. 5/3.

Murray, Paul. 1999. "Truth and Reason in Science and Theology: Points of Tension, Correlation, and Compatibility," in *God, Humanity, and the Cosmos: A Textbook in Science and Religion*, Southgate, Chris (ed.). Edinburgh: T & T Clark.

Neville, Robert Cummings. 1992. *The Highroad Around Modernism*. Albany: SUNY Press.

Nichols, Aidan. "'Non tali auxilio': John Milbank's Suasion to Orthodoxy," in *New Blackfriars*. 73/861.

Nielsen, Kai. 1987. "Searching for an Emancipatory Perspective: Wide Reflective Equilibrium and the Hermeneutical Circle," in *Anti-Foundationalism and Practical Reasoning*, Simpson, Evan (ed.). Edmonton: The Academic Press.

Parusnikova, Zuzana. 1992. "Is a Postmodern Philosophy of Science Possible?," in *Studies in History and the Philosophy of Science*. 23/1.

Peacocke, Arthur R. 1984. *Intimations of Reality: Critical Realism in Science and Religion.* Notre Dame: University of Notre Dame Press.

Percesepe, Gary J. 1991. "The Unbearable Lightness of Being Postmodern," in *Christian Scholar's Review.* 20.

Pieterse, Henk. 1989. *Gary Comstock's Two Types of Narrative Theology: An Evaluation.* University of Port Elizabeth (unpublished paper).

Pieterse, Henk. 1996. "The Revisionist Theology of David Tracy: A Postmodern Challenge." Ph.D. dissertation: University of Stellenbosch.

Placher, Willam C. 1989. *Unapologetic Theology: A Christian Voice in a Pluralist Conversation.* Louisville: Westminster/John Knox Press.

Polkinghorne, John. 1991. *Reason and Reality.* Philadelphia: Trinity Press International.

Proudfoot, Wayne. 1985. *Religious Experience.* Berkeley: University of California Press.

Proudfoot, Wayne. 1991. *"Regulae fidei* and Regulative Idea: Two Contemporary Theological Strategies," in *Theology at the End of Modernity: Essays in Honor of Gordon Kaufman.* Davaney, Sheila Greeve (ed.). Philadelphia: Trinity Press International.

Puddefoot, John C. 1994. "Resonance Realism," in *Tradition and Discovery: The Polanyi Society Periodical.* 20/3.

Quine, Willard Van Orman. 1951. "Two Dogmas of Empiricism," in *Philosophical Review.* 40.

Quine, Willard Van Orman. 1969. *Ontological Relativity and Other Essays.* New York: Columbia University Press.

Reichenbach, Hans. 1938. *Experience and Prediction.* Chicago: University of Chicago Press.

Rescher, Nicholas. 1988. *Rationality: A Philosophical Inquiry into the Nature and the Rationale of Reason.* Oxford: Clarendon Press.

Rescher, Nicholas. 1992. *A System of Pragmatic Idealism.* Vol. 1. Princeton: Princeton University Press.

Rescher, Nicholas. 1993. *Pluralism: Against the Demand for Consensus.* Oxford: Clarendon Press.

Rolston, Holmes. 1987. *Science and Religion.* New York: Random House.

Rorty, Richard. 1979. *Philosophy and the Mirror of Nature.* Princeton: Princeton University Press.

Rorty, Richard. 1982. *Consequences of Pragmatism: Essays 1972-1980.* Minneapolis: University of Minnesota Press.

292

Rorty, Richard. 1989. *Contingency, Irony, and Solidarity*. Cambridge: Cambridge University Press.

Rosenau, Pauline Marie. 1992. *Postmodernism and Social Science*. Princeton: Princeton University Press.

Rossouw, G. J. 1993. "Theology in a Postmodern Culture: Ten Challenges," in *Hervormde Teologiese Studies*. 49.

Rossouw, G. J. 1995. *Life in a Postmodern Culture*. Pretoria: HSRC Press.

Rottschaeffer, William A. 1985. "Religious Cognition as Interpreted Experience: An Examination of Ian Barbour's Comparison of the Epistemic Structures of Science and Religion," in *Zygon*. 20/3.

Rouse, Joseph. 1987. *Knowledge and Power: Toward a Political Philosophy of Science*. Ithaca: Cornell University Press.

Rouse, Joseph. 1990. "The Narrative Reconstruction of Science," in *Inquiry*. 33/2.

Rouse, Joseph. 1991a. "Philosophy of Science and the Persistent Narratives of Modernity," in *Studies in History and the Philosophy of Science*. 22/1.

Rouse, Joseph. 1991b. "The Politics of Postmodern Philosophy of Science," in *Philosophy of Science*. 58.

Rouse, Joseph. 1996. *Engaging Science: How to Understand Its Practices Philosophically*. Ithaca: Cornell University Press.

Russell, Robert J. 1989. "Cosmology, Creation, and Contingency," in *Cosmos and Creation*, Peters, Ted (ed.). Nashville: Abingdon Press.

Sanders, Andy F. 1995. "Traditionalism, Fallibilism and Theological Relativism," in *Nederlandisch Teologisch Tijdschrift*. 49/3.

Schrag, Calvin O. 1985. "Rhetoric Situated at the End of Philosophy," in *Quarterly Journal of Speech*. 71.

Schrag, Calvin O. 1989. "Rationality Between Modernity and Postmodernity," in *Life-world and Politics: Between Modernity and Postmodernity*, White, Stephen K. (ed.). Notre Dame: University of Notre Dame Press.

Schrag, Calvin O. 1992. *The Resources of Rationality: A Response to the Postmodern Challenge*. Bloomington: Indiana University Press.

Schrag, Calvin O. 1994. "Transversal Rationality," in *The Question of Hermeneutics*, Stapleton, T. J. (ed.). The Netherlands: Kluwer Academic Publishers.

Schrag, Calvin O. 1995. "Reminiscences of Paul Tillich: The Man and His Works," in *NAPTS Newsletter*. 21/1.

Schrag, Calvin O. 1997. *The Self After Postmodernity.* New Haven: Yale University Press.

Schreiter, Robert J. 1997. *The New Catholicity: Theology between the Global and the Local.* New York: Orbis Books.

Scott, Janny. 1996. "Postmodern Gravity Deconstructed, Slyly," in *The New York Times,* May 18, A1, 22.

Shults, LeRon. 1993. "Integrative Epistemology and the Search for Meaning," in *Journal of Interdisciplinary Studies.* 5/1.

Sokal, Alan. 1996a. "A Physicist Experiments with Cultural Studies," in *Lingua Franca.* 6/4.

Sokal, Alan. 1996b. "Transgressing the Boundaries: Towards a Transformative Hermeneutics of Quantum Gravity," in *Social Text.* 46-47/1&2.

Sokal, Alan; Bricmont, Jean. 1998. *Intellectual Impostures.* London: Profile Books.

Solberg, Mary M. 1997. *Compelling Knowledge: A Feminist Proposal for an Epistemology of the Cross.* Albany: SUNY Press.

Soskice, Janet Martin. 1988. "Myths, Metaphors, and Narrative Theology," in *Proceedings: 7th European Conference on Philosophy of Religion.* Utrecht: Utrecht University.

Stenmark, Mikael. 1995. *Rationality in Science, Religion, and Everyday Life.* Notre Dame: University of Notre Dame Press.

Steuer, Axel D. 1987. "The Epistemic Status of Theistic Belief," in *Journal of the American Academy of Religion.* 55/2.

Stoeger, William R. SJ. 1988. "Contemporary Cosmology and Its Implications for the Science-Religion Dialogue," in *Physics, Philosophy, and Theology: A Common Quest for Understanding.* Russell, Robert J.; Stoeger, William R. SJ; Koyne, George SJ (eds.). Notre Dame: University of Notre Dame Press.

Stone, Jerome A. 1992. *A Minimalist Vision of Transcendence: A Naturalist Philosophy of Religion.* Albany: SUNY Press.

Stout, Jeffrey. 1981. *The Flight from Authority: Religion, Morality and the Quest for Autonomy.* Notre Dame: University of Notre Dame Press.

Thiel, John E. 1994. *Nonfoundationalism.* Minneapolis: Fortress Press.

Thiemann, Ronald F. 1987a. *Revelation and Theology: The Gospel as Narrated Promise.* Notre Dame: University of Notre Dame Press.

Thiemann, Ronald F. 1987b. "Radiance and Obscurity in Biblical Narrative," in *Scriptural Authority and Narrative Interpretation,* Green, G. (ed.). Philadelphia: Fortress Press

Thiemann, Ronald F. 1991. *Constructing a Public Theology: The Church in a Pluralistic Culture.* Louisville: John Knox Press.

Tilley, Terrence W. 1995. *Postmodern Theologies: The Challenge of Religious Diversity.* Maryknoll: Orbis Books.

Toulmin, Stephen. 1985. *The Return to Cosmology: Postmodern Science and the Theology of Nature.* Berkeley: University of California Press.

Toulmin, Stephen. 1990. *Cosmopolis: The Hidden Agenda of Modernity.* New York: Free Press.

Tracy, David. 1981. *The Analogical Imagination.* New York: Crossroad.

Tracy, David. 1992. "Theology, Critical Social Theory, and the Public Realm," in *Habermas, Modernity and Public Theology,* Browning, Don S.; Fiorenza, Francis S. (eds.). New York: Crossroad.

Trigg, Roger. 1977. *Reason and Commitment.* Cambridge: Cambridge University Press.

Trigg, Roger. 1993. *Rationality and Science.* Oxford: Blackwell.

Trigg, Roger. 1998. *Rationality and Religion.* Oxford: Blackwell.

van Fraassen, Bastiaan C. 1989. *The Scientific Image.* New York: Clarendon Press.

van Huyssteen, J. Wentzel. 1987. *The Realism of the Text.* Pretoria: UNISA.

van Huyssteen, J. Wentzel. 1988. "Inference to the Best Explanation? The Shaping of Rationality in Theology," in *Paradigms and Progress in Theology,* Mouton, Johann (ed.). Pretoria: HSRC Press.

van Huyssteen, J. Wentzel. 1989. *Theology and the Justification of Faith: Constructing Theories in Systematic Theology.* Grand Rapids: Eerdmans.

van Huyssteen, J. Wentzel. 1993. "Critical Realism and God: Can There Be Faith after Foundationalism," in *Intellektueel in Konteks: Opstelle vir Hennie Rossouw,* van Niekerk, A. A. (ed.). Pretoria: HSRC Press.

van Huyssteen, J. Wentzel. 1993. "What Epistemic Values Should We Reclaim for Religion and Science? A Response to J. Wesley Robbins," in *Zygon.* 28/3.

van Huyssteen, J. Wentzel. 1997a. *Essays in Postfoundationalist Theology.* Grand Rapids: Eerdmans.

van Huyssteen, J. Wentzel. 1997b. "Should We Be Trying So Hard to Be Postmodern?," in *Zygon.* 32/4.

van Huyssteen, J. Wentzel. 1998a. *Duet or Duel? Theology and Science in a Postmodern World.* London: SCM Press.

van Niekerk, A. A. 1990. "To follow a rule or to rule what should follow?," in *Knowledge and Method in the Human Sciences,* Mouton, J.; Joubert D. (eds.). Pretoria: HSRC Press.

van Niekerk, A. A. 1992. *Rationaliteit en Relativisme: Op Soek na 'n Rationaliteitsmodel vir die Menswetenskappe.* Pretoria: HSRC Press.

Ward, Graham. 1992. "John Milbank's Divinia Commedia," in *New Blackfriars.* 73/861.

Watts, Fraser. 1998. "Science and Theology as Complementary Perspectives," in *Rethinking Theology and Science: Six Models for the Current Discussion,* Gregersen, Niels; van Huyssteen, J. Wentzel (eds.). Grand Rapids: Eerdmans.

Wavel, Bruce B. 1980. "The Rationality of Values," in *Zygon.* 15/1.

Wegter-McNelly, Kirk. 1996. *Making Sense of Pluralism.* Graduate Theological Union Berkeley (unpublished paper).

Werpehowski, William. 1986. *"Ad Hoc* Apologetics," in *Journal of Religion.* 66.

Wiles, Maurice F. 1986. *God's Action in the World.* London: SCM Press.

Wilson, Edward O. 1998. *Consilience: The Unity of Knowledge.* New York: Knopf.

Index

297

Index